Margaret Stokes

Three Months in the Forests of France

A Pilgrimage in Search of Vestiges of the Irish Saints in France

Margaret Stokes

Three Months in the Forests of France
A Pilgrimage in Search of Vestiges of the Irish Saints in France

ISBN/EAN: 9783337294601

Printed in Europe, USA, Canada, Australia, Japan

Cover: Foto ©Lupo / pixelio.de

More available books at **www.hansebooks.com**

Three Months in the Forests of France

A PILGRIMAGE IN SEARCH OF VESTIGES OF THE IRISH SAINTS IN FRANCE

With numerous Illustrations

BY

MARGARET STOKES

HONORARY MEMBER OF THE ROYAL IRISH ACADEMY, ETC., ETC.

Amor mi mosse che mi fa pariare.

LONDON

GEORGE BELL AND SONS

1895

Dedication.

TO THE FRIENDS WHO FORM THE

CHURCH HISTORY CLASS

IN THE

LITERARY SOCIETY OF ALEXANDRA COLLEGE,

DUBLIN.

PREFACE.

I NOW present a second instalment of the series of letters from the continent commenced in 1892, relating to the missions of the Irish Church in the sixth and seventh centuries. The scene has changed from the valleys and heights of the Apennines to those forests on the plains of France where Columban led the first mission from Ireland, and Fursa the second; and to the localities most connected with their memories, whether in the Southern Vosges and Department of the Haute-Saône, or in Picardy and on the borders of the rivers Marne and Oise.

Since the story of St. Fursa's life which appears in the following pages was signed for press, I have met with the following legend of a characteristic incident in his life, the beauty of which will, I trust, prove sufficient excuse for its insertion here at the last moment. There was a young nun who waited on St. Molaisse of Leighlin, who loved and was beloved by a clerical student. She tells her lover to flee from the wrath of her master. "It is enough," she says, "that I should be ruined" (*as lor, ar si mu mhudhugudh sa*). St. Molaisse curses her, and deprives her of heaven. She dies in childbed, and is buried in a bog outside the church and graveyard. Her lover devotes himself to saving her soul from hell. He builds a hut by her grave, and every day he recites seven times the Beatus and the Psalms, and he performs a hundred prostrations. After a year her spirit appears to him, blesses him, and declares that she is almost rescued, and that the Beatus has helped her most. The story ends thus:

"Once, then, Fursa the Pious came to the church and beheld the service of angels (between heaven and the grave in the bog). 'Well, O Molaisse,' saith Fursa, 'what saint is there in the bog?' 'An idol is therein,' saith Molaisse, 'a diabolic nun.' 'Look, Molaisse!' saith Fursa. They both look, and they beheld the service of the angels ascending from the grave to heaven.

"Thus the nun's body was taken out of the bog and buried in the graveyard. And Fursa took the cleric under his protection; wherefore he afterwards became a holy man, and went to heaven.

"So that the Beatus is better than any prayer for saving a soul from devils."[1]

The fame of St. Fursa (Fr., Furcy), who is still honoured as the Patron of Lagny and of Péronne, does not, as in the case of St. Columban, rest upon the importance of the schools and monasteries founded by him so much as on the fact that his visions of heaven and hell are among the first and most interesting of that circle of visions which culminate in the Divina Commedia of Dante. Such apocalypses are not confined to Christianity, and in a forthcoming work of Mr. David Nutt, the reader will soon have an opportunity of comparing those of our Irish seers with their forerunners, the non-Christian visitants of the other world, such as are given in the voyages of Bran, son of Febal, of Maelduin, of Connla and others.

Believing, as I do, that the main interest of this volume lies in the fact that it contains Fursa's vision, and that the whole subject of this strange chapter in the history of our native literature is too little known to the general public, I begged of my elder

[1] See "Lives of Saints, from the Book of Lismore," translated and edited by Whitley Stokes, D.C.L., Preface, p. x.

brother to allow me to enrich my little book with a reprint of his translation of Adamnán's "Vision of Heaven and Hell," fifty copies of which had been privately printed in Calcutta thirty-five years ago.[1] In granting my request he has but added one more to the many debts I owe him.

I have also to offer my grateful acknowledgment to my kind friend the Rev. Christopher McCready, for placing at my disposal his literal translation of the visions of St. Fursa, from the Codex Salmanticensis, now at Brussels, which is given in a condensed form at page 87 of this volume. Finally, I have again to thank the President of the Royal Irish Academy, Dr. Ingram, who, in the midst of his laborious life, has found time to revise my proofs.

[1] See also "Fraser's Magazine," February, 1871, p. 184.

CONTENTS.

CONTENTS.

LIST OF ILLUSTRATIONS.

INTRODUCTORY LETTER.

Carrig Breac, Howth,
January, 1895.

DEAR E.,

IN the Preface to the letters I wrote you when on my pilgrimage in search of vestiges of the Irish saints in Italy, you will have seen that one object I had in view was "to find a clue to the origins of Irish art, and to discover the reason for the development of certain styles in Ireland;" and it then seemed probable that the result of further expeditions of the same kind would be the discovery of "connecting links between Ireland and North Italy, through Gaul, by the Loire and Brittany, and along the Rhine, through Holland and Great Britain to Ireland." I am now inclined to modify this view; for, if we search for such origins in the parts of France most frequented by Irish travellers and settlers, the result is that we arrive at localities about the middle of France and the bed of the Rhone rather than along the Loire and in Brittany.

It is still quite uncertain at what period the art of enamelling was first practised in Ireland, and some writers are inclined to the belief that it originated in the British Isles. The subject is discussed in a paper read by Dr. Valentine Ball before the Royal Irish Academy, and Dr. Anderson[1] is quoted as maintaining that the home of the art was in Britain. However this may be, it is

[1] See "Proc. of Soc. of Antiquaries, Scotland," vol. vii., p. 45.

held, by the first authorities on the subject, that in the time of Septimius Severus (*circa* 200 A.D.) the art of enamelling was not practised either in Italy or Greece, and a Greek teacher, Philostrates, who gained admission to the imperial palace at Rome, described the enamels on the horse trappings of "the barbarians who live in (or by) the ocean" as an entirely new art to him. Whoever the "barbarians" were, there is a passage in Strabo (lib. iv., ch. 5) in which glass is mentioned, in connection with the trade with Britain, which seems rather to imply that it was imported to Britain from Gaul. The linguistic evidence on the history of enamel in Ireland in the first centuries of the Christian era, communicated to Dr. Ball by my brother, Whitley Stokes, seems to say that in Ireland, at all events, it was an importation. The Irish word "Cruan" is explained in O'Davoren's "Glossary" (p. 71) as follows:

> "Cruan, *i.e.*, a kind of the old art-work from abroad. *Cruan, i.e.*, the red (kind), and *Créduma, i.e.*, the yellow. *Maithne, i.e.*, yellow, and green, and white."

Whether originally imported, or an entirely native art, enamelling appears to have been extensively practised in Ireland, as is proved by the fine examples in our museums of antiquities, found in this country and of native workmanship. No more remarkable discovery of enamel in its crude state has ever been made than the rough block of red enamel, first recognized as such by Dr. Ball, which was discovered in the Rath of Caelchu on Tara Hill, brought there, or made there, probably before A.D. 565, when Tara was abandoned as a royal residence.

Wherever the first origin of the art may be found, there is no doubt it was largely practised in Gaul in the Merovingian period, and especially in the 1ère Lyonnaise and the district round Autun.[1] It seems, from what may be gathered from the legends of the first Christian students and teachers from Ireland in the fifth and sixth centuries, that they congregated in this central part of France. The school of Germanus at Auxerre was the school of St. Patrick,[2] Brioc,[3] Michomer,[4] Isserninus (Irish Fith),[5] who, with St. Lupus of Troyes, are said to have accompanied Germanus into Britain. Brioc returned to work in Brittany, Michomer to labour with St. Lupus in the district of Troyes and Langres, while Patrick and Isserninus worked and died in Ireland. It was about the year 432 that St. Patrick returned for the second time to Ireland, having received episcopal consecration from a Gaulish bishop as a missionary from the Gaulish Church, and was supplied with Gaulish assistants. He is described by Tirechan as arriving at certain islands (probably the Skerries) "attended by some Gauls, and by a multitude of holy bishops, presbyters, deacons, exorcists, ostiarii, and lectors, besides students." He is also said to have brought with him

[1] The ancient name of this city of the Aedui was Augustodunum, Mons Bifractus—Bibracte—now Mont Beuvray, which lies in the suburbs of Autun. It stands in the Ville de France, on the Arroux (Saône-et-Loire), and the enamel workshops of Bibracte, with their furnaces, crucibles, moulds, and polishing stones, and with crude enamels in their various stages of preparation, have been recently excavated from the ruins of the city destroyed by Cæsar and his legions. This Bibracte must not be confused with Bibrax, the Oppidum Rhemorum of Cæsar ("Bell. Gall.," ii. 6), about the identification of which there has been much discussion. It was probably on the site of the village of Bruyère near Laon.

[2] "Autissiodorum nomen erat civitatis cuius St. Germanus erat superior et nobilis antistes." See "The Tripartite Life of St. Patrick," ed. with translation by Whitley Stokes, D.C.L., LL.D., 1887, Rolls Series, pp. 26, 416, 420, 503, 510.

[3] "Acta Sanctorum" (Boll.), tom. i., Maii i, pp. 91, 94.

[4] *Ib.*, tom. iii., Aprilis xxx.

[5] "Trip. Life of St. Patrick," pp. 342, ll. 1-24; 344, l. 3. "Annals of Ulster," A.D 468.

"many relics, and books in plenty, given him by Pope Sixtus, who showed much kindness to Patrick."

Such imported books and relics, many of which may have been enshrined, were probably examples of the arts of writing, illumination, and metal-work practised in Burgundy and Neustria in the beginning of the Merovingian era. In the ecclesiastical history of France the names of other Irish visitants at this early period occur, such as Mansuetus, who became first Bishop of Toul in the fifth century; and there is a passage in the writings of Heric of Auxerre where he describes the Irish Michomer as visiting "all those towns which were in the country of the Aedui, whose capital was Bibracte," *i.e.*, Autun.[1] He ended his days as a recluse near Langres. From these evidences of early intercourse with Burgundy, it may not be thought rash to assume that we find an explanation of Columban's subsequent mission there in the reign of King Gontran. Then, in 590, Rachanarius, a disciple of Columban's at Luxeuil, became Bishop of Autun, and established the Columban Rule there, and the youths of Autun, Langres, Lyons, Châlons-sur-Marne attended the school of Columban at Luxeuil for instruction.

"Ancient Gaul," says Paul Lacroix,[2] "in spite of its disasters, still retained, in certain parts of its territory, men, or rather groups of men, in whose hearts the cultivation of art still remained a living principle. This was the case in Provence, round the archbishops of Arles; in Austrasia (Metz), near the throne of Brunehaut; in Burgundy, at the Court of King Gontran. Most of the works, and even the names of these artists, are now lost, but history has recorded the movement." Gregory of Tours appears to be the principal authority on the subject. He tells how, when King

[1] See "Acta Sanctorum," tom. iii., Aprilis xxx.

[2] "The Arts in the Middle Ages and the Renaissance." By Paul Lacroix, p. 256.

Clovis renounced paganism and asked to be baptized, "this intelligence was the greatest joy to St. Remi. He orders the sacred fonts to be prepared, the streets to be overhung with painted cloths, the churches to be ornamented with hangings." When the abbey church of St. Denis was consecrated "its walls were covered with tapestry, embroidered in gold and ornamented with pearls." These tapestries were long preserved in the abbey treasury. St. Remi (born at Laon, A.D. 439; died 533, January 13th) gave an impetus to Christian Art in many ways. He endowed the bishopric of Laon, placing the noble Guenebald, a man skilled in profane and sacred learning, over it, as well as over the bishoprics of Tournai, Arras, and Cambrai. He possessed a silver table decorated with sacred subjects. He gave to Rheims a silver chalice, ornamented with several images, which was sold in Hincmar's time for the ransom of captives taken by the Normans.[1]

The example of this great bishop may have given an impetus to early Christian Art which spread to Ireland. An extract from the life of one of our Irish pilgrims at this date will illustrate the kind of hospitality and protection which St. Remi was always ready to extend to these strangers.

The old biographer, writing of Ireland, adds:[2]

"From that island, I say, seven brothers started on a pilgrimage for the love of Christ. They were men of great piety and virtue. These men, Gibrian,[3] Helan, Tressan, Germanus, Veranus, Habranus, Petranus, and three sisters, Frauda or Francla, Portia, and Possena.

---

[1] Another chalice, but one which appears to be of later date, is shown as a chalice of St. Remi in the treasury of the church of Notre Dame, Rheims, which, after having appeared in the Cabinet of Antiquities, was returned in 1861.

[2] Boll., "AA. SS.," February 27th and October 3rd.

[3] The village of St. Gibrien, near Châlons-sur-Marne, takes its name from this Irish saint, whose relics were finally enshrined in the church of St. Remi at Rheims. See "Acta Sanctorum," tom. ii., Maii viii.

"When they reached St. Remi, father of pilgrims, he received them with hospitality and kindness; and, learning their sacred purpose, determined to choose suitable places for their dwelling on the river Marne, where they might visit and help one another. They did not live only on the charity of those whom the pious president had commended them to, but also on their own industry and the labour of their hands, in accordance with the customs of the religious bodies of Ireland. This life, united to wonderful holiness and constant prayer, won for them a great love among the natives of the country. The holy priest Helan selected for himself the village of Buxiolum, on the Marne, a spot rich in meadows and vineyards, of soil not less fertile than that of the neighbouring lands. In this place he, living for many years a life of sobriety, piety, and justice, instructing the people, and forming in them the habits of faith, piety, and morality, after a life of rectitude, at length *quievit in Domino.*"

An Irish pilgrim, who adopted the name Amandus, returning from Italy through Gaul, was granted land by St. Remi and Clovis I., on which he founded a church, at Beaumont (Pulcher Mons), where, on his death, Remi ordered his tomb to be erected, and his oratory to be replaced by a larger stone building.[1]

Fifty-five years after the death of St. Remi, St. Eloi, the patron saint of jewellers and farriers, the great Bishop of Noyon, was born in a villa named Cadaillac, six miles from Limoges. He not only founded and endowed churches, but the exquisite works with which he is recorded to have enriched them were wrought by his own fingers. "His hands," says St. Ouen, "were finely formed, and his fingers long." He also wrought splendid

[1] See Boll., "AA. SS.," tom. iii., Jan. xvi. In the account of the building of this church we meet with a variety of the same legend of the miraculous transportation of stones by dumb animals, that we have in accounts of the building of San Frediano at Lucca (see "Six Months in the Apennines," p. 72), but at Beaumont, two doves, instead of oxen, tow the stones across the river to their destination.

furniture for kings' palaces, made coins and medals, while he entered into the labours of the common smith. He founded the monastery of Solignac, near Limoges, and the ancient church of St. Paul-des-Champs, at Paris, in 634, remarkable for its lofty, narrow, tapering bell-tower, and originally intended as a hospital for the poor and for pilgrims. The roof of this church was remarkably high, and covered with lead. He also built the church of St. Martial, in Paris. As a worker in gold and silver he wrought the shrine of SS. Germain, Severian, Piat and his friend Chrysole, Quentin, Lucien, Geneviève, Colombe, Maximien, Lolien, and Julien, Denis, Fursa, Brice, his greatest work being the shrine of St. Martin at Tours, and the shrine of SS. Crépin and Crepinien at Soissons. The friend of King Dagobert I., he is said to have wrought for him a throne of gold; and for Clothair to have made two state chairs of gold. He was also Master of the Mint in Paris under Clothair II., Dagobert I., and Clovis II., and fourteen coins have been identified by the learned numismatist, M. Dancoisne, as struck by St. Eloi.

If it can be established that St. Eloi, all through his career, from his youth in 590 to his death in 659, was associated with Irish missionaries and a visitor in their monasteries, may we not find indications of the school in which our Irish artificers learned their arts of filagree and jewellers' work? His dearest friend, Ouen—called also Dadon—had been baptized by St. Columban when the Irish saint, after his banishment from Luxeuil, was resting in the house of Ouen's father, Autharius, at Eussi (Bussy, Busiacum), on the Marne. He was treasurer to King Dagobert when Eloi, the young goldsmith from Limoges, appeared in court. When Eloi, in course of time, embraced a religious life, Ouen or Dadon, "whom he cherished as his soul," followed in his footsteps. Eloi then proceeded on a mission to Brittany, where King Judicael was the reigning monarch. When, by the force of his goodness and mercy, he had won over this wild people to peace, he returned to King Dagobert, and entreated that he would grant him the lands of Solignac in the Limousin, where he desired to found a monastery *upon the plan of that of Columban at Luxeuil*, as Montalembert has noted in the following words:[1]

> "Il faudrait surtout raconter la fondation de Solignac faite en Limousin par Saint Eloi. Elle eut lieu peu de temps après le concile de Mâcon. Son illustre auteur, qui avait visité les principaux monastères de la Gaule et avait reconnu que la régularité monastique n'était nulle part observée comme à *Luxeuil*, déclara qu'il la voulait absolument conforme au plan et à la regle de *l'abbaye modèle qu'il avait rencontrée dans les Vosges* et à laquelle il la subordonna directement."

The monastery of Solignac was capable of receiving a hundred and fifty monks, whom he placed under the Columban Rule. "There [*i.e.*, at that place] is at this time," says St. Ouen, in his biography of Eloi, "a great company adorned with all the flowers of various graces. There are also many artificers skilled in divers arts." And he goes on to describe how "it was surrounded by an enclosure (not, indeed, a stone wall, but a bank, with hedge and ditch, *sphaerico muro non quidem lapideo; sed fossatum sepe munitum*) about a mile and a quarter in circumference."

As monks from every side crowded to his monastery, Eloi, "impelled by the desire to enter still more thoroughly into the life of holy men," repaired to Luxeuil. Columban's disciple and successor, Eustace, was then Abbot of Luxeuil. He became the friend of Eloi, who often went to visit him afterwards. "You should see him," writes Ouen enthusiastically,[2] "how he entered that monastery; first falling prostrate on the ground, then walking forward with bowed head and downcast eyes, he

[1] Montalembert, "Les Moines d'Occident," vol. ii., p. 572.

[2] Audeonus, "Vita St. Eligii," lib. i., c. 21.

approached the monks with gravity, honouring each in turn with a low salutation, and piously entreating their benediction." Nor did he quit them without carrying away a morsel of their bread, which he accepted as a benediction, and valued as a costly gift. So long as the bread remained incorrupt he would take a small fragment day by day, as if he thus partook of the Holy Communion. Eloi was brought into close contact with the Irish mission in Picardy and Flanders, commenced by St. Fursa and his companions, in the following manner:—One of the disciples of Columban, named Achaire, was promoted to the bishopric of Noyon (Noviomagus Vermanduorum), in Ville de France, Department of the Oise. When he died in 639, St. Eloi was named his successor, while Ouen became Bishop of Rouen. Noyon lies within easy distance of Péronne and Lagny, of both of which churches St. Fursa was patron. Fursa had landed in France three years before St. Eloi's consecration, and the mission of Eloi in Flanders was henceforth carried on simultaneously with that of Ultan and Foillan, and the other Irish followers of Fursa. He, too, with Fursa, became a dear friend of Queen Bathilde. He also met with Erchenwald the mayor, who proved so true a friend to Fursa; though Ouen, the biographer of Eloi, does not paint this functionary in such favourable colours as those in which he appears in the life of Fursa. Eloi outlived Fursa nine years; but at the death of the Irish saint we learn that a shrine was prepared by him for Fursa's relics, and that he was assisted in the work by Autbertus and Medardus, and that when Eloi approached the church porch, bearing with him the precious shrine, Erchenwald met him with due honour, and prepared a tabernacle under which the shrine was temporarily placed. The Venerable Bede adds that these things happened four years after the death of Fursa. But this shrine, and all the other splendid works attributed to this artist saint, have disappeared. The few examples of art contemporary with Columban and Fursa that I can here show you are two illuminated letters taken from MSS. formerly belonging to the abbeys of Luxeuil and Beauvais, and three gold pieces coined by Eloi. Fig. 2 is taken from the famous Gallican Lectionary of Luxeuil, fol. 172, MS. of the seventh century, used by Mabillon for his work on the Gallican liturgy, and now preserved in the Bibliothèque Nationale of Paris (see

Fig. 2.—GALLICAN LECTIONARY, LUXEUIL.

Appendix). Fig. 3 is from Homilies of St. Augustine, A.D. 625. This manuscript belonged to the church of Beauvais. It is now in the bibliothèque of the Château of Troussures (Oise). Mabillon believed it to date from the time of the coming of Columban, A.D. 585 or 586, and M. Léopold de Lisle has endorsed his opinion. Figs. 4 and 5 represent two golden coins struck in Paris in the time of Clovis II., and the name Eligius appears on the reverse, who was apparently none other that St. Eloi himself, who was Master of the Mint under Clothair II., Dagobert I., and

Clovis II. I am indebted to the kindness of M. Henri de la Tour, head of the Coin Department, Bibliothèque Nationale in Paris, who, with great skill and pains, has made casts from these coins for me, from which these photographs are taken. They are Nos. 686 and 693 of the magnificent collection of Merovingian coins in the Cabinet de France. Fig. 6 represents one of a hoard of coins found in the parish of Crondal, Hants,

Fig. 3.—HOMILIES, ST. AUGUSTINE, LUXEUIL.

belonging to a series of *tiers de sol* or gold *triens* of the French kings of the first race, and the coin is read by Mr. Akerman, "PARISIUS FIT," *rev.* "ELEI MONET," and Mr. Lefroy suggests, that possibly the termination of the upper bend of the cross in a double pastoral crook is an allusion to the sacred character of St. Eligius.[1]

[1] See "Numismatic Chronicle," vol. x., New Series, p. 168. M. Prou, "Catalogue des Monnaies Mérovingiennes de la Bibliothèque Nationale, 1892," in 8vo., pp. xlviii., xlix.

A Merovingian coin of this date was also found in Ireland, near Maryborough, it has been engraved in the journal of the Kilkenny Archæological Society (2nd Ser., iv., p. 245), and Mr. Graves has given the following account of it.

"*Obv.*, Blundered legend. Helmeted bust, to the right.

"*Rev.* '+ MELLIONE,' a cross with a graduated base. In *field*, two pellets and two quatrefoils; weight 22 grains."

M. de la Tour has written to me respecting this coin. "I send you a rubbing and a squeeze of No. 419 of the Bibl. Nationale.

Fig. 4.—CLOVIS II.

Fig. 5.—COIN OF ELIGIUS.

Fig. 6.—MEROVINGIAN COIN FOUND AT CRONDAL.

This coin was struck at Mans. It is probable that the coin found at Maryborough, also stamped '+ MELLIONE' is identical with this, Cenomanus being the ancient name for Le Mans." Conjectured by Mr. Madden. The broken letters on the obverse were probably "Cenomanis," which have been misread "LEI . . . NNIS."

It will be seen at once from these examples that they belong to a school of art wholly independent of Celtic influence. Here and there throughout my journey I observed in local museums an occasional bell or clasp, or even rudely carved stone, that had an Irish character, but whether such antiquities were brought into Gaul from Ireland, or whether similar objects in our Irish museums were importations from Gaul in the fifth century, it would be difficult to determine. In the museum of Amiens an old iron bell, exactly similar to the bells of our Irish saints, is still preserved, and, as will be seen from the illustration, it is not of cast metal, but simply a sheet of iron folded, not soldered, but fastened together with rivets. Another bell, also of a Celtic pattern, I found in the museum at Péronne, which came from Offoy, an old church some miles to the south-east. Such is the bell described by Didron, in the museum of Cologne, said to have belonged to St. Cumbert; such also was the bell of St. Godeberte, at Noyon; and another in the museum at Arras, found in L'Aveyron, a tributary of the Tarn, in the south of France; and another at Stival, in Brittany. Perhaps it was because such objects were of no intrinsic value that they were spared, while the golden and jewelled shrines were stolen.

It would appear as if the importation of bells into Ireland by Gaulish missionaries was a common occurrence, but we must remember that the intercourse between the two countries was reciprocal. "By crowds the readers resort thither, carried over by ships," says Aldhelm, writing about the time of Fursa's death; and he adds, "The country of Ireland, rich in those learning, and flourishing in the fertile pasturage of students, resembles the star-bearing heaven, adorned by the quivering of brilliant constellations." "These crowds of Gaulish students," writes Haureau, "sought the Irish shores in order to win back again from their pupils of former times the learning they had lost themselves." And along with others went Agilbert,[1] who "for the pleasure of reading the Scriptures abode not a little while in Ireland;" and when he returned to the Continent, about the

[1] Bede, "Eccl. Hist.," bk. iii., c. 7.

year 664, he so amazed the church in Gaul by the extent of his knowledge, that, at the death of Importunus, they hastened to make him Bishop of Paris.

At the death of Sigebert, brother of Clovis II., the government of his kingdom fell into the hands of Grimoald, his mayor, who, in his ambition to secure the throne for his son, Ildebert, determined on banishing Dagobert, the child of Sigebert. He sent him secretly to Ireland, and it is recorded that the boy was educated in the monastery of Slane in Meath. When he had grown to manhood, Erchenwald, the mayor, and the staunch friend of St. Fursa, unable to endure the injustice done to the young prince Dagobert, took arms against the usurper Ildebert, whom he defeated; while his father, Grimoald, was seized, imprisoned, and finally beheaded. His enemies thus destroyed, Erchenwald recalled the young Dagobert from Ireland, and he at first received a part of Austrasia from Childeric II. He (Dagobert) reigned for five years after the death of Childeric, and at his death (A.D. 718) his body was interred at Choisy, while his memory was revered as that of a martyr at Stenay, the capital of Bar, in the diocese of Trèves. Ill-fitted for the throne by his early training in the quiet of an Irish monastery, he was powerless to quell the tumult in his

Fig. 7.—IRON BELL.
Museum, Amiens. Found in the river Aveyron.

long misgoverned kingdom, and the motto surrounding his medal is:

"Mecum voluto eventus belli varios."[1]

Such incidents as these are examples of the constant intercourse between Ireland and Gaul before the eighth century, the existence of which is further evidenced by the co-existence of many similar customs in both countries. Thus the anchorite life, and the habit of the early Christian bishops and pastors of seeking solitude and retirement for a time, dwelling in caves and deserts, is illustrated by the traditions of the cave of Columban, near the summit of the mountain over Annegrai, the cave of St. Walbert, and his subterranean chapel among the limestone rocks in the forest of Luxeuil, and the cave of St. Gobain in the forest called by his name. The question as to whether wood or stone was the material used by such early church builders in the erection of their churches has been a matter of debate among antiquaries, abroad as well as at home, when dealing with the foundation of such abbeys and monasteries as Luxeuil,

Fig. 8.—IRON BELL.
Museum, Péronne. Found at Offoy.

[1] F. Eudes de Mezeray, "Hist. de France depuis Faramond," vol. i., p. 117 (1643).

Grandval, and St. Imier. The exact correspondence of St. Eloi's first monastery at Solignac with the Irish cashels, as well as that of Columban at Annegrai, is very striking indeed. It is expressly stated that Eloi surrounded the monastery with a bank and a ditch, the same method of enclosure as that which existed in Ireland.

There is ample evidence in the following pages of the prevalence of the custom among early Christians of building their sanctuaries either on the sites of pagan temples, or within the disused ramparts of a pagan encampment. Thus the Abbey of Luxeuil was built on the site of a temple of Diana; and the monastery was within the walls of a Roman encampment, and among the débris, the fallen columns and mutilated statues of a former religion. The monastery of Annegrai, and the church of St. Fursa, at Péronne, were erected within the ancient castellum or fort of the mayor, while at Burghcastle, in Suffolk, the grand Roman fort, inside of which Fursa planted his monastery, stands clear and bold to the present day, though no trace of the monastery itself remains.

The correspondences that exist between the oldest French churches and those of Great Britain and Ireland, open too wide a field for a work such as this. I can only touch upon the fact that there are certain peculiarities universal in Ireland, and often occurring in England and Scotland, which may also be met with in those parts of France most frequented by our Irish monks. For instance, the occurrence of the square end in the chancel, so universal with us, in preference to the rounded apse derived from the basilica, is found in the northern provinces of France. The chapel of Vieux-Pont en Auge, in the Department of Calvados, is exactly on the ground-plan of an Irish church; the same may be said of St. Quirin, at Vaison, and Beauvoisin, while at Namps au Val, near Amiens, there is an old church which, in more points than one, bears a striking resemblance to our Irish Romanesque churches. It has no transepts; the chancel and little square apse remind one of the ground-plan of Cormac's chapel. There are bold pilasters at the corners. The west door, like that of Kilmalkedar, is arched, and beneath the arch there is a lintel formed of a huge monolith pentagon, forming a sort of pediment. The lintel of the side door is also a monolith.

The personal relics of the saints mentioned in this book are the mazer, or wooden drinking-cup of St. Walbert; the staff of St. Fursa; the bell given to him by an angel; the girdle of St. Fursa, long preserved in Suffolk; while, for implements, a wooden ruler, an iron wedge for splitting logs, spades, and rakes, and sickles are mentioned. None of these, save the mazer, appear to have survived the successive robberies of the monasteries, where many such memorials were once preserved.

The animals named in these legends are bears, oxen, swine, boars, doves, and swans. Algisus is directed to the spot where his church is to be built by the guidance of a dove; the Bishop of Tuam to the site of an abbey in Mayo by the flight of three swans.

Wells are said to spring forth miraculously at the touch of the saint's staff, and their waters are held to the present day to preserve their salutary effect. The diseases named as being curable by such, are the various ailments of little children, if washed in them on the eve of the Ascension or Whitsun Eve; or skin diseases and rheumatism. The practice of hanging offerings at such wells also prevails all over France. It is specially noted here as found at the well of St. Deicola at Lure.

Other superstitions are related also, and legends common to both countries, such as the special efficacy of medicine taken from St. Walbert's cup; the fragrance that is distilled from the bones of saints; the appearance of three lights, a sign of death; a non-consuming flame surrounds the birth of a saint; a column of fire guides Gertrude through the forest. The identity of the legend of the hump-backed fiddler of Knockgrafton with that of the "Bossu de Fontenoy" is very interesting, and that of the suspension of a saint's robe on sunbeams; and the mystic ships, with no human hand to steer them, rudderless and oarless, which track the pathless sea, and ascend great rivers, holding on their course against the current, are all varieties of legends we have found in Ireland and Italy.

The question as to the nature of the vessels in which the early inhabitants of our islands ventured forth upon the ocean must always be an interesting one. Mr. Cecil Torr, in the opening of his work on "Ancient Ships," observes that whereas in the Mediterranean Sea the nations inhabiting its shores filled the sea with oared vessels, and oars became the characteristic instruments of navigation, and their arrangement the chief problem in ship-building; on the other hand, the nations of Western Europe, and dwellers by the ocean, devised sailing vessels of different types for voyages on the Atlantic, and oars gradually gave way to sails. In the legends of St. Brendan, vessels with three sails are described. Adamnan mentions no less than nine kinds of vessels as in use among the Scots in his day. Yet it seems as if they might be classed under three heads. First, ships that were built; secondly, currachs covered with skins; thirdly, boats of solid wood hollowed out of the stems of trees. They are styled *navis oneraria*, *barca*, *caupullus* or *coblach*, *curuca*, *navicula*, *scapha*, or *cymba*, or *cymbula*, *olnum*, and *navis longa*. In the life of St. Brendan, from the "Book of Lismore," when the saint starts in search of the island from which he had seen trains of angels rising to the sky, two kinds of vessels are spöken of in the account of his embarkation; and, in one instance, vessels built of wood, and not merely hollowed out of trees, are referred to. St. Brendan orders three vessels to be built, "with three rows of oars to each ship, and three sails of hides and thirty men in each ship."[1]

[1] See "Lives of Saints, from the Book of Lismore," p. 253, edited, with translation, etc., by Whitley Stokes, D.C.L. Oxford, Clarendon Press.

"Three vessels the sage sailed
 Over the wave-voice of the flowing sea;
Thirty men in each vessel he had
 Over the storm of the crested sea."

And we learn afterwards that these first vessels were covered with hides. When he first returns, after having failed to reach the angelic abode, his mother, Ita, says to him,[1] "The land which thou art seeking from God thou wilt never find in those dead stained skins, for it is a holy, consecrated land, and men's blood hath never been spilt therein, howbeit," she saith, "let wooden vessels be built by thee, and it is probable that thus thou wilt find the land later." He then builds in Connaught "a great marvellous vessel."[2] In this "built" vessel he embarks with all his household and his people,[3] among whom wrights and smiths are specially mentioned, and they bring therein a cargo of various plants and seeds.[4]

In Adamnan's "Life of Columba" the *navis oneraria* is spoken of as a vessel capable of containing parcels of light timber for building a dwelling-house. We get an idea of the aspect of these boats from a passage in the life of Columba where the sailors are said to hoist their sails in the form of a cross.[5]

"When they were returning to Hy with a cargo of wood for building ships, it is said 'the sailors having raised the sailyards in the form of a cross, and having spread the sails upon them, we put to sea.'"

---

[1] See "Lives of SS. from the Book of Lismore," p. 253, edited, with translation, etc., by Whitley Stokes, D.C.L. Oxford, Clarendon Press.

[2] This vessel, we must conclude, was regularly built, not hollowed out of a tree, and not wicker, covered with skins.

[3] "Lives of the Saints, from the Book of Lismore," p. 257.

[4] Ibid., p. 106.

[5] Reeves, "Columba," p. 178. Such a vessel marks one of the purely Christian types of Gnostic gems illustrated by King, which we have chosen as the stamp for the binding of this work.

The word *barca* is used to describe the vessel in which a captain and his crew, having sailed from Gaul, arrived at Cantyre.

Ware has some observations on the boats of the ancient Irish; he says they made use of wicker boats covered with cow-hides, not only on rivers but sometimes in their navigations on the open sea. These little barques were called by them currachs.[1] A similar boat to this is mentioned in a manuscript life of St. Brendan, and termed *navicula*, being a currach or boat brought to Columba across a river which was so shallow that men could ford it on foot. The *cymba*,[2] or *cymbula*, was a skiff or boat, a frail vessel such as that in which Columba is said to have embarked in a storm on Lough Ness, but this had sails which carried him against the wind. So we see that, occasionally these currachs were furnished with sailyards, sails, and ropes, as well as oars; and Adamnan relates that St. Cormac made use of such a boat, with a covering of skins, in his third voyage.[3] Probus, in his life of St. Patrick, speaking of MacFil, Bishop of Man, says that when he was at sea in *navi pellicea*, *i.e.*, in a boat made of skins, the wind being from the north, he was cast upon the Island of Man. Gildas, in his epistle concerning the destruction of Britain, says, "The rude droves of Scots and Picts throng hastily out of their currachs in which they were transported across the Scythian Channel" (*i.e.*, the Irish Sea). "They sew skins to skins and

[1] Lucan ("Pharsalia," bk. iv., l. 136) describes such boats of osiers:

"The bending willow into barks they twine,
Then line the work with skins of slaughtered kine."

And he adds that with such boats the Venetian fishers float through the marshes of the Po, and the Britons navigate the ocean.

[2] *Cymbæ*, according to Mr. Cecil Torr (*op. cit.*, p. 112), were vessels of a type invented in Phœnicia; but Latin authors applied the name to any boat.

[3] Reeves, "Columba," p. 169.

plough the pathless seas in furthest parts with keels of leather," is the description given by Festus Avienus about the beginning of the fifth century.

On one occasion when Cæsar was at war in Arragon, and when he was hemmed in between the rivers Segre and Cinca, and his bridges were destroyed by a violent storm, he ordered his soldiers to make ships of the kind that his knowledge of Britain a few years before had taught him. First, the keels and ribs were made of light timber, then the rest of the hulk of the ships was wrought with wicker work and covered over with hides. See Cæsar's "Comm. on the Civil War," book i., li.

We find details given as to the making of these currachs in second life of St. Brendan.[1]

> "They made a very light barque, ribbed and fenced with timber, and covered it with raw cow-hides, and on the outside they daubed all the jointings of the skins with butter, and put into the vessel materials for making two other boats of other skins, and provisions for forty days, and butter to prepare or dress the skins for the covering of the boat, and other utensils necessary for human life. They also fixed a tree in the midst of the barque, and a sail, and other things belonging to the steering of a boat."

With respect to the third class, the boats of solid wood, or those hollowed from the stems of trees, we find that the Irish custom seems to have resembled that of the Gauls, who were described as hollowing out the trunk of a tree, either an oak or an alder, as in Dryden's translation of Virgil we read:

> "Then first on streams the hollowed alder swam."[2]

---

[1] See "Notes to Metrical Life of St. Brendan," p. 5, and notes p. 58 (Thos. Wright, Percy Society), for another version of this curious description of a very primitive ship.

[2] Virgil, "Georgics," i., 136.

Such vessels as these would be the *naves longae* of the Irish, the long ships made of pine or of oak which were brought from Ireland to Iona by Columba, loaded with building materials; or the boat described by Oengus the Culdee as that in which the humble Egbert is described as crossing the sea. "He came over the great sea: unto Christ he sang a vigil, in a coracle without a hide around it."[1]

Hitherto the main interest in our studies of these lives of our early Irish missionaries has been confined to the light they cast upon the customs and primitive conditions of life in early Christian times. A new feature, and one bearing on the history of Christian literature, is presented in this volume in the visions of heaven and hell seen by St. Fursa, patron of Killfursa in Galway, and of the churches of Lagny and Péronne in France. Such visions, apocalypses, and allegorical poems form one of the most striking features in ancient literature. Springing from the heart and brain of man at moments when the thoughts are with the dead rather than the living, and the desire to pierce "behind the veil" seems irresistible, we find in many of these writings the most profound religious convictions of the day, while no small amount of imaginative power is brought to bear upon the subject. Octave Delepierre seems to have been the first to collect together such of these visions as were not merely developments of the poetical faculty, but also were objects of religious belief, and which were only seen by persons convinced of their reality, not mere mystic romances. Among these he enumerates the visions of St. Salvius (A.D. 584), related by Gregory of Tours; that of the monk Drihthelm, A.D. 696, related by Bede; of Wettinus in 824; of St. Anschar, A.D. 865; Alberic, A.D. 1150; Tundal, A.D. 1149; Owen Miles, A.D. 1153, and Thurcill, 1206. To these names we may add the Irish Brendan (died A.D. 576)

[1] See "Calendar of Oengus." By Whitley Stokes, LL.D., Dublin, 1880.

and Adamnan. I shall now endeavour to indicate the main points of interest, as compared with those of Fursa, which seem to illustrate the growth of various ideas regarding the state of the soul after death.

There is a distinct development, a growth and a decay, in the character of these visions in the course of centuries. Their primitive simplicity is modified by the growing familiarity with classical imagery as the writings of the ancients become more widespread. At first they were more of heaven than of hell, but after the ninth century a strongly-marked change is perceptible in the spirit of the dream; it darkens, or glows, with the lurid light of hell. In details of torture and of misery in a future life, men used these visions as instruments of terror, or even of personal vengeance, and, searching in the literature of the far distant past, they drained the very sources of Greek and Latin mythology for images of dread. When this new phase presents itself the vision becomes a form of poem which embraces all kinds of human misery, giving expression to the rage of the oppressed against the oppressor; and it is also often used as a means of conveying political, moral, and theological doctrine.

In 824, A.D., Wettin, a monk of Reichenau, anticipates Dante in the introduction of historical characters into his vision; thus Charlemagne is seen tortured for having given way to luxury. Allusions to contemporary events occur in certain visions after this date, such as we find in that related by Berthold to Hincmar, and evidently composed to serve the purposes of the latter. Political questions were dealt with in the vision of Raduin, the monk of Rheims, and when we arrive at the thirteenth century, in the vision seen in the year 1206 by Thurcill, native of a village near London, a new element appears. Thurcill, living at Fidstude, was devoted to rustic labour and hospitality when Julian l'Hospitalier appeared to him. Then his soul is separated from his body, and he goes through all the trials of purgatory. The new elements in this story, which in time became marked features in the mystery plays, are those of the spectacle, the *mise-en-scène* of the Court of the Prince of Darkness, and the element of the humorous, which give an amusing side to the horrors of the infernal pains.

Hitherto these seers of visions have been out of the body, and only visitants in the spirit to the land of spirits, but in the twelfth century, in the story of Owen Miles, we find it said that he visited hell in the flesh, his soul not being absent from the body, and returning to it as in other instances. His tale is more one of mystic romance than of hallucination, like that of the monk of Evesham.

It is most important to note the transitions to a new phase of belief in the conditions of the soul hereafter, such as may be traced by a comparison of the visions of Fursa and that of Drihthelm,[1] the latter coming some years after the former. While Fursa is immediately borne upwards by angels to enjoy the light and music of the heavenly choir, Drihthelm is drifted away to a region in the north-east, a vast valley, deep, and infinitely long, where, thinking himself in hell, he is told by his miraculous guide that he is only in purgatory. Flame, upon one side, with icy mountains and insufferable cold, hail, and snow, upon the other, where he beholds the souls of men tossed by a stormy wind on every side. Passing through the valley, he enters a land

[1] Drycthelm—Drihthelm—a landowner dwelling at Cuningham in Northumbria (Mon., "Hist. Brit.," 260; and Stevenson's "Note on Bede," "H. E.," v. 12.), who is said to have died in the middle of the night, and to have revived at dawn. While separate from the body he had visions of purgatory—Gehenna, the place of imperfect happiness, and the vicinity of the celestial kingdom. He is said to have been so profoundly impressed by this experience that the whole course of his life was altered. He left home and lands, and breaking through all earthly ties, became a recluse in a cell near Melrose.

of darkness at the far end. This is hell, at the side of which he is left alone by his angel guide, and in the depths of which he perceives bubbles like black globes being tossed upwards, and tortured souls flying hither and thither like sparks; while the air is filled with a horrible stench, and he hears the noise and din of jeering laughter, mingled with the lamentations of devil-tormented souls.

It is believed that the vision of St. Fursa occurred about thirty years before that of Drihthelm, and it will be acknowledged that it is quite as memorable as any one of those here cited. The construction of the piece is interesting. The time is limited to three days, as with our Lord's visit to Hades, and, as in the case of another Irish vision, that of Tundal of Cashel. Paragraphs 4 to 6 contain the vision of heaven in the first day. Paragraphs 7 to 14, the vision first of hell and second of heaven, till midnight of the third day. Contrary to the usual custom of mediæval visions, heaven occupies the principal place in Fursa's dream, there being, in fact, two scenes in heaven to one in hell. The principal episode in the hell vision is the dispute of the guardian angel with Satan. This argument begins at paragraph 10 and ends at paragraph 13, when the Lord pronounces judgment, and the adversary is conquered. The three attendant angels who protected Fursa in hell, rejoicing in his victory, are surrounded by a great light, and he is instantly transported to heaven (paragraph 13), when the ministration of angels on earth is explained to him. This is followed by the apparition of the two teachers of his youth, Meldan and Beoan, one of whom preaches on the backslidings of the clergy, the other on the inner life. The return of the saint to earth is related in paragraph 23, when he must again pass the fires of hell on his way, and he receives the blow the mark of which remains throughout his earthly career as proof of the reality of his miraculous experiences.

The love of music is singularly manifest throughout these visions of Fursa. At the first moment of his rapture the saint is described singing an evening hymn as he walks homeward, leaning on the arm of his friend. When transported to heaven he hears an angel leading, followed by a chorus, singing psalms and hymns (paragraph 4), "Ibunt Sancti de virtute in virtutem," and "Exierunt obviam Christo;" paragraph 5, "Videbitur Deus deorum in Syon;" paragraph 14, "Hosanna Sanctus Deus Sabaoth." It is said that his soul was filled with these sounds of unspeakable joy, upborne by the song, and his spirit was restored by the melody of heaven. That such acknowledgment of the elevating power of music should come from a writer of the seventh century in Ireland need not surprise those who are familiar with our ancient Irish melodies, such as "Erragon More," from the glens of Antrim, or the chants to which our Ossianic fragments have been sung in the present century. It is known that even Dante, in some long-lost work, referred to the antiquity of music in Ireland, as he is quoted by Vincentio Galilei in the following passage on the harp:

> "Fu portato d'Irlanda à noi questo antichissimo strumento (*commemorato da Dante*) dove si lavorano in eccellenza et copiosamēte; gli habitori della quale isola si esercitano molti e molti secoli in essa," etc.[1]

This incidental mention of the name of the great Italian poet leads us on to the question as to the possibility of his having met with these Irish visions of heaven and hell. It has been allowed that the lately recovered vision of St. Peter and those of Paul, Clement, Salvius, Wettin of Reichenau, and Alberic of Monte Cassino, are links in the long chain of Christian writings which culminated in the Divine Comedy. Is it too much to

[1] V. Galilei, "Dialogo," p. 143. "Harpa venuta à noi d'Irlanda."

hope that Ireland may be thought to supply fresh links in this memorable chain, since in Irish Christian literature we have no less than five visitants to Hades who have left a record of their revelations: Brendan, Fursa, Adamnan, Tundal, and Owen Miles. The Venerable Bede, who dwells with much reverence on the history of Fursa and his visions, is one of the writers whom Dante specially honoured. He speaks of him in his ninth Epistle. 7, when writing in scorn against the theologians who gave their whole time and study to the forged decretals he says, "deserting Augustine and Gregory, Ambrose, Dionysius, and Beda, men who sought God as their end and best good;" and in the tenth canto of the "Paradiso" he places Bede in the fourth heaven, that of the sun, as forming one of the wreath of blessed spirits standing there with Thomas Aquinas and with Boethius, etc.

> "Vedi oltre fiammeggiar l' ardente spiro
> D' Isidoro, di Beda, e di Riccardo,
> Che a considerar fu più che viro."

In the writings of Bede Dante very possibly made acquaintance with the name of St. Fursa. However, if we note as interesting a few parallelisms which occur in his great work and those of his Irish forerunners, it is not that we would impute any plagiarism to him, but that we may perceive that his poem is no sudden and spontaneous growth; but that, on the contrary, it is linked to an entire cycle of older works, and the result of permanent conditions of thought regarding a future life, and faith in the eternity of the soul, which time cannot destroy. One of the most striking of these parallelisms is to be found in the description in the "Purgatorio" of the river in the forest, where Dante meets the Countess Matilda, which resembles the river in the voyage of St. Brendan when he and his monks came into the "Londe of Byheest" (*i.e.*, Promise), where "all the trees were charged with ripe fruit and herbes full of flower, and at the last they came to a ryver, but they durst not go over." There came to the river a fair youth who gave them gracious greeting, and told them they had gained sight of the land they sought, the earthly paradise; but he sent them away laden with fruits, since "the water of that river divides the two worlds, and no man in this life may cross to the other side." The fruits he gives ripen all the year round, it is eternal day, eternal spring. In like manner Dante finds himself on the brink of an impassable river. He beholds a fair nymph standing on the opposite bank who tells him that that place was prepared for man as pledge and earnest of eternal peace. Here is perpetual spring and every fruit may ripen, fruits that grow upon no other soil, sown in seed wafted by the winds of Paradise.[1]

Between the visions of Dante and Fursa occasional correspondences may also be traced, as, when the devil quotes Scripture in his arguments with Fursa's angel, we are reminded of Dante's "fools," who "reflected back the Scripture image by distortion marred."[2] And when the guide shows Fursa the fire that burns to consume the sin of fraud, we remember the words of Virgil to Dante, when he tells him that the souls in the seventh circle are accursed who are guilty of

> "Fraud, that in every conscience leaves a sting."[3]

The third fire which burns in Fursa's vision for the stirrers-up of strife, corresponds to the third cornice in Dante's purgatory, where the sin of anger is purged.[4] In the address of Meldan, speaking to Fursa among the heavenly host, he declares that the anger of the Supreme Judge is chiefly kindled against spiritual

[1] "Purg.," c. xxviii., l. 30.
[2] "Par.," c. xiii., l. 123.
[3] "Hell," c. xi., l. 55.
[4] "Purg.," xv., xvi., l. 24.

teachers and leaders, in terms that at once remind us of Dante's condemnation of the Church, who

> "Mixing two governments that ill assort,
> Hath missed her footing, fallen into the mire,
> And there herself and burthen much defiled."[1]

And when Beoan warns Fursa to keep himself a faithful steward, and to purge his nature of all desire of gain, we are reminded of the admonition in Dante:

> "Such cleansing from the taint of avarice[2]
> Do spirits converted need."

Another very remarkable parallel occurs in the passage of Meldan's address: "Let the teachers of the Church be slow to excommunicate, lest they should sustain the accused in his fault, and render the soul barren that might, if fed with spiritual food, have become fruitful," while Dante says:

> "War once had for his instrument the sword,
> But now 'tis made, taking the bread away,
> Which the Good Father locks from none;"[3]

meaning, that it is one of the evils of his day that excommunication, or interdiction of the Eucharist, is employed as a weapon of warfare.

Delepierre,[4] having referred to the theory of Bottari and many other Italian critics, that Dante undoubtedly derived the general plan, as well as many of the details of his work, from the vision of Alberic (A.D. 1170), declares that, in his opinion, on the

[1] "Purg.," c. xvi., l. 129. [2] *Ibid.*, c. xix., l. 115.
[3] "Par.," c. viii., l. 123.
[4] "L'Enfer, Essai philosophique, par Octave Delepierre," p. 63.

contrary, if the great poet was indebted to any preceding work, it was rather to Tundal of Cashel (A.D. 1149) than to Alberic that we are to turn for his source.[1]

"Cette Vision de Tondal est peut-être la plus célèbre de toutes, et fut traduite dans la plupart des langues de l'Europe. Par ses détails, c'est une autre 'Divine Comédie' en prose. . . . . Il est même des passages où, le mérite du style à part, Tondal présente des images plus terribles et plus justes."[2]

It is, however, the opinion of Dean Plumtre[3] that there is no ground even for imputing to Dante any conscious reproduction from the works of those who had preceded him in recording their visions of the Unseen World. "His position is simply that of one who, like all great poets, is the heir of the ages that have preceded him. The supreme artificer uses all materials that he finds ready to hand. Whatever was grotesque, horrible, or foul in the mediæval conceptions of the Unseen World, no less than what was pure, bright, transcendent in its beauty, was likely to find its way into his treasure-house of things new and old, and to be used by him in the spirit of his own, and not of a later, generation."

An exhaustive study of the various incidents in the conceptions of hell and Satan, of heaven and the angels, that appear in these pre-Dantesque works would be of the deepest interest, but

[1] Tundal—Tungalus. Dungal, or Donngal, was probably the real name. The name Donngal, as borne by a king of Cashel, A.D. 851, occurs in the "Annals of the Four Masters." The vision is said to have been written (? copied) by an Irish monk for an abbess in South Germany, who lived A.D. 1149, in the reign of King Stephen of England (Delepierre, pp. 64 and 78): and Prosper Marchand states that John 22nd based on the work of Tundal his doctrine that the faithful would not enjoy his beatitude, or the sinner suffer his chastisement, till after the last judgment.

[2] See "L'Enfer," p. 63.

[3] See "Commedia and Canzoniere of Dante Alighieri," translated by E. H. Plumtre, D.D., Dean of Wells, pp. 371, 373.

time and space will only allow us to consider a few of such which are common to those particular visions already named.

Thus we find that among the many points of resemblance between the incidents of Dante's hell, and those of these earlier visions, may be noted the Bridge of Dread by which the gulf is spanned. In the vision of Wettin of Reichenau (A.D. 824), we read of the bridge that led from the arid plain to the high marble mountains over the river of fire; and in the vision of Tundal, the long plank, but one foot in width, which spanned the dark abyss, whose depths resound with cries of tortured souls amid clouds of sulphurous smoke. This incident occurs also in the visions of Owen Miles and others, and the idea is borrowed, says J. Labitte, from Persian theogony, whence it has passed into the Koran. It is one of the first traces of the invasion of Oriental legend into the bosom of Christian tradition in the middle age.

Whitley Stokes has drawn attention to a similar incident in his notes on the "Vision of Adamnan" (see Appendix, "Vision of Adamnan").

The conception of hell with all these Irish seers differs essentially from that of the Scandinavian writers, in which fire and heat have no part. Their conception is of a hell of ice and snow, tempests and frozen torrents, and this is thus painted by Shakespeare.

> "To reside
> In thrilling regions of thick-ribbed ice,
> To be imprison'd in the viewless winds,
> And blown with restless violence round about
> The pendent world."[1]

In Adamnan's hell we have a wall of fire, a river of flame. In Fursa's, four fiery furnaces. Nor is the conception of the devil

[1] "Measure for Measure," Act iii., Sc. 1.

Scandinavian. The iconography of the devil in the Middle Ages, as we learn it in such frescoes as those of the Campo Santo at Pisa, and on the walls of Byzantine churches, is so strikingly similar to the pictures drawn by these Irish writers that we are tempted to assign to them a common origin. These devils are black, long-necked, scranny, pot-headed, unclean, horrible, flying shadows flitting through flame; and the devil is called the Adversary, the old Accuser, and compared to a crushed snake with an envenomed head, followed by satellites who quote Scripture, and whose words distil a viper-like poison.[1]

Again, in the conception of heaven, the mediæval ideal of an inclosed space, hedged round by a very great and lofty wall without any aperture, occurs in Drihthelm's poem, while in that of Fursa no mention of walls or hedges is to be found. Heaven is seen as a flowery plain, with shady bowers in full sunshine, and the air full of harmonious voices mingling with the exhalation of a thousand perfumes.

In the vision of St. Sauve, recorded by Gregory of Tours, as occurring in 584, which precedes that of Fursa by about twenty years, we find that the revelation was much more of heaven than of hell; but his heaven is also an inclosed place, entered through a shining gate with golden floor. A great multitude, whose voice was as the voice of many waters, stand upon its golden floor, in the midst of ineffable light; and his body is so fed on perfume that he needs neither food nor drink. Another vision of heaven is given by Anschar at Corbie. With him the blessed were clothed in radiant clouds taking the form of the human body; and here a beautiful incident in the vision of Fursa is repeated, when a voice full of melody and sweetness is heard to say, "Return to earth, and stay till purified by martyrdom, and then come back to us;" and the writer adds, "my angel guide looked on me tenderly

[1] See "Christian Iconography," Bohn, vol. ii., p. 126.

as a mother gazes on her sleeping child, and my soul returned to its earthly habitation."

By the angels of Fursa's vision we are again reminded of the iconography of the Campo Santo; they appear as winged hands and winged faces, whose bodies are invisible, lost in dazzling light, or winged birds with human faces.

> "As more and more toward us came, more bright
> Appeared the bird of God."

Besides the bodiless winged heads, there are three angels who protect and guide St. Fursa on his way through hell, and his approach to heaven. We may believe them to have been endowed with noble form and countenance, in their presence the flames of hell can do him no hurt, and one of them, armed with shield and sword, who goes before, is Michael. We cannot remember any passage in early Christian poetry showing a finer ideal of the mission and the ministry of angels than that (in c. 14) which is conveyed in the angel's answer to Fursa, when he, rapt in the beauty of the heavenly music, as it swells upon his ear, says, half in wonder, half in envy, "It is great joy to hear these songs." To whom the angel of the Lord replied: "We may not often hear them. We are the ministers of man, and we must toil and labour in his service, lest demons destroying human hearts should make our labour vain." This calls to mind a passage in the "Vision of Adamnan" where the seven thousand angels are described who spread their light and radiance through the heavenly city, and to whom the mission is given to minister to those who do not reach that city, but who yet are predestined to attain its blessedness. These men the angels haunt, "changefully and restlessly, in heights and in hills, in moors and in morasses, till doom shall come to them." Even thus are those hosts and their assemblies, and a comrade angel in lowliness and attendance on every single soul that is therein.

And now I must ask you to forgive me for the undue length to which this letter has run. My only excuse is the great desire I feel that I should leave no point neglected which may awaken your interest in a subject that has been a source of pure delight to myself; and none the less so because I have learned that the more we search into the past history of the inhabitants of Great Britain and Ireland, their arts and customs, the more we perceive the unity that prevailed among them; and that it is because their occasional differences were the exception, not the rule, that historians have hitherto given such differences undue prominence.

Although the nature of my subject has compelled me to confine myself to Ireland, yet you will find many indications throughout these pages of the friendly intercourse, the unity of aim, similarity of customs that prevailed in Ireland, Scotland, and England in the seventh century.[1] If Anglo-Saxons visited the schools of the west of Ireland, Irishmen in their turn travelled to East Anglia, and entered into the labours of the early teachers of Christianity there. When the Irish Mauguille retires to his hermitage in Picardy, it is the British Wulgan from Canterbury who crosses the sea to soothe his later days. If an Irishman be the patron of Péronne, yet Irish, Scotch, and English together frequented the monastery there, through subsequent centuries, and were all classed by the natives of the place under the one word British; while to this day that part of the town they occupied is called the British quarter, and the old gate through which these travellers entered is styled Porte de Brétagne. And while we exalt the beauty of our early Irish art, it must never be forgotten that the Gaulish patron of art, St. Eloi, had Teilo the

[1] It is known that Aldfrid, King of Northumbria, when in exile, was educated in Ireland (*circa* 685), and, while living there, was named Flann Finna. A very ancient Irish poem said to be written by him in praise of Ireland is still extant. See "Story of Early Gaelic Literature," by Douglas Hyde, LL.D., p. 17.

Anglo-Saxon as partner in his labours, and his assistant in those wonderful works in jewellery and metal-work whose fame has descended to the present day. This Teilo succeeded Eloi as Master of the Mint, and ended his days with Eloi, labouring as a Christian missionary at the same time, and in the same fields, as St. Fursa and his companions. It is well to keep these facts in our mind if we would be saved from that spirit of exclusive patriotism which seeks to exalt our own country at the expense of our neighbours. It is while keeping clear of all such narrow tendencies that I again invite you to follow me in thought to those foreign scenes where the influence of Ireland for good was strong in the distant past. We must gather up the threads of my story where I laid them down in the scenes of Columban's life in France, and I ask you now to come with me to the forests of Luxeuil and Ardennes.

LIFE OF ST. COLUMBAN IN FRANCE.

CIRCA 574-595.

November 12th.

AUTHORITIES.

The monk Jonas of Bobio, "Life of Columban." "Life of Columban," by an anonymous writer, see Fleming's "Collectanea," p. 244. "Mirac. S. Columb. transumpta ex MS. Codice Bibl. D. Thuani in suprema Gallicarum." Colgan, "A. SS. Hib.," 117, 157, c. 12; "Trias Thaum.," 88, c. 98, 113, 110. Gregory of Tours, "Hist. des Francs." Guizot, "Coll." i. 11. Fredegarius, "Chron. Gallic. Rer. Script.," ii. Guizot, "Coll. des Mém.," ii.

THE reader will remember that when writing five years ago from Italy about the traces of Columban still to be found in the Apennines, I was compelled, by the nature of my subject, to curtail my notes on that portion of his life spent in Gaul before he entered Italy, my primary object then being to trace the vestiges of these Irish missionaries in Italy, as it now is to seek for such in France. We must therefore return to that period in the life of Columban when he and Deicola dwelt in Burgundy, and founded the churches of Annegrai, Luxeuil, Fontaines, and Lure.[1]

The fame of the baths of Luxeuil in the Department of Haute-Saône is said to date from a very remote period. Long before Julius Cæsar came into Gaul the virtue of its waters had been discovered by the people of Sequania, as the district in which it stands was named. It was in the year 58 B.C. that the Roman general chose the fertile plains of Sequania as winter quarters for his legions. The Roman dominion, then commencing in Gaul, lasted for about five centuries. The native proprietors of the land were renowned for their wealth, their rich

[1] See "Six Months in the Apennines," pp. 112-117.

possessions stretching from the mountains of the Jura in smiling plains, watered by broad rivers, and beautiful in their varied culture. In the second and third centuries Christianity slowly penetrated to these districts, and insensibly extended its branches to Autun, Besançon, Dijon, Langres, Châlons, Toul, Metz, Trèves, and Strasburg. Although, at first, Rome ruled by force alone, yet the Sequanais were gradually won over, more by the softening effects of civilization than by arms, while the Romans associated them in the rights of citizens, and in political dignity, even opening to them a seat in the Senate.

The first half of this long period was comparatively prosperous and happy, but the second was one long series of terrible disasters following on the Germanic invasions. The progress of Christianity was arrested, and all development paralyzed. In the second half of the third century (A.D. 260-268) the Rhine was crossed by the barbarians, and all the provinces on the borders of the river, especially Sequania, were devastated. Then A.D. 275-276 seventy-five Gaulish cities fell before Germanic tribes, who for two years unceasingly ravaged the country. A.D. 293-297 came another swarm of Germans, who were met at Langres, and afterwards in the field of Windisch, by the Emperor Constantius Chlorus. In the years 304, 350, 355, 357 successive invasions took place, when Besançon was ruined, Sequania depopulated, and the enemy penetrated to Lyons. In 378 the lands of Sequania are described as one vast solitude, in which no trace of the reign of the Emperors was to be found. Two more invasions followed, and then, in 451, the advance of Attila dealt the final blow to the province of Sequania.[1]

Like the desolating march of a hurricane his wild hordes swept all before them in their advance. Religious teaching died out among the hunted, scattered people to whom hearth and home were known no more, and the historians of Sequania can find no colours black enough in which to paint their dark and mournful picture. Besançon, Luxeuil, Mandeure, Seveux, and a number of other cities were nothing then but heaps of cinders.' The ranks of the clergy were thinned, churches and schools levelled to the ground, all effort at instruction ceased, and no attempt

[1] "Histoire des SS. de Franche Comté," vol. i., p. 12, Besançon.

was made to restore these ruins. If Faith still breathed, yet all religious service was abolished, as Jonas[1] has witnessed: "Gaul, where, then, either by reason of the number of foreign invaders, or on account of the negligence of the governors, religion and virtue were almost held to be abolished."

Luxeuil (Luxovium) was one of the first places conquered by Attila and his Huns. The Roman garrisons along the eastern frontier of Gaul, too feeble to resist so formidable a foe, retreated to meet and concentrate their forces beyond the Loire, and, joined by the Franks and Visigoths, these armies ranged themselves under the banner of Aetius, the Roman commander. The ruin of Luxeuil was complete. The enemy was attracted to its defenceless walls by rumours of the former celebrity of the town, of the wealth of its inhabitants, and the splendour with which the Romans had invested it. The moat was filled up, the walls were scaled, and the Huns, masters of the city, giving the reins to their wild passions, pitilessly massacred the inhabitants, burnt their temples, and broke their idols. This struggle, unlike that with the Romans, found no peaceful solution, led to no further development. The saying arose that the grass once trodden by the feet of Attila's horse never was green again. The country became one vast desert, the forests spread beyond their fences, while within the ruined city the marbles that had once adorned their thermæ and gymnasium, the statues of the gods that had been worshipped in their temples, now cast to the earth, were overgrown with brambles, or buried in the débris of her ruined walls; and soon all traces of culture, science, art, and even of religion, disappeared, while the people roamed half naked amid the wreck, and still trembled at the name of Attila.

Paganism thus gradually regained its ground, and this condition of things seems to have remained unchanged at Luxeuil till Columban reached Sequania in the year 574. In no other part of the province had the passage of the barbarians wrought more profound and ineradicable change than here, at the foot of the Vosges mountains, on the border-land of Austrasia and Burgundy, where lay this vast extent of country covered by forests, and almost solely peopled by wild animals; and in this

[1] The biographer of St. Columban. "Vit." c. xi.

one city of Luxeuil, once so flourishing, founded by the Celts, re-established by the Romans, enriched by its salutary thermal springs, which had now become but a heap of shapeless ruin.

When Columban reached this country there stood in a valley, some fifteen miles distant from Luxeuil, the ruins of an ancient fort named Annegrai, and on the summit of the mountain, now dedicated to St. Martin, rose a Gaulish temple to Diana, near the wood of Jupiter. The fort, or Castrum Anagrates, was enclosed by strong walls. Jonas, the friend and biographer of Columban tells us, "it had once been protected by very strong fortifications; wild animals used to resort there." Here, amid mountains, barren rocks, and forests, the Irish missionary and his companions established themselves about the year 574, and remained till he founded the monastery in the more central and less secluded situation of Luxeuil.[1]

Here Columban wrought many wonderful cures through the power of his prayers; here he and his brethren endured starvation, and were only saved from death by feeding on wild fruits and herbs. In his wanderings through the mountains that surround this valley he found the cave near the summit of a hill to which he was wont to retire, having driven away the wolf which had made it its lair. Here he struck the rock and opened the fountain that is still held sacred by the peasants around.

But as his school at Annegrai increased in numbers the saint was encouraged to found another in a more central situation, and less difficult of access. A glance at the map of M. Le Clerc[2] will prove to us why Luxeuil was the place of his choice. The meeting of many Roman roads at this point, and the communication by water in the neighbourhood, made it a fitting centre for a great school. One road extended north to Plombières, where there were also ancient baths, and south to Vesontio (Besançon), the capital of the Sequanaise. It followed the Breuchin river (Brixia) to the suburban village of Baudoncourt, where the pavement of the road was lately discovered in the garden of the Mayor. From Baudoncourt it passed south to

[1] For the events of Columban's life at Annegrai, see "Six Months in the Apennines," pp. 114-125.

[2] "La Franche Comté à l'époque Romaine," p. 127, par Ed. Le Clerc, Besançon, 1853.

Villeneuve, and the fourth Roman entrenchment near Villers-les-Luxeuil, where the rampart is still in places some nine feet high; from Vesoul, due south to Quenoche, where there is an ancient entrenchment. At Vesoul there stood a Roman camp and temple of Cybele. At a place called La Motte, there was on the road a temple of Mars, and, in the ruins of a priory, at the foot of a hill, a stone was found, which once formed the keystone of the church door, and bore this remarkable inscription:

"Non amplius Marti, sed Christo Deo vero."

The road then passes on to Rioz, and between this and the point at which it crosses the river Ognon, it appears as a causeway, six feet six and a half inches high, then enters the long narrow valley leading to Voray. Here its traces are visible, and Roman ruins scattered through the woods mark its direction. Having crossed the Ognon, it passes in a straight line to Miseray. At Mailleroncourt a branch goes in a direct line due west to Port-sur-Saône, the famous *Portus Abucinus*, whence water communication was carried on by the Saône, the Rhône, and the Mediterranean, to Rome itself. In the words of Strabo:

"Whoever fixes his attention on the disposition of these territories will see that it is not the result of mere chance, but of a special providence. For the Rhône is navigable for a long distance upwards by ships with heavy cargoes, which they distribute throughout various countries, since the rivers which fall into the Rhône are also navigable, and capable of floating heavy burdens. The Saône and its tributary, the Doubs, will also receive such cargoes." [1]

The town of *Portus Abucinus* was the last on the river following it towards its source.

The most ancient literary evidence that we possess of the existence of these Roman towns is to be found in the life of St. Columban, written by his friend Jonas. Thus, in the following passage he describes Annegrai, and how the saint quitted it for Luxeuil (Luxovium).

Columban stayed "in a great wilderness called Vosagus, in which there was once a camp,[2] now in ruins, to which ancient

[1] Strab., "Géogr.," l. iv.
[2] Castrum. "Vit. S. Col. (Surius)," Nov. 21, t. vi., p. 533.

tradition gave the name Anagrates. And when the saint reached it, although the places were wild, and notwithstanding their extreme solitude and the hindrance of the rocks, yet here he settled with his people. . . . He found that this camp had once been protected by very strong fortifications, and was eight miles, more or less, distant from the place above mentioned [*i.e.* Luxeuil]. Wild animals used to roam there. . . ."

Then turning to Luxeuil he says: "Eight miles, more or less, distant from the place above mentioned was that which in ancient times they called Luxovium. A camp in the desert amid vast walls, but these now gone to ruin in old age."[1] And he adds, "Here there used to be warm baths [lit. waters], built with extraordinary magnificence, and there were many stone statues there, to which the pagans had formerly rendered a profane and criminal worship, honouring them with execrable ceremonies, *execrabilibus eas cærimoniis prosequentes*."[2] And again he says: "Here the groves were thick with crowds of stone images, which the heathen in old times used to honour with wretched worship and profane rites." "But," he adds, "then [*i.e.*, at the time when Columban settled there] there were only wild beasts, bears, buffaloes, and wolves; they were to be found in numbers."[3]

So also in the life of Columban's disciple, Agilus,[4] we read of Luxeuil as that "Castra vasta" enwalled in the desert, and then in ruins to the very ground.

The truth of these things related by Columban to his friend Jonas more than twelve hundred years ago in the valley of the Apennines where he told the story of his life, is proved by such examples of the ancient art of Luxeuil as I have illustrated here.[5] From a depth of six feet six inches, and beneath a layer of cinders

[1] According to the legend of St. Gall. "*Locus muris antiquitus septus, sed jam vetustate collapsus.*"

[2] This passage is quoted by M. Breuil ("Mém. de la Soc. des Antiquaires de Picardie," xxii., p. 61), as indicating that the Burgundians in the time of St. Columban had introduced the worship of the waters of Luxeuil into their devotions, and in this instance finds the first vestige of the worship of medicinal waters on the soil of France.

[3] Jonæ Bobiensis, "Vita S. Columbani," cap 17. In "Act. Bened.," 2, 12, 13.

[4] "Vit. S. Agili," ch. 2, "AA. SS.," Aug. 27th.

[5] See also E. Desjardin's "Monum. des Thermes Romains de Luxeuil," Paris, 1880.

and charcoal, forming, as it were, the winding-sheet in which these figures were embedded, have come forth statues, bas-reliefs, tombs, and marble busts, broken capitals and shafts of columns,

Fig. 9.—GALLO-ROMAN TOMB FOUND AT LUXEUIL.

arms, medals, bronze statuettes, embossed tiles, and clay vases of various forms; and second to none in interest are the various inscriptions found on tombs and pillar stones.

As works of art, however, these Gallo-Roman monuments are far surpassed in beauty and nobility of character by a bust now stored in an upper room, amid much rubbish, in the Hôtel de Ville of Luxeuil. It was discovered during recent excavations, the head separated from the shoulders, but without other serious injury. This bust has not yet been identified; the method of wearing the hair has given rise to the suggestion that Lucius Verus was represented here, but on this question I have the following opinion from Sir Frederic Burton:

"That bust cannot, in my opinion, represent Lucius Verus. The handsome, vicious and utterly abandoned profligate whom Marcus Aurelius raised to be his associate on the throne, had features entirely different from those of the bust, as seen in the photograph. The coiffure and growth of the slender beard give indeed at first sight a certain sort of resemblance to the heads of Lucius Verus. But these things were the fashion of the times of the Antonines. The heroically sized head of Lucius Verus, which is a superb piece of sculpture, now in the Louvre, is the type of all the other busts of Lucius Verus, but finer than the rest. A marked feature in all is the shape of the eyebrows, which, lowly arched on the outer sides, curve suddenly downwards to the root of the nose, and meet there, giving a very peculiar character to the face. Very picturesque, but not morally promising in man or woman."

As will be seen from the photograph, no sudden curve down to the nose from the eyebrow is visible in this bust, and there is a remarkable distance between the eyes and nose. Whoever the original of this portrait bust may have been, the paramount interest and profound import of this discovery beneath the soil of Luxeuil remains the same (fig. 10).

There is a story in the face that might appeal to any earnest man, irrespective of his creed. If Columban saw this face, and the thing is not impossible, was his untrained eye wholly incapable of beholding in its expression that which might indeed have awakened his deepest sympathy? The profound sadness born of the failure of all earthly hope, the earnest searching after a higher revelation, seem to have left their mark here. If he saw this laurel-crowned head, half hidden in the ruins of the gymnasium, did he only rank it with those other statues that he speaks of as "objects of wretched worship and profane rites"? Or did he behold the struggle in which he was engaged under a new and different light? Here, his was the rude, untutored mind, as compared with that

Fig. 10. – BUST FOUND AMID RUINS OF GYMNASIUM, LUXEUIL.

before him. And yet in his heart lay the power that was to satisfy those yearnings, and bring hope where despair had entered in.

When Columban had once established his monastery within the precincts of this ruined Gallo-Roman castrum, he proceeded to the composition of his Rule, as I have already described;[1] and when this Rule had been for some years in practice, and the fame of his monastery spread throughout the kingdom of the Franks, the native bishops observed with jealousy that these Irish teachers adhered to the old Jewish and Roman cycle which they had received with Patrick, ignoring the fact that the Roman Church had altered the time for the observation of Easter. So much has been written by all historians of the Irish Church on this Paschal controversy that it is not necessary to enter into the particulars of it here. It created great hostility among the native bishops to the Irish missionaries in Luxeuil, and drew forth several letters from Columban, which are still extant, addressed to a Frankish synod and to Pope Gregory I. In this we see the struggle in the old man's fiery nature to have been a severe one between a passionate clinging to his native customs and traditions, and the equally passionate devotion to his Master's religion of brotherly love and submission. "Let us live here in Gaul," he said, "in like peace with you as we hope to live in eternally in heaven; but if it be God's will that ye drive me from this wilderness whither I have come so far for the sake of Jesus Christ, I shall say with the prophet, 'If for my sake this great tempest is upon you, take me up and cast me forth into the sea.'"

In addition to this controversy came the still more terrible struggle with immorality and tyranny in which he was finally driven from the country. It was his hard fate to have lived through the worst period of the Merovingian wars, and to have come in contact with Queen Brunehilde at that period in her life when ambition and unbridled passion had overcome the nobler instincts of her nature.

Her husband, Sigibert, had been slain by the poisoned daggers of Fredegonda's hired assassins; Brunehilde, his widowed queen,

[1] See "Six Months in the Apennines," p. 117.

had been imprisoned; their young child, Childebert, proclaimed King of Austrasia when his mother, having effected her escape after a prolonged struggle, turned the scale against her hated rival. Fredegonda put her own step-children to death by poison, torture, and the stake, and was even accused of having connived at the death of her husband, Chilperic. Brunehilde took her husband's nephew Merovig in marriage, who was slain, as some thought, by the connivance of Fredegonda, his step-mother. At the early death of her son by Sigibert, her grandchild succeeded Theodebert in the government of Austrasia, and his brother Theodoric became King of Burgundy. During their minority Brunehilde reigned over both kingdoms. She lived at first with Theodebert, till driven into Burgundy, where she gave herself up to conspiracy, and even fomented an unnatural warfare between the brothers Theodebert and Theodoric. In her passion for sway she would have continued to govern both her sons, and both their kingdoms, but Theodebert had found a wife who had secured his affection, and Brunehilde was banished from that court. She then came to live with Theodoric, and succeeded in taking the reins of government out of his hand, all the more easily because this young king was given over to dissipation and all the vices of his age, and he, caring only for pleasure, handed all the duties of his government over to Brunehilde, who, in order to gratify her own lust of power, encouraged him in his weakness instead of striving to arouse his sense of honour and virtue.

The good dispositions and religious training Theodoric had received in youth, were not, all at once, extinguished by such vices. And these good influences were sustained by the high esteem in which he held St. Columban, then living within the borders of his kingdom of Burgundy. Him he both loved and reverenced, and he was often guided to acts of mercy by his counsel and intercession. Hence he sought his presence frequently, either calling him to his court, or repairing himself to the monastery where he communed with him. The saint took advantage of these kindly dispositions, not only for the benefit of his monks and the spiritual welfare of the people and Church, but also from consideration for the king himself, and, strong in that liberty and freedom of the Gospel which is the heritage of saints, he was never weary of rebuking the king's vices, and striving to open his eyes to the weakness of his conduct. Thus he showed him how scandalous in the eyes of all his subjects it must be to know, that instead of having an honourable wife, and one worthy of his race, he should keep low women in his court, by no one of whom he could ever give to his kingdom a successor worthy of the esteem and love of his people. With these and other arguments Columban strove to influence the king's mind, until he at last induced him to wed the Princess Irmengarde, daughter of Bertericus, King of Spain.

The noble gifts and rare virtue of the new queen were enough to win the heart of Theodoric, and the suspicions of the ambitious Brunehilde were aroused, which led her to fear that through the influence of Irmengarde she would lose her place in the government of the kingdom. History does not record all the arts she used to blacken the character of the queen, and to alienate the affections of the king from his wife, but the fact remains that she succeeded in doing so. In a short time the tender affection inspired by his young wife in Theodoric's heart turned to unconcealed hate, and repudiating her within a year, he sent her back to her father, and returned to his evil ways.

Columban, who up to this time had watched the infirmities of Theodoric as a true friend, did not desert him in his fall, and, finding that no loving exhortation had power to recall him to the right path, he denounced his life of sin with all the fervour of a Hebrew prophet, and the fire of an Apostle. Finding the king's nature was now saturated with evil passion, he did not fail to thunder forth on more than one occasion that *Non licet tibi habere uxorem fratris tui* which the Baptist had already sounded in the ears of Herod, and ended by announcing to him that never should one of his children, born in sin, reign in his stead. But notwithstanding these bold denunciations, which harrowed the king's mind, Theodoric ceased not to love and to respect the holy abbot who still came often to his court to admonish and rebuke him. The constancy of such mutual affection between the king and Columban was displeasing to Brunehilde, who dreaded lest the influence of the saint should lead him to recall his banished wife, Irmengarde, and thus put an end to her own rule. Therefore she set to work to render him also odious to the king, and the historian Jonas has preserved for us the account of her success.

One day the saint arrived at the Court of Bucheresse (a royal palace between Châlons and Autun). Brunehilde seized the occasion to introduce four children to him, the natural sons of Theodoric, as she desired him to give them his blessing. For she argued thus: either he will bless them, and by so doing will contradict all his previous declamations, or if he refuse I shall have good cause in hand wherewith to excite the anger of the king against him. She did not deceive herself. The saint asked what she desired as regarding these children. "They are the king's sons," answered the aged queen; "I present them now that they may gain thy benediction." The saint refused, and, speaking in the voice of a prophet, he said, "Know that these children shall never reign, for they are the fruit of dishonest passion."

Brunehilde, furious, withdrew, and the saint departed. As he left the palace, the building was shaken to its foundations, and it seemed as though they would be buried in its ruins. No sooner had he crossed the threshold than he heard a roar like thunder in the palace which filled the people in its outer court with terror, yet did not shake the spirit of the evil queen. She still cast new toils around the king, and plotted for the disgrace and banishment of the saint from court. Yet she treated him with all appearance of esteem, so as to conceal the venom of her hate. Although she knew that Columban admitted none but men within his cloister, yet she demanded entrance at the gate. The saint, as she expected, refused her admission. She complained to the king that she had been insulted, and gave orders that no communication should be held with the monastery, nor should anything be given to the monks.

Columban, learning these things, sought out the king, whom he found at Epoisses (a palace between Avallon and Semur), which place he reached in the evening. Contrary to his usual practice he refrained from entering the palace. Word was brought to the king that the man of God stood at the gate.

"Better," said the king, "to come to the saint's assistance than to offend God by insulting his servants." Then, conscious on the one hand of the hatred of Brunchilde for the saint, and, on the other, wishing to greet him in kindness, and unwilling to draw down the chastisement of God upon his head for doing his servant wrong, he ordered that a regal repast should be carried outside to the saint. This being done, Columban demanded the meaning of this show. The servants of the palace answered, that it was a feast prepared for him by order of the king. The food was rejected indignantly. "God refuses the gifts of the impious. Never shall His servant's mouth be soiled by forbidden fruit, not in his own house, neither in the house of another. I shall not soil my mouth with the meats of those who forbid the servants of God to enter their doors or those of others." Thus saying, he seized the cups and vases and flung the wine upon the ground and scattered the rest in fragments. The servants, in their terror and astonishment, hastened back to the king, and prayed that he would induce the saint to enter the palace. So that, next morning early, Brunehilde and the king went to the servant of the Lord, calling on him to pardon the outrage, and promising to amend their ways. Columban, thus soothed and hopeful, once more returned to his monastery, but it was not long before he learned that the penitence of these royal personages was but the effect of momentary terror, since Brunehilde only conceived a still more ardent hatred for the saint, and a stronger desire to stifle the voice that was raised against her ambition, and Theodoric returned to his evil ways.

The abbot, believing that he could not now succeed by his own personal influence in turning them from infidelity and crime, resolved to write in a strong tone of indignation, and menace the king with excommunication if he did not amend.[1] The imperious Brunehilde, rather than repent, seized on this act as another incitement and means of irritating the mind of Theodoric against the saint. She guessed that it would only help to inflame the monarch's anger, and she roused all the foremost men at the court as well as in the kingdom, so that all

[1] According to the ancient discipline of the Church, whoever had the power (*facoltà*) of confession, also held that of excommunication, but only in the inner tribunal (*ma solo nel foro interno*). It may also be understood, that this only meant exclusion from public preaching and the reading of the diptychs in the Canon of the Mass.—Gianelli, "Vita di San Colombano," p. 79. Torino, 1844.

cried out against the saint. She even attempted to seduce the bishops, and, affecting a great zeal for religion, she led them on to believing that they should no longer tolerate the presence of a man who followed foreign rites, and thus promoted schism in the Church.

Notwithstanding this dark and prolonged conspiracy, it was not easy to induce Theodoric to drive such a man as Columban with violence from his kingdom, one who had so clearly enjoyed the protection of heaven.

Complaints then arose on all hands of the custom he introduced of denying seculars admission to the cloister; and the native monks, with Brunehilde and her minions, determined finally to go in a body and compel the saint to break this rule in the observance of his institution, under peril of banishment from the kingdom.

Columban tried to show them why it was not desirable to yield this point to laymen, who were often without religion, and therefore not suited for such intimate daily communion with monks; that he had never been accustomed to it, nor did he believe it advisable; but he approved of exercising all duties of hospitality, and in his own monastery there were apartments set aside for the reception of all conditions of men. The king, taking part in the dispute, not seeming convinced by these wise explanations, answered, "If you wish for my goodwill, open the doors to all." "And I tell you," said the saint, "if you force an entrance into this place, the privacy of which has hitherto been respected, henceforth I will accept neither your gifts or your favours; and if you come here to destroy our monasteries and to violate our rules, know that your kingdom will fall, and your race be annihilated." [1]

Theodoric, breaking through the enclosure, had already reached the refectory. But the abbot, imperturbable and strong in spirit, was not to be thus slighted, nor did he yield. "Know, sire," he repeated, addressing the king, "that if thou comest here as one who intends to disturb the peace of the servants of God, and to conspire against their discipline, soon shall thy kingdom

[1] It appears that it was the ancient practice, though not observed by the monks of Burgundy, to refuse admission to seculars in the inner cloisters of the monasteries.—Della Torre, "Vita di S. Colombano," cap. vii.

be torn away from thee, and thine inheritance be snatched from thy race."

Thus, for the first time did the saint prophesy his tragic end to the king, in words which were soon to be verified. These threats, uttered in a prophetic and menacing tone, arrested the king; he did not dare to continue his progress, and he drew back with trembling steps.

But Columban, in the heat of his fervid passion, ceased not to threaten and rebuke as he followed him in hot pursuit, till at last the king turned on him and said, "It is clear to me that thou, Columban, art seeking still another benefit from me. Thou dost hope to gain the crown of martyrdom from my hand, but thou shalt not have it. No, I am not so senseless as to let myself be drawn into so great a crime. I have a wiser plan for you, and since you will not suffer the society of laymen here, I will see that you return back to that land from whence you came." Then all the court echoed the king's words with applause, saying they would no longer endure a man among them who refused them free admission to his cloisters. Such words were powerless to move the holy abbot, who then proclaimed, in presence of the king, that he would never leave his monastery till he was driven thence by force, since he was placed there by the will of God.

The king seeing how firm and resolute the saint was, did not wish to answer him again. But he was fixed in his determination to drive him out of his monastery, and charging Baudulfus, one of the nobles of his court, to conduct the saint to a new institution at Besançon, he angrily departed.

Columban was attended by Domoalis, or Dogmael, on the way to Besançon, where he was to await the further orders of the king. The great soul of Columban had lost nothing of its courage and its peace. On reaching the city he was told that its prisons were filled to overflowing with criminals condemned to death; and his first act was to walk to the prison doors, which opened miraculously at his approach, and he entered in to preach the Word of God to its immates. The prisoners, converted, vowed that if ever they were restored to liberty they would expiate their sins by a better life. On this Columban desired Dogmael to loose their chains; scarcely had the young monk touched them than they broke asunder and fell to the ground. Then Columban bathed their feet with his own hands, and bade them go confess their sins in church.

The rumour of these things soon spread through the city, where Columban was already known. He had long been the friend of St. Nicetas, then the Bishop of Besançon, who welcomed him with every sign of his esteem and love, eager to console him, rejoicing in his converse with him, so that to Columban, when under his

Fig. 11.—HILL OF THE CITADEL.

roof, it seemed rather that he had entered into heaven than into exile.

Nicetas had commenced his duties as head of the church of Besançon at about the same time as Columban at Luxeuil, and when the buildings of the Irish monastery there were completed, Nicetas came by invitation of Columban to pronounce a solemn benediction on the undertaking. It was Nicetas who restored the church to Besançon, and destroyed its heresy; for after the town had been sacked by Attila the episcopal see was transferred to Nyon, a small town on the lake of Geneva, and the Burgundians had introduced the Arian heresy into Besançon, the old seat of Christianity. Therefore the experiences and difficulties encountered by these two friends, each in their separate sphere, were much alike. Both were enthusiasts, disinterested and lofty in their aims, both gifted with eloquence, preachers of the Word, and faithful servants of the same Master.

But Columban still sighed after his monastery, nor could the friendship of Nicetas or the regard of the citizens console him for the absence of his own children ; and going out one Sunday to the summit of the hill on which the town was built, now the site of the Citadel, he looked across the plain towards Luxeuil, just visible on the horizon (fig. 11). The road was clear, no obstacle visible, yet he waited till midnight lest any witness should suspect and should betray him. Then descending to the town he bade the faithful Dogmael follow him, and in secret took the road to Luxeuil, where they arrived to the astonishment and joy of the disciples.

Theodoric and Brunehilde were infuriated when the report of this event reached their ears. By counsel of the queen, the king ordered one of his officers to seize the saint in his monastery and again lead him into exile, but this time he was to be sent back to Ireland.

Henceforth the saint crossed her path no more. Led out of Gaul by the Loire he re-entered it by the dominions of Clothair II., who gave him an honourable reception, and he passed through the north-east of France, as we have already related,[1] to the Rhine, ascending the river to Switzerland, and thence made his way to Italy.

The fate of the terrible queen who had driven him into banishment was far different from his. Brunehilde was at last utterly deserted, hated by the Austrasian nobles, while regarded by priests and people with horror as the persecutor of the saints; and yet so shocking was the barbarity with which she was treated that our sympathies are awakened for her in the end. We ought not to forget that the use she had made of the money she had wrung from her subjects by extortion and cruelty was not without glory and

[1] See "Six Months in the Apennines," p. 138.

grandeur. She had founded numerous churches and monasteries and schools. She had favoured the mission sent by the Pope for the conversion of the Anglo-Saxons; but then, in order to make head against Clothair, she had called in German aid, and she therefore died the death of a traitress. She, the aged queen, the daughter, sister, mother, grandmother of a long line of kings, was taken and fastened by the hair and tied foot and arm to the tail of a wild horse, which was set free, and dragged her to pieces. As Michelet writes, so profound was the impression left by her long reign that the memory of the Roman Empire itself in Gaul seems to have been weakened, and the people ascribe to this famous Queen of Austrasia a number of monuments which were in reality Roman. Remains of Roman roads still met with in the north of France are called Chaussées Brunehaut; and, near Bourges, the Château Brunehaut is shown; at Estampes her tower may still be seen; near Tournay there is the Stone of Brunehaut; and the Fort of Brunehaut near Cahors on the road from Orleans to Toulouse; while a huge sarcophagus is still shown in St. Martin's Church at Autun as the tomb of Brunehilde.

This last monument consists of the fragments of various Roman monuments. It is formed of massive slabs of black marble veined with white, of great antiquity, the lid of which, judging by its form and material, must be the work of a period anterior to that of the Merovingians. The coffin is of white limestone taken from another tomb, and the little columns of dark grey marble which support it, have evidently been derived from still another source.[1]

[1] See "Mém. lus à la Sorbonne," tom. I. Bulliot, "Notice sur un Sarcophage en marbre blanc du Musée d'Autun."

LETTERS FROM LUXEUIL,

WRITTEN TO THE FRIENDS WHO FORM THE CHURCH HISTORY CLASS IN THE LITERARY SOCIETY OF ALEXANDRA COLLEGE, DUBLIN.

Maison Jouffroi,
Luxeuil,
Haute-Saône,
April 25th.

DEAR E.,

AT last I have reached Luxeuil. I left Laon and reached this charming old town at half past two o'clock. As I approached Columban's country I tried to realize what its aspect must have been in his day. This is not so easy here as it was in Bobio, where the everlasting hills stood around in their unchanging majesty. Here, where all was forest once, we have wide plains extending to the horizon, and long straight roads bordered with lines of tall poplars, but this is only to the south and west; in other directions the forests of the Jura still hold their ground, and the woods to the north of Luxeuil are an outlying portion of these forests. In former days they were interspersed with lakes and ponds. Among the Celts such lakes were consecrated to divinities, and the worship of the god of waters is often found associated with that of woodland nymphs. Thus the woods around Luxeuil were held sacred, and pagan ceremonials practised in them down to the Middle Ages, and the name of the river Breuchin, on which the town is built, is derived from Brixia, a Celtic goddess of waters. The forest of St. Walbert, which extends to the north of Luxeuil, is a portion of that ancient forest

Fig. 12.—LUXEUIL FROM THE FOREST.

which once covered the western slopes of the mountains of the Vosges, where they meet the Jura range, and which, having once scaled the summits of the Jura, descends into Switzerland on the other side. Sitting on a height on the outer edge of this forest of St. Walbert, the eye ranges over a vast horizon, to the north-east of which rise the mountains of the Vosges, and the rounded summits of the Ballons Servances, and the mountain above Annegrai, with its chapel of St. Martin standing clear against the blue sky; then along the fertile plain watered by the river Breuchin, to where rises in the far distance, like a tiny islet in a sea of verdure, the perpendicular height crowned by the chapel of St. Roch. The golden green of the meadows, and the purplish tinge of the fields of luzerne, are relieved by the dark fir-trees stretching in horizontal bands across the scene. Here the houses of Luxeuil begin to appear, most picturesque in the variety of colour and form of their roofs. Rising from the midst of the town, to the right, is to be seen the old church tower built by Abbé Jean de la Palud in 1527, the original spire of which was destroyed in 1680. This is the sole survivor of the three fine belfries which once rose above the old church of Luxeuil. In the immediate foreground lie the two cemeteries of the town; the numerous crosses and groups of cypress-trees in that of the Christians make it easily distinguishable from that of the Jews with their plain headstones. I thought it was interesting to see the two graveyards thus side by side, and only divided by a low partition wall, overgrown by moss and bramble. In the centre of the large open fields that extend below the point on which we stand, a plain stone cross has been erected to mark the place where missions have been held, and open-air sermons preached from time to time (see fig. 12).

The road that enters the fir-wood near this point, and which may be seen winding through the trees towards the mountains, passes along the valley of the Breuchin, skirting the bases of the hills till it reaches Annegrai. This is the road by which we must travel when we start to explore the oldest remaining traces of Columban's first settlement here. Leaving Luxeuil by the Rue des Vosges, and travelling along this road, we pass the villages of Corvereine and Raddon, till we come to the ancient Celtic tumulus of Amage. We then reach the village of Sainte-Marie-en-Chanois, or Saint Mary of the Oak-wood, where we begin the walk up the mountain to the chapel, the cave, and the holy well of St. Columban. I got a little girl for my guide, and climbed the mountain by a steep stony path till we reached the oak-wood which still covers its summit. The child told me she was sorry I had not come the week before, when the good curé of Sainte-Marie-en-Chanois led a grand procession of the villagers and peasants from the valley, with banners and pictures, up the mountain to the chapel of St. Columban. "And why on that particular day was this procession?" I asked. "To pray the saint to intercede for rain; the season has been so dry."

Here is an instance, I thought to myself, of a survival of a middle age custom common to the inhabitants of both northern and southern Europe, where the Virgin, or some special saint, is implored to intercede for rain. Such a procession was held near Liège, about 1244, when the solemn chanting of the *Salve Regina* was followed by a torrent of rain which scattered the multitude of worshippers.[1] In Servian songs the Virgin's name is thus often allied with that of the prophet Elias, who among the Slavs is endowed with the attribute of the Thunderer, holding in his hands the lightning and the thunder and controlling the rainfall on the earth, so that he can close the clouds of heaven to guilty man.

We were now on the narrow path which runs along the summit of the hill to the cave or hermitage of Columban, and my little guide gathered me some bits of a wild plant, a myrtle, which crept along the ground, and which she called "the *brin belu* of St. Columban," adding the pretty legend of how once, when the

[1] See M. A. Breuil, "Mémoires des Antiquaires de Picardie," xiii., p. 88.

saint was climbing to his hermitage, after long fasting and prayer, he sank fainting on the ground, and his eye caught sight of the crimson berry, on eating which he was restored. Two different varieties of broom, now in full blossom, clothe the sides of this hill. The path finally descends towards a ravine, and at a distance of about a hundred feet we came upon the cave, a

Fig. 13.—CAVE OF ST. COLUMBAN, NEAR LUXEUIL.

hollow, overshadowed by a great mass of rock, and surrounded by trees, from which Columban is said to have expelled a wolf, who quietly left his lair at the saint's command. To the right of the cave is the rock which Columban cleft, causing a spring of water to flow forth to satisfy the thirst of his faithful servant, Domoalis.[1] I climbed to this point, and found a clear spring in

[1] See p. 16, *supra*, and "Six Months in the Apennines," pp. 112, 116, 117. The name appears in various forms in the legends of Columban: Dogmael, Domoalis, Italian Domiziale, Donald.

the depths of the hollow. Here the peasants still come to fetch the healing waters for their sick and dying (figs. 13 and 14).

In a chapel raised at the side of this well these miracles are

Fig. 14.—HOLY WELL OF ST. COLUMBAN.

still commemorated (fig. 15). Here the saint came when he wished to leave his brethren for a time, and sought for solitude and meditation; and the legend relates that squirrels and doves sought shelter in the folds of his cowl, that the birds in the trees around mingled their voices with his, and nestled in the palm of his hand. Wild beasts retreated before him, and one bear is said to

Fig. 15.—CHAPELLE FONTAINE DE ST. COLUMBAN.

have left the carcase of a stag when the saint told him that the monks of Annegrai required the skin of his prey for their shoes.

Descending the mountain again, we continued on the road

Fig. 16.—THE VALE OF ANNEGRAL.

towards Faucogney, till we reached the point where it branches off towards the vale of Annegrai. Great was my disappointment when I found that no trace of the old church remained here. It stood upon a knoll in the middle of the valley, not far from the banks of the river Breuchin. Around the base of this knoll,

Fig. 17.—CASHEL OF ANNEGRAI.

which is now a ploughed field, runs an ancient wall, evidently of the same character as that which enclosed the monastery of Glendalough and the *cashels* which surround most of our early monasteries in Ireland. Like them, this also was built of unhewn stone, without mortar, and is still six feet high in places (fig. 17). I observed two low, square-headed apertures on the external face of this wall, and the peasants told me that these lead to subterranean passages through which a man may creep until stopped by stones, earth, or water, with which they are filled. Within the last few years, when they were ploughing the field, they came upon a number of sarcophagi, all of which have since been destroyed, except two. One of these, which I found on the road, had been half broken by the ignorant men by whom it had been disinterred, and who threw it over the wall to get it out of the way. The other is in good preservation, and serves the purpose of a water-trough beside the spring which supplies the village, which seemed to be a very ancient well, and was surrounded by a circular wall. From the form of these sarcophagi, narrower at the feet than at the head, it is quite clear that they were used as Christian tombs. I could get no information as to whether bones were found in them. The answer to my question was, that "bones were found everywhere about," and so this is all that remains of the first monastery of Columban, which in the course of two or three years grew to such great extent that six hundred monks are said to have collected here, and the hive had to be transported to the more central site of Luxeuil.

Maison Jouffroi,
Luxeuil,
April 27th.

DEAR F.,

I confess to feeling some disappointment at finding how few and far between are any Christian monuments here that can be said to belong to the period of Columban's sojourn in this country. However, to-day's expedition led me to explore a subterranean church which there seems no reason to doubt was contemporaneous with the saint, and beside which was the hermitage of a successor of St. Columban, Walbert, before he became head of the monastery at Luxeuil. My object is now to deal with the monuments I find here in chronological order, and this is the oldest monument I have seen, next to the Roman remains and the fragments I have noticed at Annegrai.

The drive was delightful; the road, stretching through the forest to the north, up hill and down vale, passes through scenes of extraordinary and varied beauty, and the brilliant sunlight illuminating the long vistas of oak, fir, and elm, relieved here and there by the silvery birch and aspen, produced a perfectly charming effect. The silence and sense of solitude increased as one approached the little village which bears the saint's name, and as the road ascended we saw down into deep, wooded valleys on either side, and now and then caught glimpses through the hills of the vast plains beyond.

Passing the village and descending into one of these wooded dells, in about a quarter of an hour we reached the hermitage, consisting of a tiny chapel, like a little rectangular tower, a subterranean chapel, and a cave formed partly by nature, partly by art, hollowed out of huge blocks of sandstone, within which is the saint's well. The exquisitely clear cool water streams forth from the jaws of a grotesque antique head, some long-forgotten river god, and falls into a great stone reservoir. On looking further into the depths of the cavern, I saw worn antique statues, in their priestly robes, piled up against these huge Cyclopean walls, strange relics of some long-abandoned cult. And at a height upon the face of the cliff above me there was a rude impassioned image of the saint in prayer, carved on an upper strata of the rock; that Christian hermit who had turned the fountain into a Holy well. This group of symbols of successive forms of worship, thus thrown together in this wild forest cave, was one of the most impressive things I have ever seen.

Leaving the cave I crossed an open space covered by a carpet of short velvety grass of indescribably brilliant green. The subterranean church bore so strong a resemblance to the chapels I

Fig. 18.—HOLY WELL IN CAVE OF ST. WALBERT.

had seen in the Catacombs at Rome, especially those in the cemetery of Sant' Agnese, that I could hardly help thinking this must be a reminiscence of one such. Here, as there, we descend by a flight of the rudest possible stone steps, which form the entrance to a rectangular chamber. This chamber measures

Fig. 19.—HERMITAGE OF ST. WALBERT.

thirteen feet four inches long by eleven feet four inches wide. At its east end is a small square chancel with rude stone benches against the wall on either side; at the eastern end stood the altar or tomb, as the case might be. This chapel is almost entirely excavated out of the rock, the inequalities of which are supplemented by very archaic-looking masonry, pierced at top by three windows, one foot nine inches high by one foot wide, two being square-headed and one semicircular, the arch scooped out of the stone. But the entire roof of this little chapel consists of a huge rock, beneath which it was excavated. The saint is said to have been a sculptor, and out of the rough mass of the living rock above him he has carved a colossal dove, with wings outspread, in an aureole, which covers the whole diameter of the roof. Was it not like a kind of invocation to Peace, thus fixing its image for ever to hover over him when he came to this retreat? These are the kind of touches that give one a clue to the secret of the marvellous growth of Christian Art, and the help men found in its symbolism.

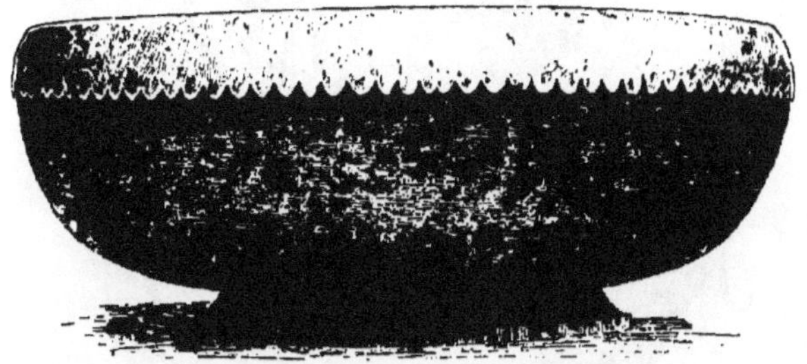

Fig. 20.—MAZER OF ST. WALBERT.

The last memorial of the saint to be mentioned is his wooden drinking-cup. This is no longer in his little oratory or by his fountain side, but is preserved with jealous care in the Séminaire adjoining the abbatial church of Luxeuil. The cup belongs to the same class of antiquities as that which I found at Bobio, the drinking vessel of Columban himself.[1] They are called *mazers*, the name being derived from the old German *màsa*, meaning a spot. A *mazer* is a bowl of spotted wood. The upper part of the cup is edged with a silver rim, and the foot contains a relic of the saint beneath a silver boss. The monks have always held

[1] See "Six Months in the Apennines," pp. 179, 280.

this cup in great honour, offering it to the veneration of the faithful within the monastery, and bearing it in their hands to the houses of the sick. There is a wide-spread belief in its curative power. The monks empty their medicines into it,

Fig. 21.—CASE FOR MAZER OF ST. WALBERT.

pronouncing a special benediction at the same moment, and the people take the remedy with faith.[1]

[1] The formula for the prayer of benediction used with the Cup of St. Walbert, and inserted in the cover of its shagreen case, is as follows:

"Adjutorium nostrum, etc. . . . . Dominus vobiscum . . . .

"Oremus. Domine Jesu Christe, Deus de Deo, lumen de lumine, salus æterna credentium, qui cæcis visum, surdis auditum, claudis gressum, necnon cunctis ægrotantibus te juste postulantibus semper auxilium misericordiæ tuæ

Maison Jouffroi,
May 29th, 1893.

DEAR M.,

I left Luxeuil at eleven this morning to visit the ancient priory of Fontaines, the third foundation of St. Columban. The town stands in the Canton of St. Loup; it contains 1,644 inhabitants. To reach it we had to drive through a portion of the same beautiful forest in which the hermitage of St. Walbert is situated. The view from the platform near the railway station is so striking, so entirely characteristic of French scenery, that I stopped for some hours to sketch it. The pretty village, crowned by the lofty spire of the priory, stands on a little hill, the base of which is watered by the river Roge, which flows down here from its source at Bressen near Faucogney in the Vosges, and changes its name to Beuchol after it has turned the mill wheels of the village so called. The present priory is only a modern building, but the foundation dates from Columban, and "this, the first priory founded in France," says Canon De Beauséjour, "now sleeps its last sleep on the banks of that same river which saw its first walls arise, and has ever since witnessed all the changes of its fortune." The hill was surrounded by a flat marshy basin until the coming of Columban and his followers,

tribuere consuevisti, quique de fidelibus tuis mira dignatione tua dicere voluisti: In nomine meo dæmonia ejicient, linguis loquentur novis, serpentes tollent, et si mortiferum quid biberint non eis nocebit, super ægros manus imponent et bene habebunt, te suppliciter exoramus ut per sacrosanctam nominis tui invocationem virginisque matris tuæ Mariæ et sanctorum martyrum tuorum Stephani, Vincentii, Laurentii, Blasii atque beati N., omniumque sanctorum et sanctarum deprecationem super hanc potionem virtutem benedictionis tuæ ✠ infundere digneris, quatenus omnes in te credentes ex ea gustantes corporis et animæ percipiant beatitudinem. Qui vivis et regnas, etc.

"Aspergatur aqua benedicta ✠."

who were the first to drain its marshes and cultivate its lands. The name it still bears, Fontaines, is derived from the number of springs in the district. When I was sketching, and as my eye followed the outlines of the long flat meadows, straight roads, and level hedgerows to the bases of the distant hills, I remembered the pretty story of Columban and his reapers, the scene of which lay in this very spot.

The saint was staying in his priory here at harvest time, and the reaping was interrupted by heavy and incessant rains, but Columban, inspired by heaven, suddenly ordered his brethren to take their sickles and follow him. He chose the four most fervent monks of his company, and bade each stand and pray at one of the four corners of the field. They were Cummian, Eunochus, Eogain, who had been three of his companions in Ireland, and Gurganus the Breton. Then Columban raised his own sickle in the face of the four reapers and suddenly the rain ceased, the clouds were dispelled, and the sun burst forth so that they could continue the reaping in joy and thankfulness; and they said of Columban as has been said of our Lord on the lake of Gennesaret, "Who is this man, that even the winds and the sea obey him?" This miracle has been celebrated by Padre D'Aquino in verses ending with these words:

> "Messorem Divum, sociosque ad iussa paratos
> Ut cernat, profert sol sine nube caput."

"The sun uprears his head without a cloud, that he may behold the divine reaper and his companions awaiting his command."

Another day, when he saw sixty of his labourers at work reclaiming these waste lands, he perceived that they were weary, and he said to them, "My brethren, may the Lord sustain ye!" and one among them answered and said, "Father, we have here but two loaves and some *cervoise*."[1] "Bring them to me," said the saint.

[1] Old name in French for a kind of bitter beer.

Fig. 22.—VIEW OF FONTAINES.

Having raised his eyes to heaven, he prayed to the Lord Christ, and blessed the loaves and the drink, and the miracle of the Master was repeated at the voice of the disciple, so that the sixty brethren ate and drank abundantly, and they carried four loaves and two measures of *cervoise* back to the monastery. Another story is told of a miracle worked in this priory when the monk Theodegesilus, while grinding corn, cut his finger so badly that the saint had pity on him, and joining the wounded finger together, he blessed it, and the monk was healed immediately. Columban is said to have wrought a somewhat similar miracle here on his servant Vinocus. This man stood watching a monk splitting wood, when a wedge of iron struck him on the forehead inflicting a terrible wound. Columban closed the flesh together firmly and then bathed it with his spittle, and the man was instantly healed. The whole district around Fontaines is full of ancient legends. The ancient name of the Canton of Fontaines, Grannum, as recorded by Lucan,[1] is of great historic interest. It is said that when Attila entered Gaul with his 500,000 warriors he ravaged all that he met in his path, only sparing those places that opened their gates to him. The people of the fortress of Grannum thought they could hold out against the conqueror, but its inhabitants were the victims of their patriotism, the greater number perished amid the ruins of their dwellings. Their bishop, Lupus, who had striven to impede the progress of Attila, became after his death the patron of those inhabitants of the place who had escaped the ravages of the Huns. Another legend relates how a church which was built here in the twelfth century was restored in the fourteenth by an architect named Breuillard, who returning one night from Conflans was attacked by robbers at the junction of the rivers Eaugrogne and Combeauté; thinking his last hour had come, he invoked Heaven, and made a vow to rebuild the

[1] Lucan, "Ph.," lib. I.

church of St. Loup (Lupus), which had fallen into ruin, if by divine grace he should be delivered from this peril. The robbers fled on the moment, and Breuillard returned to St. Loup. Faithful to his vow, he built the choir of the church at his own expense, and, besides, contributed his last penny to the building of the nave and tower. The origin of another of the chapels here, called Boisle-saint, is said to have been as follows. A young nobleman from Fougerolles was surprised by a storm while hunting a bear; he recommended his soul to the Virgin, and made a vow to raise a chapel in her honour. Immediately the heavens grew calm, and in due course of time the chapel was built in accordance with the vow. Such are the legends that have gathered round this priory. Well worship is also practised here, and people afflicted with eruptive diseases are bathed in the waters of the holy well of St. Laurence. Pilgrims come from a great distance, and, having invoked the blessing of the patron in the little chapel beside the well, they then wash their faces and hands in its waters.

Having finished my sketch I walked down the hill leading to the river, and up the main street of the town to the little inn opposite the priory. The landlord sent a message to the curé that I wanted to see the interior of the church, and he immediately came out of his garden and showed me most kindly over the building. It is a Gothic structure of graceful proportions, and the east window is of good stained glass. Here we see St. Columban represented holding the plan of his church in one picture; in the second, Columban directs the draining of the marshes. St. Columban is again represented in a modern painting in a chapel to the north side of the altar. In the background we see his monastery, and he holds the following scroll in his hand:

"Locum quæsit, aliudque Monasterium construit . cui Fontanas nomen indidit."

"He sought a place and built another Monastery, which he named Fontaines."

Beneath Columban's figure we read:

"Ne. cessa. pro nobis clamare ad Dominum. ut Salvet. nos."

"Cease not to cry to God for us that He may save us."

I had to leave Fontaines with a feeling of great disappointment, having found nothing of any great interest there, except indeed the general aspect of the place and the surrounding country, some of the charm of which I have tried to convey in my sketch. Our next expedition must be to the church of Lure, where Columban left Deicola when he himself was banished from Luxeuil.

I shall have to tell you his legend first, that you may sympathize in my desire to trace his footsteps.

LEGEND OF ST. DEICOLA (ST. DESLE).

AUTHORITIES.

"Vit. S. Deicol. Boll. AA. SS.," January 18th. "Mém. Hist. sur l'abbaye et la ville de Lure," par l'abbé L. Besson.

THIS saint was a native of Leinster, and first became a friend of St. Columban at Bangor in Down, where he was distinguished for his learning and piety, and Columban conceived a great love for him. One day he said to Deicola, "How does it happen that your face is always shining with joy, and nothing seems to trouble your soul?" And Deicola answered, "It is because nothing can ever part me from my God." Though an older man than St. Columban he followed him on his pilgrimage, and lived with him at Annegrai and at Luxeuil. In the year 600, when St. Columban and his Irish monks were expelled from Luxeuil, St. Deicola hoped to be able to follow his master into banishment; but he had not gone more than a few miles along the valley of the river Ognon, when his strength broke down at a place called Vepras, near the town of Lure. He was an aged and infirm man at this time, and, throwing himself at the feet of St. Columban, he prayed him to let him finish his earthly pilgrimage among the trees of the forest in which they found themselves. The sorrow of Columban was very great at the thought of leaving his oldest friend, and one whom he so honoured, alone in the wilderness; but, setting the will of God before his own, he answered, saying, "May the Almighty Lord, for the love of whom you have left your native land, grant that we meet before His face in heaven." At these words St. Deicola, knowing that the hour of parting had come, fell upon Columban's neck, and said, "May the Lord bless you all the days of your life with all the blessings of Jerusalem." Then St. Columban went on his way, and St. Deicola remained in the forest alone. It was in a vast expanse of country, only peopled by wild animals; tract beyond tract of marshy and uncultivated ground. Here, without human help, but sustained by his sure faith, Deicola cast his care upon the Lord, and then plunged into the woods to seek a place where he might build his house. He remained without food or drink until the next morning. Kneeling on the ground, he struck it with his staff, and a fresh stream of water sprang forth, from which he drank. He then rose up refreshed, and continued his way until he reached a clear space in the forest, where a herd of swine were feeding. The swine-herd, who was in charge of them, was startled at seeing this old man, of unusual height and noble presence, clad in a strange costume, come forth from the wood. He said, "Who are you, and whence do you come? What do you seek in these wild places, coming thus without guide or companion?" "Fear nothing, my brother," said Deicola; "I am a traveller and a monk, and I ask you in charity to show me a place where I may build my cell." The swine-herd replied that he only knew of one spot, called Lutra (Lure), a very marshy place, where he would have plenty of water. "But I cannot be your guide," he added, "for my herd would stray away in my absence." Deicola looked at the swine-herd, and answered, "Here, my son, take my staff, and fix it in the ground, and it will take thy place with the swine, and guard them till thy return." So saying, he planted his staff in the ground, and the swine crouched in a circle round it. The swine-herd followed the old man, and led him to the site he had spoken of, where the saint fixed his tent beside a well. When the swine-herd returned to his herd he found them as he left them, grouped around the staff.

The solitude of the saint was broken one day by a visit from King Clothair II. This prince, now head of the Frankish monarchy, had gone out hunting in the ancient forest of Sequania, and was in pursuit of a huge boar, who sought refuge in the cell of the old monk. The beast, terrified and panting, crouched at the feet of Deicola, as if in search of pity and protection, and the saint, laying his hand upon his head, said to him, "Since thou hast sought charity here, thou shalt find safety also." He then went and stood at the door of his cell; the pack of hounds came on at full speed, baying loudly, but suddenly stopped before the door, as if they were afraid to advance. The huntsmen hurried to tell the king; who approached that he might see this miracle. When he learned that Deicola was a friend of Columban, whose name he had always honoured, the king left off his hunting that he might sit some while in the cell of the old recluse. He asked, "What are your means of living, and how do your brethren fare in such a wilderness as this?" "It is written," said St. Deicola, "that they who fear God shall want for nothing. We are poor, it is true, but we love and serve the Lord; that is of more value than much riches."

Some time after this event King Clothair made a solemn grant to this rising community of all the forests, pastures, and fisheries possessed by the fiscal in the neighbourhood of Lure; to these he added a town named Bredana, with its church and vineyard of St. Antoine.[1]

When Deicola (Desle) first settled here, he found that there was a church dedicated to St. Martin, on the summit of a neighbouring hill, to which the lord of the district, Werfarius, had appointed a priest for the holy office, and to this sanctuary Deicola went by night to offer praise and prayer to God, and each night that he approached the door was opened by angels for him. But the priest in residence was displeased when he heard this, and said to his congregation, "I will remain here no longer because of this itinerant monk. He lies hidden in the forest all day, and then comes forth at night, and by some unknown enchantment the door of this temple opens at his approach." The people advised patience, saying, "The truth will come to light some day. If this monk's power be of God we cannot hinder him; if it prove otherwise, we shall treat him as an impostor, and drive him pitilessly forth from our land."

So Deicola (Desle) continued to pray in the church of St. Martin by night, and the fame of his miracles and holy life inflamed the anger of the priest against him, so that he closed the doors and windows of the church with thorns and branches;

[1] "Vit. S. Deicola," cap. v. St. Antoine lies east of Lure in the Canton of Champagney. The chapel is still visited by pilgrims from Alsace.

nevertheless, the saint kept on his nightly vigil without hindrance. The priest appealed to the lord Werfarius, who was of a cruel and angry temper, and who was then living in his castle of Analesberg, or Lawesberg, near Châlonvillars, south-east of Belfort. He commanded that Deicola should be seized and chastised; but no sooner had the order gone forth, than the prince was seized with a mortal illness and died. His wife Berthilda, seeing the hand of God in this, sent to entreat the saint, whom her husband had unjustly condemned, to come to her aid.

When Deicola arrived he was weary and heated by the long journey, and seating himself, he took off his cloak. A servant advanced to lay it down, when suddenly it was seen suspended in the air, hanging on a ray of sunlight that had penetrated into the chamber. Seeing this, Berthilda threw herself at his feet, and praying for her husband's soul she sought to repair his cruelty to the saint by endowing his church with land and with the Church of St. Martin. Thus enriched, a spacious monastery arose at Lure in a few years, where men of one heart and one soul kept up the *Laus perennis* night and day, and spent their days in labour and in prayer. Two churches, one dedicated to St. Peter, the other to St. Paul, were added to the buildings.

When all these things were accomplished Deicola, feeling his end approach, called his follower Colombin and his monks to his side, and they took the last Sacrament together; then he spoke to them in wise and touching words, bidding them of all things to remember charity, and with fervour to strive against the difficulties that beset the way to heaven. Having parted from each of his children with a loving embrace, he fell asleep on the 18th of January, A.D. 625, and his disciples buried him with honour in the place where he had died, in the Oratory of the Holy Trinity.

The saint seemed to live again in his follower Colombin, and the fame of Lure was spread throughout Franche Comté and into the Vosges and Alsace. And thus it was that St. Deicola laid the foundations of this great abbey of Lure, which ultimately became one of the richest abbeys of France, and which twelve centuries later numbered princes of the Roman Empire among its abbots.

LETTERS FROM LUXEUIL.

LURE.

Maison Jouffroi,
May 25th, 1893.

DEAR H.,

I STARTED early yesterday on an expedition in search of any existing remains that can be found of St. Deicola in Lure. The drive led through the forest, which is celebrated for the beautiful legend "La Lyre de Citers." They say that after dawn the sound of a lyre is heard through the trees which is a thousand times sweeter to listen to than the song of a nightingale. The attraction of this fantastic harmony should be resisted as if it were a siren's voice. When you hear the sounds you should instantly close your ears to them and fly in the opposite direction to that from which these magic chords proceed, for if you take one step towards the enchanted instrument you will be drawn by an irresistible force to follow it on and on. Wondrous things are told of those who have submitted to its powerful charm. The strangest visions have appeared to them. To their eyes the forest becomes carpeted with flowers which shine like diamonds. The branches of the trees turn to gold and silver, and through their vistas the forms of beautiful women are seen to emerge, while the very air seems to vibrate with the sounds of the invisible lyre as they swell and fall in the distance in waves of enchanting harmony. But all these objects, sights, and sounds are intangible and fleeting. If you wish to gather the flowers, to embrace the dryads, to seize the sweet lyre, then flowers, nymphs, and lyre all fly before the hand stretched out to reach them ; the beauty of the vision vanishes at the first burst of broad daylight, and the melodious songs of night are succeeded by mocking laughter, while the traveller who has let himself be carried away by the deceitful sounds of this forest lyre finds himself entangled in thorny bushes in the midst of a dreary marsh.

Leaving this haunted forest, the road from Luxeuil crosses the plain of Baudoncourt, and for some distance runs along a small tributary of the river Lanterne called the "Stream of Famine," for the legend is that its waters only move in years of want, and remain stagnant in times of plenty. When I reached Lure I found it to be a cheerful little town containing about four thousand inhabitants. The fine monastery founded by St. Deicola was destroyed during the French revolution (see Fig. 23). It stood at the side of the parish church, but its place is now filled up by private houses. The sous-préfecture now occupies the eighteenth-century buildings that were the last foundation of the monastery of St. Deicola. The church was rebuilt about 1770, and I found the interior so very dark that I had scarcely light to photograph the chapel and altar of St. Deicola which stand at the south of the chancel. Above the statue of the saint upon the altar I perceived in the dim light what seemed to be a good picture of the saint, but I was much disappointed to find no antiquity existing here connected with the patron, although the cult of St. Desle is popular all through the district. A little book containing his office, with the legend of his life, is sold in every stationer's shop. The "Cantique de St. Desle," is sung in all the churches to the air of "Pitié, mon dieu." When I inquired for the holy well of the saint, I found there were two such to be seen, but at a distance of some miles, and as they lay in opposite directions I could hardly hope to visit both on this occasion. I hired a carriage and drove some distance, first skirting the forest, and then into it as far as the road extended. We stopped at last at a forester's house, and I learned that I must finish the expedition on foot. I hired a little boy as guide, as the driver could not leave his horse, and we had a delightful walk, winding through the dense wood on a green, mossy path. At last we came out on an open space by the side of a little lake surrounded by trees casting their perfect reflec-

Fig. 23.—MONASTERY OF LURE, LUXEUIL.
(*From old engraving.*)

tions in the still water. In order to reach the holy well we should be obliged, as I thought, to cross the lake, for whenever I asked the boy where lay the "Fontaine de St. Desle," he pointed across the water. We hailed a man in a flat-bottomed boat, who paddled us out on the lake, past a tiny island, and then stopped in the middle of a sheet of water, "Voilà la Fontaine," said the boatman. I looked round in every direction, along the banks and into the wood, but could see no sign of well, rock, or stone, among the ferns, and moss, and tangled grass. "Mais, c'est ici! c'est là dessous!" he cried impatiently; and then I looked again and saw that his oar was pointing, not to one side or the other, but downwards, and looking into the clear depths below I saw, *not* a submerged church as they see in Lough Neagh, but a submerged holy well! The great grey rugged rock, from whose cleft side the waters had so freely flowed that they grew into a lake which seemed to shield rather than to hide it beneath its glassy surface. A crystal shrine indeed, and framed in borders of emerald green enamelled with wild flowers.

I went to Lure again to-day to search for the second holy well of St. Deicola (Fig. 24). It lies to the north of the town, in the Commune of St. Germain, where there are the remains of an old Roman road to be seen.[1] We drove past houses which struck me as being singularly primitive examples of masonry, although of recent erection. They are built of wattles and logs of wood, rough and untrimmed as they come from the woods, the interstices filled in with rough plaster. I soon had to leave the carriage and make my way, for an hour or more, along a narrow path through the forest, often forcing my way through the trees and brushwood till at last I reached a wide open glade, upwards of a mile in circumference, which evidently in damp weather is nothing but a vast marsh. I found a French bog more tiresome than heavy sand to walk on, with no resistance whatever, no stools or hummocks to give firm footing here and there as in our good old Irish bogs! At last we reached the well of St. Deicola, which is still a place of pilgrimage, and its waters are held to be peculiarly beneficial for children's diseases. The well is surrounded by branches of trees, on which offerings are hung by the parents of the sick children, who come here to fetch its healing waters for their little ones. I saw a tiny child's dress, two little

[1] This road was probably that taken by Columban when leaving Luxeuil for Besançon. It still exists, a well-paved causeway, between St. Germain and Baudoncourt.

baby caps, one of embroidered muslin, various towels and pinafores, and a rosary with crosses. Many of these things had evidently been hanging there a long time, others seemed quite fresh, and they were tied so tightly to the branches that though the storm might tear them it could not remove them. My

Fig. 24.—WELL OF ST. DEICOLA.

thoughts went back to the well at Straffan in Kildare, where I had last seen such offerings hung.

As I was making my sketch of this calm pool, the one spot of colour reflecting the blue overhead, its peculiar outline reminded me of the Irish name of Cormac's well at Tara, "the Dark Eye," [1] and the fringe of rushes round its edge, like eyelashes reflected

[1] See Whitley Stokes, "Prose Tales in the Rennes Dindsenchus," "Revue Celtique," vol. xv., p. 285.

in its clear depths, only strengthened the resemblance. Wells are so named in other countries besides Ireland. The Spaniards have "Los ojos de la Guadiana;" in the Ariège there is the Eicheil, signifying "Watery Eye," and the source of the Garonne is Ouiel, and in the Pyrenees the name is extended to flowing streams and moving waters.

The worship of waters seems to have arisen from the idea of purification by water. Before the introduction of Christianity the Pagan inhabitants of Northern Europe believed in sanctification by water, the ceremony was called *Vatni ausa*, to sprinkle with water. In Christian countries wells were placed under the protection of different saints, and the cures obtained by the water were supposed to come through the intercession of the saint, certain waters being held good for fever, others for mania, others for blindness or diseases of the eye. It would be a curious question whether the name of the saint, his personality, his special powers and attributes, or the events of his life and death had any connection with the nature of the evils which the waters of his well were supposed to alleviate. As, for example, it is the case that in France the wells placed under John the Baptist are good for epilepsy; those under the protection of St. Agatha are good for sore breasts; the waters of the holy well of St. Hubert, in the Ardennes, cured hydrophobia in men and beasts.

That wells and rivers are the dwellings of gods and genii is a notion common to many races, and Monsieur l'Abbé Santerre traces the origin of the worship of waters to Genesis, when, at the Creation, it is said, "the Spirit of God moved upon the face of the waters." However this may be, the idea of eternity will always be connected with the Ocean, the eternal motion an emblem of the living soul in nature.

Have you ever asked yourself what is the charm that one is conscious of in such communities of custom, and such survivals from immemorial time that seem still to bind the human race in one, no matter how far they drift apart? In England, on the road to Benton, a village near Newcastle-on-Tyne, a fountain like these of Ireland and France may still be seen, and still the bushes that surround it are hung with rags, so that it is named Rag Well. In Scotland rags and garments are hung beside the waters very frequently. The sufferer who seeks alleviation for his ills in such healing waters offers a portion of his clothing,[1] holding that in so doing he parts with his disease, which has attached itself to his rags. At Lure, and in some other parts of France, the pilgrims use a form of imprecation on him who ventures to untie the string of his offering until it falls through rot or damp.

The Church seems to have striven from the earliest times to keep these practices under restraint. At the Council of Arles, held in 452, the decree was issued, that should the faithful light torches and worship trees, wells, or stones, and the bishop neglect to abolish this custom, he ought to know that he is guilty of sacrilege. St. Eligius,[2] in a sermon referring to such practices, common among the Vermandois and in Santerre, says, "Cease to light torches at stones or wells or trees, and to make vows there. *Nullus Christianus ad fana vel ad petras vel ad fontes vel ad arbores luminaria faciat aut vota reddere praesumat.*" It is not only by their practices at holy wells that the peasantry round Lure remind one of the Irish. At St. Antoine—a church we have mentioned above as the gift of Clothair II. to Deicola—the pilgrims who visit leave little crosses behind them, blessed medals, flowers, coins as tokens of their visit. And there is an ancient wooden statue, much worn and defaced, in the chapel, which, like the figure of St. Molaise, in Inismurray,

[1] On the transference of disease to inanimate objects, see "Lives of Saints, from the Book of Lismore," pp. 287-361, ed. and trans. by Whitley Stokes, D.C.L.

[2] Life of St. Eligius (Eloi), by St. Ouen, Part II., chap. 3.

co. Sligo, is still honoured as the image of their patron Antoine.

The story of St. Deicola's cloak[1] hanging suspended on a sunbeam finds it parallel in the legend of St. Brigit, when she is said to have received a visit from Brendan, the traveller, who wondering at the fame of her miracles, came out of the west to see her.[2]

"Brigit came from her sheep to welcome Brenainn. As Brigit entered the house she put her wet cloak on the rays of the sun, and they supported it like pot-hooks. Brenainn told his gillie to put his cloak on the same rays, and the gillie put it on them, but it fell from them twice. Brenainn himself put it, the third time, with anger and wrath, and the cloak staid upon them."

In the folk lore of this district, also, I met with a fairy tale called "Le Bossu de Fontenois," which is a variety of the Irish fairy tale of Lusmore, the humpbacked fiddler, who, while resting on the rath of Knockgrafton, heard the fairies within singing these words, "dia Luan dia Mort, dia Luan dia Mort," meaning Monday and Tuesday; and at first he was pleased with the song, but in time, weary of the monotonous repetition of the same words, he skilfully blended into the song a new phrase, "agus da Cadine," meaning, "and Wednesday also," for which he was whirled into the midst of the delighted fairies, who rewarded him by removing his hump and restoring him to his friends. The version of this legend in the Haute-Saône is as follows:

"On raconte à ce propos qu'un samedi, vers minuit, il y a de cela bien longtemps, un pauvre tailleur d'habits de Fontenois, petit et bossu, s'en revenait de Dampierre, où il avait travaillé de son état, lorsque,

[1] See p. 44, *supra*.

[2] See "Three Middle Irish Homilies," ed. and trans. by Whitley Stokes, Calcutta, 1877.

passant sur le pont de la Linotte, il entendit aux alentours du pont, dans le bas, un bruit étrange, singulier, qui l'effraya d'abord; des voix criaient: '*C'est demain Dimanche! c'est demain Dimanche!*...' Le tailleur, d'humeur assez gaie, s'avisa de répliquer en disant: '*Et après-demain Lundi! et après-demain Lundi!*' Il avait à peine fini de parler que déjà il était entouré d'êtres bizarres, aux formes les plus fantastiques, qui, sans lui laisser le temps de se reconnaître, les uns le tirant par le bras, les autres le poussant par derrière, l'entraînèrent dans une danse infernale.

"Quand ils eurent fini, le chef de la bande, un assez bon diable, se mit à dire bien haut: '*Que sa bosse disparaisse!*' et, en même temps, le frappant sur le dos, du coup il lui enleva sa bosse qui vint rouler par terre. Ce service rendu, il lui dit de continuer son chemin, ce que notre homme fit aussitôt.

"Rentré à Fontenois, il alla le dimanche se montrer dans le village; mais personne, tout en disant le reconnaître à sa figure, ne voulut croire que c'était lui, tant il était inouï qu'il put être autrement que bossu.

"Mais s'il eut de la peine à persuader son monde, il fut cependant pris au mot par un autre bossu de Fontenois qui se promit d'aller tenter la même aventure. Il y alla en effet un samedi, jour de sabbat, à l'heure de minuit, à l'heure où les diables faisaient un vacarme d'enfer, tout autour et au-dessous du pont. Comme le tailleur, il entendit les mêmes paroles: '*C'est demain Dimanche!*' auxquelles il répondit sans hésiter: '*Et après-demain Lundi!*...'

"Ces mots à peine dits, il fut assailli de tous côtés, par une foule de diables et de sorciers, qui se ruèrent sur lui, le renversèrent, le remirent sur ses pieds, puis se le rejetèrent les uns aux autres. Enfin l'un d'eux, le plus diable de tous, revint sur lui avec la bosse du tailleur dans ses griffes, et la lui appliqua fortement sur le dos,—ce qui, ajouté à la bosse qu'il avait déjà par devant, lui en fit deux, avec lesquelles il s'en retourna tout confus à Fontenois."[1]

I fear I have given you too much of Lure and its fairy legends,

[1] In the collection of Breton legends by Souvestre the tale of Torubouzouk is closely related to these legends of hunchbacks.

and its memories of Columban's old friend, Deicola. In my next letter I shall return to more serious work, and tell you something of the Abbey Church founded by Columban at Luxeuil.

Luxeuil,
May 27th, 1893.

DEAR B.,

I think I have told you already that there is a tradition at Luxeuil that the abbey was founded by Columban over the débris of a temple of Diana. The saint dedicated his church to St. Peter,[1] and it appears from a letter of Columban's that it was consecrated by a bishop named Aidus. He speaks in this letter of *altare quod sanctus Aidus episcopus benedixit.*[2]

It would be interesting to divine some details of the original building, as to its form, material, dimensions. St. Columban calls it *altare*, an altar; the author of the life of St. Gall says *oratorium*, an oratory. Perhaps, as Mons. Fabert[3] has suggested, it simply consisted of an altar, covered in, with a great portico in front, under which the monks were ranged during divine service. Then we may ask as to the material, whether was it wood or stone? Some assert that it must have been wood, because they hold that down to the tenth century churches in this part of the country were always built of wood. But the "Acts of St. Gall" prove that in the time of St. Columban they built in stone, and this is confirmed by the ruins of Grandval,[4] and St. Emier.

[1] The author of the "Life of St. Gall" says, speaking of Columban and his followers, "Invenerunt locum muris antiquis septum, calidis aquis rigatum, sed jam vetustate collapsum, qui vulgo Luxovium vocabatur. Ibi oratorium in honore beati Petri construentes, mansiunculas in quibus commanerent fecerunt."—"AA. SS.," Boll. Oct. 16.

[2] "Bibl. veter. Patrum," XII., p. 349.

[3] "Notice sur l'Église et l'Abbaye de Luxeuil," par M. de Fabert, 1845.

[4] "Mémoires de la Société d'émulation de Doubs."

Then as to its dimensions. Canon de Beauséjour[1] conjectures that they were considerable, because there were six hundred monks in the monastery besides numerous pupils in the school; but it does not therefore follow that there was any one building of great size in which they were lodged. It is more likely that these Irish monks followed their native custom of erecting a number of huts in groups around and about the oratory, either inclosing them in a cashel or making use of the old Roman walls as shelter and protection. Within this sanctuary the bodies of St. Columban the younger, a kinsman of the founder, and of St. Eustace, the second abbot, were interred. Ebroin, the mayor of the palace, and St. Leger, Bishop of Autun, were confined here for misconduct. Theodoric, the grandson of Brunehilde, worshipped at this altar. Clothair II., obedient to the last instructions he received from Columban, took the monastery under his protection, enlarged its boundaries, and enriched it with gifts.

This first building, however, could hardly have existed more than a century. A new church was erected by Chilperic II., who reigned from 715 to 720. Almost immediately after, and still in the eighth century, it underwent its first serious attack. The cloisters were desolated "by the Vandals," according to some ancient chroniclers, but, no doubt, by those Saracens to whom Charles Martel dealt the final blow at Poitiers. The monks were massacred, and the church remained in ruins until it was restored in 817 by Ansegisus, and endowed by Louis le Débonnaire. He raised the height of the building, repaired the roof, and enriched the treasury with gifts of precious ornaments and sacred vessels of great value, completing the exterior by the restoration of the portico which united the building to the chapel of St. Martin.

It is further stated in the chronicle of Fontenelles that Abbot Ansegisus employed an artist named Madalulfo to paint frescoes

[1] See "Notice de l'Église de Luxeuil," par M. l'Abbé de Beauséjour. Luxeuil.

on the walls of the refectories and dormitories of the abbeys of Luxeuil and St. Germain Flaix. These works were carried on between the years 817 and 823.[1]

After the abbacy of St. Ansegisus there is no further mention of the church till the ninth century, when, in the year 888, the monastery was attacked by the Northmen. They killed Prior Tetelmus, put all the monks to flight, and pursued the abbot, St. Gibart, to Martinvelle, where they shot him with arrows. But though they destroyed the monastic buildings, the church still remained for a century longer, so that it survived the terrors of the year 1000. Confidence being restored, it was resolved to rebuild the monastery, and a Romanesque structure, the work of the Abbot Gérard II. (A.D. 1049), succeeded that which had been remodelled and enlarged by St. Ansegisus. In 1201 the monastery was burnt by Richard de Montbéliard, when he invaded the south of Burgundy. The church and all its monastic buildings, titles, privileges, charters, and archives, became the prey of the flames. But in the course of time this disaster was repaired and a new monastery and church were erected. The monastery only lasted till the seventeenth century, the church is the one that we see here now.

The exterior of this building, although shorn of much of its ornament, still preserves many features of interest, such as the pinnacles of the flying buttresses, the gargoyles of the apse, the modillions and corbels on the cornices of the chapels and transepts, and finally the little round staircase tower at the north side of the transept. But the monument has been terribly mutilated. Of the three bell-towers by which it was crowned, only one remains. Of the two destroyed, one was at the junction of the northern side aisle and the transept; the other, which raised its square tower over the columns of the transept, was taken down at the beginning of this century. The tower which remains, and is

[1] See D'Achery et Mabillon, "Vita S. Anseg."

Fig. 25.—ABBEY AND PRESBYTERY OF LUXEUIL.

represented in my view of Luxeuil,[1] was added to the church in the year 1527 by Jean de la Palud, who by his additions altered its character to that of the sixteenth century, as we see from its windows, and raised a lofty spire of wood which was famed throughout the country for its elegance. This spire was destroyed by lightning in 1680.

I was disappointed to find that no trace remains of the tower which Dr. Petrie refers to in his work on the "Ecclesiasical Architecture of Ireland," pp. 376, 377, where he quotes the following passage from Mabillon's "Iter Germanicum."

"*Luxovium.* Cernitur prope Majorem Ecclesiæ Portam Pharus, quam Lucernam vocant, cujus omnino consimilem vidi aliquando apud Çarnutas. Ei usui fuisse videtur, in gratiam eorum, qui noctu ecclesiam frequentabantur."

The tower stood in the Place St. Martin, but judging from what I could learn of its form, it appears to have belonged to a totally different type of tower from the Irish bell-house (Cloicteac). It bore much more resemblance to a lighthouse, and the lower portion was quadrangular.

It is impossible to say anything more about the exterior of this abbey, on the south, east, and west sides it is so built up, and its outline so hidden from view by the buildings that crowd around it. The only side from which it is now visible was once occupied by the Chapel of Our Lady, and we must remember that the architects of this church had to confine their object to the necessities of monastic service and the exigencies of the other previously erected buildings of the monastery.

The interior of the church is very solemn and impressive. The lofty nave with its triforium and low-roofed side aisles dimly lighted; its great transcepts with chapels oriented, so that looking down the church eastward the eye rests on five altars at

[1] See p. 21, *supra*.

Fig. 26.—CLOISTERS OF ABBEY OF LUXEUIL.

a time; and its chancel of most unusual length, measuring, as it does, fifty metres long and thirty-seven metres wide, which was once completed by an apsidal chapel now destroyed, all combine to form a picture at once striking and impressive.

We should not fail to observe an interesting feature in the apse of this church which is also found in Cormac's chapel on the Rock of Cashel, that is, the deviation of the axis towards the north.[1] This is plainly visible from the case of the organ, at the west end; the deviation from the straight line is certainly about six feet six inches.

Many abbacies and old cathedrals present a similar deviation either to north or south. Writers of the Middle Ages give neither sense or reason for this fact, and modern archæologists have tried to explain it in various ways. To some it is the expression, in the ground-plan of a cruciform building, of a mystic idea suggesting the inclination of the head of Christ upon the cross. According to others it is a simple accident arising from the necessities of circumstance and place. Canon de Beauséjour, in his account of the building, gives it as his opinion that in the case of the church at Luxeuil there are certainly material reasons for such deviation. The apse was evidently an addition of later date than the nave, and many difficulties arose in its adjustment to the rest of the building. Allowance had to be made for the buildings already flanking its sides, some of which were still standing, and others to be rebuilt on their ancient foundations.

It is worthy of observation that churches in which this peculiarity appears are all reconstructions upon ancient foundations amid buildings that have dominated and interfered with the new construction. We must remember also, that bishops and abbots, when rebuilding their churches, for the sake of economy preserved either the nave or the apse of the earlier building, but afterwards, when it came to rebuilding that portion which they

[1] "Notes on Irish Architecture," by Lord Dunraven, vol. ii., p. 72.

Fig. 27.—INTERIOR OF ABBEY OF LUXEUIL.

had preserved, they found many difficulties in fitting the new and old together. Viollet-le-Duc,[1] who is one of the best opinions on the subject, remarks, "The exact adjustment of the axis is one difficulty, and there is infinite chance of making a mistake."

Fig. 28.—ELEVATION OF ONE BAY OF NAVE.

There is room for belief that these deviations of the choirs of our churches proceed from inevitable irregularities in the grouping of monuments erected at different times. If we could name any two instances of churches completed at one time instead of at different periods, in which the apse and chancel had the same inclination to one side, we might then be tempted to adopt the theory of a symbolic intention. Until then we must adhere to the opinion of M. l'Abbé de Beauséjour, p. 19.

In some ways the style of this church is essentially monastic, and this accounts for the disposition of the doors, the form of the transept, the position of the chapels, and the dimensions of the apse. Distinct characteristics of the Burgundian school are perceptible throughout in the style of the architecture.

Yet it is not uniform, the lower and older portion of the

[1] "Dict. d'Architecture," art. *Chœur*.

building is Romanesque, the upper and later being Pointed; the first was executed in the thirteenth and part of the fourteenth century, and we need not wonder that the Romanesque style is still found prevailing in Luxeuil at so late a date. It is the fact that in the remote provinces of France the Pointed style was very slow to develop, and the Benedictines clung longer than the other orders to the Romanesque or round arch.

Fig. 29.—ROMANESQUE WINDOW, LUXEUIL.

It is in the side aisles that most traces of the Romanesque style are preserved. They are a little heavy, but simple and impressive. There is a fine Romanesque porch (fig. 30) in the south aisle, though its effect is marred by a modern superstructure or attic; and also a pretty Romanesque window (fig. 29) in the same aisle. There are interesting columns with transition capitals in both aisles (figs. 31 and 32), and when we study such columns, with their broad bases, with straps and hollow mouldings, their double arches, without any moulding, their capitals with square plinth and corbels adorned with human and animal forms, as well as rudimentary foliate designs, and when we place beside these features this little semicircular headed window in the south aisle, a last example of those bay windows once so common, we cannot but acknowledge that the beginning of the Pointed or Ogive style still continues to be stamped with a Romanesque character.

It was owing to the exertions of the wise and enterprising Abbot Odo de Charenton that the work was completed in 1330, and his memory will ever live in association with this building. By his direction every servant of the abbey was employed in its construction. Some prepared the mortar, others, who happened to possess carts or other means of transport, brought stones and wood, and all material necessary for the undertaking. Nor did any one of all this crowd complain of such painful toil, since religion inspired them, and they knew that they laboured in God's service.

Fig. 30.—ROMANESQUE PORCH.

"Praying, the mason lifted course on course
Unpaid, to breast the storm of centuries,
And flash the dawn unrisen o'er golden plains."[1]

Added to this, Odo had a strong sense of the beautiful; even though it must be allowed that the proportions of the choir are excessive, and that it seems, as it were, lost in the depth and distance of the building, yet the effect of the whole is most imposing. The architect's name was Renaud de Fresnes St. Mémez, and we may quote the following lines bequeathed by Dom Guillaume de Queuve, a monk of the sixteenth century, which record the original settlements.

[1] Aubrey De Vere.

"Heudes[1] abbez, lequel paya à maistre Renaud de Fresnes-Sainct-Mémez, maistre mansons de l'œuvré du mostier Saint Pierre de Luxeu, à cause de l'œuvre du mostier, de trois ans passés, la somme de trois cents livres estev. et prébende entière de pain et de vin et de général. Ensemble roubbe d'escuier, baillez et délivrez par ledict sieur en l'an mil IIIe et xxx le dimanche après la Nativité de Notre Dame. Alors Jehan de Gohenans était secrétaire."[2]

Fig. 31.

The stained glass windows give additional beauty to this interior, and I found on examining them that scenes from the lives of St. Columban and his followers are illustrated in them.

The first subject in the window on the left of the apse is that of St. Columban teaching his Rule to his companions; the second, Columban miraculously multiplying the corn for the support of his monks; the third, St. Lua, one of Columban's early companions in Ireland, following his master on his journey; fourth, Columban surrounded by wild animals tamed by the sound of his voice; fifth, Columban the younger speaking to the birds who nestle in his hood. Then follow scenes from the lives of some of his foreign disciples, until we reach the eleventh subject, which represents St. Gall in his retreat in the depths of the forest; and the thirteenth, Deicola (Desle) receiving the Pope's Bulla.

Fig. 32.

Some archæological fragments of the older buildings are still

[1] *i.e.* Eudes or Odo.

[2] Dom Grappin, MS. Hist. de Luxeuil, in library of abbey.

preserved in the north transept, the most remarkable of which is a statue of St. Peter, life-size, and seated on a folding-chair with lions' heads and claws at the terminations of the arms and feet (fig. 33). He wears the robe, alb, stole, maniple, chasuble lifted on the arms, pointed shoes and a conical tiara on the head, with pendants falling behind. He holds a book in the right hand and two keys in the left. The chronicles of the abbey have been searched in vain for any reference to this figure. Dom Grillo, writing in the eighteenth century, says, "This statue having been mutilated at the time of the Revolution, and thrown outside the church, was used by the *gamins* in the street as a target for their stones, until, in 1875, it was rescued and placed where it now stands, between the tombs of the two restorers of the abbey."[1]

Fig. 33.—ST. PETER, LUXEUIL.

The havoc wrought by the mob, during the French Revolution, at Luxeuil, can hardly be realized unless we read the long list given by M. l'Abbé de Beauséjour of treasures, once in possession of the monastery, taken from the ancient inventories of the abbey. Numberless relics of Columban, Eustace, and Walbert; silver armshrines, reliquaries, crystals, a silver statuette of St. Columban, rings, enamelled

[1] Odo de Charenton and B. S. Clerc.

crosses, chalices etc., all have disappeared; nothing now remains but the wooden bowl of St. Walbert. The fine abbatial crosier was discovered, during the repairs of 1862, in a grave, buried with a skeleton. This was the tomb and crosier of Aymon de Mollain, who died A.D. 1382. It is of enamelled copper of exquisite workmanship, the socket ornamented with foliate designs and gilded figures; the knob is divided into four medallions filled by angels with outspread wings, the curve at the top enamelled like the socket; the crest, denticulated, is wound twice round, then bursts into flower at the end, and its large lily blossom fills the central space. This beautiful object was sold by the municipality of Luxeuil to the museum of the Louvre where it may still be seen (fig. 34).

Our list of the antiquities of the church of Luxeuil should include the tomb of the blessed Angelôme, which, though destroyed in the Revolution, is still faithfully recorded in a drawing made about the year 1700 by M. Vinot. This monument dated from the year 854, and when the sarcophagus was profaned and smashed in 1792, M. de Fabert, who was witness of the proceedings, saw the bones that had lain undisturbed for 898 years enveloped in fragments of brownish stuff, the débris of an ancient religious garb. The skeleton was almost perfect, but the head had been enshrined elsewhere.

The destruction of the library of Luxeuil Abbey was the most mournful episode in the history of the town. In the year 1789 the suppression of convents was the order of the day. The effect of the great revolutionary movement of the 14th of July was felt all through France. At Luxeuil the people rose *en masse* and collected at the side of the town which is washed by the river Breuchin, and scaled the barricades in a moment. The monks, who had trusted little to the townsmen for protection, had already taken flight. The peasants pouring into the abbey, whose gates were open, first rushed upstairs to the

Fig. 34.—CROSIER OF LUXEUIL.

library, persuaded that the books were title deeds. They threw them in numbers from the window into the garden below, where they made a bonfire of them. Others were torn up and used to ram the guns of the army of Sambre and Meuse. Thus disappeared among other precious works, the "Chronicon Luxoviense," the MS. treatises of Adso, and the collection of ancient ceremonials used by Mabillon in his "Liturgy of the Gallican Church."

However, some precious ancient manuscripts, which escaped the general wreck, have turned up from time to time since the Revolution, five of them are now in Paris, four in the library of the British Museum, London, and one in the collection of Baron de Marquery, and one was in the collection of the late Sir Thomas Phillips. In addition to these, we must not omit to mention a copy of St. Augustine, which, according to Mabillon, belongs to the year 625, and the existence of which had been communicated to him by Godfrey Hermon, Canon of Beauvais; also a geometry of Boetius, copied in 1004 by the monk Constant, and deposited in the library of Berne; also a Gospel acquired by M. Didot, which had attracted the attention of M. de Bastard.

I have seen the five MSS. in Paris. The fragment of the Gallican lectionary is written in Merovingian minuscule of the seventh century. This precious manuscript contains the lessons from the Prophets, the Epistles and the Gospels read at the Mass, and other offices on the principal festival days. Also the lesson for the Eve of Epiphany, the life and passion of the Blessed Martyr Julian, the lessons for All Saints' Day, and for the day of SS. Peter and Paul. The beginning of this folio is decorated by a narrow band of interlaced design, but the top of the page has been ruthlessly cut by the binder. Fishes occur more frequently than any other animal in the decoration, and there is also a good deal of single line spiral design (see Appendix).

We must now leave the church of Luxeuil, though I fear I have given no idea of the charm and interest that hang round this old building. The dim, quiet, low-roofed aisles flanking the majestic nave, the double ranges of columns that support the vault whence its arches spring, the lofty transepts and the subdued warm light, varied by the colour of the stained glass windows, all combine to awaken the sense of devotion and mystery.

And the same may be said of all connected with the church; the same exquisite taste and perfect repose seem to characterize the services, and, to my foreign eye, to set it on a different level from most continental churches. Never shall I forget the evening weekly services, commencing at eight o'clock, during the month of my stay here, when the music had a character peculiarly its own, when the choir, mainly of female voices, sang their hymns to native melodies, old French religious *cantiques*, sweet simple airs, with the true ring in them below the graceful surface. Night after night the church was filled, and when the crowds poured forth into the quiet moon-lit streets, and friend met friend and sauntered home through the Gothic cloisters, and beneath the ancient walls and carved stone balconies of the Hotel de Ville, and the Maison Jouffroi, or lingered in the arcades of

Fig. 35.—FONT AT ST. SAUVEUR.

the Maison François 1er, I could not but feel that to the poor citizens of Luxeuil this house of prayer was also a house of rest and refreshment for body and for soul.

We must not leave Luxeuil without noticing the fine old parish church of St. Sauveur, standing on the bank of the river Breuchin, just outside the town. A strange legend is recorded by Jonas of Bobio with reference to its early history. It is said that when the fame of the holiness and the miracles of St. Columban was noised abroad, and had attracted crowds of monks to his school, they found in time that he was not the

ST. PETER. ST. PAUL.

Fig. 36.

first teacher of Christianity who had come into that district, but that a solitary priest had once appeared there, who strangely re-appeared on St. Columban's advent. He was named Vinodocus, and came as a second Melchizedek with bread and wine; and having administered these to the Irish saint, he then blessed his work and disappeared into the forest that formerly covered the district where the church of St. Sauveur now stands; which church always remained, up to the time of the Revolution, the parish or mother church of Luxeuil.

The present building is comparatively modern, but there are

ST. ANDREW. ST. JAMES.

Fig. 37.

some few traces of the former church still left in it. Among these are the figures here represented, on a curious old font in the baptistery, at one side of the door. The subjects sculptured on this font were: (1) The Baptism of Christ; (2) The Crucifixion of Christ; (3) The Pietà (Mother with the dead Son); and (4) Christ in Glory. The subsidiary subjects are statuettes of St. Peter with his keys; St. Paul with his sword and book; St. Andrew with his cross; and St. James with his pilgrim's scrip and staff and book (figs. 35-37). Unfortunately an accident happened to

Fig. 38.—ST. ANNA AND THE VIRGIN.

my illustrations of the Baptism and Glorification of the Saviour, so these subjects have been omitted. The font is supported by four recumbent lions, and measures four feet in height by three feet in diameter.

Another relic of mediæval sculpture is now preserved in the garden of the Infirmary. It represents St. Anna teaching the Virgin to read, and is full of a quaint yet tender charm. It came from the ruins of the Église de Ste. Anne in the Rue de Canne, formerly a *dépendance* on the abbey, but all trace of which is lost (fig. 38).

From the year 595 to 700 Luxeuil continued to be the centre of intellectual life in the Frankish dominions; the Frankish kings protected her; their churches drew their patrons and bishops from her monastery, their nobles sent their children to her schools. The lists given in the Appendix will show the names of the holy men who went forth as missionaries from her walls, and the churches where they planted the Columban Rule.

One hundred and five monasteries in all were founded by the disciples of St. Columban, whether in France, Germany, Switzerland or Italy. After the foundations of Annegrai, Luxeuil, Fontaine, and Lure, the great monastery of Remiremont, under St. Amé and Romaric, may be numbered as the fifth Columban foundation in the southern portion of the Vosges (see Appendix).

The Columban Rule was carried into Picardy by St. Valery, St. Omer, St. Bertin, St. Mummolin, and St. Valdolenus. Valery was the gardener of the convent at Luxeuil, and in the legend of his life we read that Columban held it as a mark of the divine favour that no flowers smelt so sweet, no vegetables were so fresh as those of his dear Valery; and when the young gardener entered the hall where Columban was expounding the Holy Scripture, he carried with him so strong a perfume of his flowers that the air of the lecture-room was filled with it, and Columban exclaimed in delight, "It is thou, beloved, who art the lord and abbot of this monastery!" When the brethren visited Valery in his cell, they found him feeding flocks of little birds, who warbled through his flowers or fed from his hand. And when the swallows flew away in fright he would motion with his hand to the monks to keep them off, saying, "My brethren, do not frighten my little friends or do them any harm ; rather let them satisfy their hunger with our crumbs."

But Valery was not the first who brought the Irish Rule into Picardy. About the year 589 two Irishmen, named Caidoc and Fricor, disembarked on the coast at the little town of Quentovic, on the mouth of the Somme, with twelve companions, and they followed the great Roman road, now called the Chaussée Brunchaut, preaching the Gospel on their way. They reached Centule,[1] and remained there some days to rest. Some say they came to France with Columban, and that when Columban resumed his journey towards the Vosges, he left behind him these two monks, that they might give instructions to the half barbarous inhabitants, and initiate them into the mysteries of the Christian religion. "They fought on," said the old chronicler, "perceiving that the inhabitants of Centule were blinded by error and iniquity, and were subjected to the most cruel slavery ; they laboured with all their strength to redeem their souls and wash them in their Saviour's Blood." But the people could not understand the language of these heavenly messengers, and they rebelled against a teaching so holy and sublime. They demanded what these adventurers, who had just escaped out of a barbarous island, could be in search of, and by what right they sought to impose their laws on them. The voice of charity was met by cries, menaces, and outrage, and the natives strove to drive them from their shores by violence, when suddenly a young noble named Riquier appeared upon the scene. He commanded silence, and arrested the most furious among the mob, and taking the two strangers under his protection he brought them into his house. He gave them food and drink, and in return they gave

[1] Now St. Riquier.

him such nourishment of the soul as he before had never tasted. He learned to know God and love Him beyond all things; and with a heart broken by sorrow for the years he had spent as an unfruitful servant, he received the assurance of his reconciliation with Heaven. Thus he, having entertained these wanderers, found that they in their turn could open to him the doors of the heavenly kingdom. He resigned all the splendour of his high estate, and laid aside his girdle of golden tissue and precious stones; his gold-embroidered purses hanging at his side; his mantles fringed with gold; his shirts of golden tissue and silken stuffs; and then he cut his long locks, the symbol of his nobility, thus proving in this act of humility that he had indeed become a servant of God. From the time of his conversion to his death he denied himself the use of meat, fish, wine, or any fermented liquors, neither did he use leavened bread or oil, but lived on barley bread, with ashes, and water. When he had taken orders he became the founder of the celebrated abbey of Centule (now St. Riquier), and the bodies of the two Irishmen from whom he had learned Christianity were interred with splendour in this church. When St. Angilbert in the year 799 restored this church, he also restored their half-ruined tombs, decorated their shrines with much magnificence, and inscribed the following verses upon them in letters of gold:

EPITAPH OF ST. CAIDOC.

"Mole sub hac tegitur Chaidocus, jure sacerdos,
Scotia quem genuit, Gallica terra tegit.
Hic Domini Christi gaudens præcepta secutus,
Contempsit patrias, mente beatus, opes.
Hinc sibi concrevit centeni copia fructus;
Et metit ætherei præmia larga soli.
Huic Angilbertus, fretus pietate magistra,
Et tumulo carmen condidit et tumulum."

EPITAPH OF ST. FRICOR.

"Corpore terreno qui cernitur esse sepultus,
Gaudia pro meritis cælica lætus habet,
Iste fuit Fricorus Chaidoco consociatus:
Quem sibi concessum Centula gaudet ovans.
Hic virtute valens despexit prospera mundi,
Et modo viventi gloria magna patet;
Quando Deo placuit, cælorum regna petivit;
Nunc Angilberti carmine fulget. Amen."

HARIULFUS, "Chron. Cent.," lib. ii., cap. xi.[1]

The relics of the two saints lay beneath this monument till the year 1070, when St. Gervinus transferred them to a silver shrine adorned with precious stones, and in this shrine also were laid the relics of another Irish saint, Mauguille, of whom we shall speak hereafter. Their festival is celebrated on June 3rd. On the road from Abbeville to Doullens, on the edge of the wood of St. Riquier (Centule), and below the slope of a smiling hill, an ancient church, majestically seated in the valley below, comes into view. It is the abbey church of St. Riquier (Frontispiece). The town rises from the foot of the church like an amphitheatre round the enclosure of its ancient walls. The great tower rises above the fertile fields around and above the summits of the distant hills and woodland glades. The little stream of Scardon which almost threatens to disappear at its very source, passes through the lower town and on towards the south-west. The old chroniclers called it Rivière aux Cardons, from the little flower cardoon. This little thread of water, rising at Bonnefontaine under Isimbard's tomb, is swelled by the junction with the river Mirandeuil or Misendeuil, a name derived from the fact that it was at this spot the ladies of St. Riquier first heard the fatal news that their husbands had fallen in the battle at Crécy. Traces of a cemetery of the

[1] See "Histoire de l'Abbaye de St. Riquier," par L'Abbé Hénocque, tome i., pp. 72-144.

Merovingian period were discovered here in the year 1869, during the excavations for buildings at the side of the town on the way to Doullens. Human skeletons with vases, some broken, some in good preservation, lay at their feet, and iron spears at their heads: these graves were oriented. A little child's skeleton was found by its mother's side, from whose ear still hung an ear-ring. Fresh excavations produced the heads of a greyhound and of a horse, iron lances and clay urns with stippled and incised patterns, glazed and dried by fire. Again, in 1860, during the formation of a road above the river Scardon, Merovingian interments were discovered with vases, lance-heads, iron hatchets and javelin points. The life of St. Riquier carries us back to the time of barbarous invasions, of which these tombs may be existing memorials. The country was conquered by Clovis I. in the year 496, and the companions of Clovis divided the Gaulish and Roman towns here, or chose those already established centres as the most favourable sites for the new order of things.

The labours of the Irish church in Picardy, commenced by these two missionaries, Caidoc and Fricor, and carried on by the disciples of Columban from Luxeuil, were destined to receive a fresh impetus from the parent country, when, a few years after the death of Valery, another mission—this time from the shores of Lough Corrib in Galway—was undertaken. Fursa and his twelve companions, who landed at Mayoc at the mouth of the river Somme, A.D. 638, are still honoured as patrons of churches throughout Picardy, Pas de Calais, the Low Countries, and the departments of Oise and Marne. It is my object now to trace the history of this second mission, which succeeded that of Columban at an interval of half a century.

The leader of this later mission is an altogether different type of character from that of Columban, who with his commanding will, and "perfervidum ingenium," resembled the Hebrew prophets in their devoted courage and their rude fierceness; while Fursa, the seer of visions of heaven and hell, was of gentler mould, nor does he seem to have been a learned man. Yet that there was a certain exaltation and touch of the divine fire in his nature cannot be doubted when he earned from his biographer, the venerable Bede, the epithet "sublime."

Fig. 39.—SEAL OF ABBEY, LUXEUIL.

END OF PART I.

Part II.

LEGEND OF ST. FURSA.

Circa 600-650.

January 16th.

Authorities.

"Acta Sanctorum Hiberniæ, ex codice Salmanticensi," edited by the Marquis of Bute, 1888. "Boll. AA.SS.," Jan. 16th. "Vita Ettonis," *ib.* July 10th. "Vita Gobani," *ib.* June 20th. Bede, "H. E." 3, 19. O'Hanlon, "Lives of Irish SS.," vol. i., p. 222. Sarah Atkinson, "Essays," p. 241.

IN the beginning of the seventh century there reigned in Munster a king named Finlog, whose son, Fintan, was beloved for his nobility and rectitude of character, as well as for his personal beauty. In his twenty-fifth year this prince visited Aed Finn, brother of the King of Leinster. Being summoned on a certain day into the presence of the Princess Gelgès, the only daughter of the king, he conversed with her for some time, then told her that he was about to leave her father's court and travel, so that he might make acquaintance with the neighbouring kings, and learn lessons in wise government from them. Now this princess had been a zealous Christian from her childhood, and constant in the daily exercise of her religion. She seized this occasion to speak to Fintan on the things of God the King of Kings. She also put before him the example of many godly rulers, that so by following them he might truly learn good government. Hearing her thus converse, Fintan was filled with love for her, which those who stood by observing, they began to think of a union between these two; but when they spoke of such a marriage to Gelgès, she answered that she was a Christian, therefore could not wed with a pagan. Her father also was opposed to Fintan, as an enemy to Christianity. But Fintan abjured his idols and became converted, and in course of time they were secretly married.

Before their child was born, the angry king, discovering her marriage, condemned her to be burnt to death, although she went to him with tears and supplications praying for his pity, and even her unborn child cried out for mercy. But no miracle could soften her implacable father, and he commanded that she should be placed upon the funeral pile. After brief prayer she was thrown upon the flames, and then, behold! another miracle. Out of the earth, at the spot on which her tears had fallen, a fountain of clear water sprang forth, while rain poured down from heaven, and so the flames were extinguished. Her garments unsinged, Gelgès stood saved, and the people, converted by these wonders, were now eager to destroy the tyrant, but Gelgès drove them back, and the king, though unconverted, gave her up to Fintan and sent them into exile.

Now Fintan had an uncle named Brendan, a venerable abbot of great wisdom, excelling in honesty, and fervent in the service of God, who had built a monastery at Clonfert, and in his old age another on Inisquin[1] in Lough Corrib, or Oirbsen as it was first called. Here, in the company of his monks, Brendan devoted himself to reading and to prayer, training to holiness many fervent disciples. To him his nephew Fintan hastened with his wife, and, with words broken with sobs, told all the sorrow of his youth, and sought a remedy from his troubles and difficulties. The venerable bishop, pitying them, led them into the guest-chamber which was reserved for strangers, and entertained them with his choicest fare, though humbler food would have sufficed their needs. On the following night, while they rested their wearied limbs, a light shone forth from heaven over the dwelling wherein they slept. So bright was it that the master of the mansion thought the whole house was in flames. Distracted with terror he hurried to the bishop, whom he found keeping his accustomed vigil, kneeling in prayer. Trembling he told what he had seen. The bishop, inspired by heavenly wisdom, felt that a celestial guard had followed his guests. He summoned his monks, and hastening

[1] Inis-meic-ichuind (the island of the son of the O'Quins, *i.e.* Meldan, successor to Brendan).

in silence to the house he saw the fire, which gave a great light but did not consume. Listening reverently he perceived that all were asleep inside, and he blessed them with the sign of the cross, and then returned on foot to his monastery. At dawn the following day the people of the country were startled to hear that Fintan, son of King Finlog, and his wife, daughter of King Aed Finn, had come into their land. Many of his relations dwelling in these parts, as well as the native princes of the country, came, bringing costly gifts, thus testifying their respect.

While these things were happening his wife Gelgès bore a son, who was brought to be baptized by the venerable St. Brendan.[1] The bishop, knowing by revelation that the Holy Spirit was in the babe, proclaimed a three days' fast, and administered the rite of Holy Baptism, calling him Fursaeus, from a Scotic word signifying virtue. This youth he not only supported with the riches of this world, but also instructed in holy doctrine and the lore of the monks. When Brendan resigned his abbacy, he placed Meldan, of the race of Conn, over the island monastery, and he became the tutor of the boy Fursa, whose father and mother then, after some time, returned to Munster.

When Fursa was still living in a cell near the church, it happened that twin children a son and daughter, relations of King Brendinus, both died at the same time. Their noble rank, and the love they had inspired, caused such sorrow to their relations, that in their struggle to secure their relics it seemed as if they would tear their bodies limb from limb. Then all the wise men of the country spoke, saying that the children should be sent to Bishop Brendan secretly, and at night; so the children's bodies were placed in a ship, which then set sail, the winds being favourable. But, notwithstanding, the vessel failed to reached its destination, and, by divine direction, went ashore near the cell of St. Fursa. The sailors lifted the bodies of the children and carried them to the door of his cell, where they left them, hastily returning to the ship. Next morning, when the young Fursa, according to custom, opened his

[1] See "Life of Brendan," May 16th, cap. 59. "Life of Meldan," February 7th. "Vita St. Endei," Mar., cap. 25. A stone fort or Caher in the townland of Ard Fintan is said to be still shown as the fort in which Fintan and Gelgès lived when they visited St. Brendan on Lough Corrib.

door that he might go to the monastery for prayer, he saw the naked bodies of the children lying on the ground. Then submitting himself utterly to the will of God, in whom all things live, with tears and supplications he called on heaven in mercy to restore life to these dead forms. His prayer was scarcely finished when from the earth the dead arose, gazing on each other in turn, and then, beholding none else save the holy man, they were filled with exceeding wonder.

Fursa led them into the church, and offered thanks to heaven throughout the day, then inquired of the children as to what might be the first desire of their hearts, and they confessed that they longed to return to their native home, since here they were in the depths of anxious misery in an unknown land, knowing neither whom to obey, nor to whom to offer their prayers. Fursa, touched to the heart by their sorrow, led them to the shore, and casting forth upon the waters the scribe's wooden ruler[1] which he carried in his hand, he bade the ruler go forth and show the way to the tender exiles' home. Then, invoking the name of the Lord Jesus Christ, who walked dry foot upon the waters, and who granted a like way unto St. Peter, he bade the children follow the ruler. Behold, a great marvel from the power of the Creator! The ruler, as though it were a reasoning being, was endowed with motion at the holy man's bidding, and the children following it without any fear, reached the port of their own home. Their friends standing on the shore, first hesitating, paused, and then were stricken with wonder when they realized that they were indeed their children, the very children whom three days before they had mourned as dead. Them they behold, swiftly gliding over the waters of the inland sea, now standing near them restored to life. The children name the blessed Fursa as their restorer, and entreat that the wooden ruler which had thus guided them through the perils of the waters might be honourably housed in the church, for the glory of God, and in memory of Fursa.[2]

[1] "Il print une reigle d'escrivent (d'écrivain) qu'il tenoit en la main." See Old French version by Jean Mielot. "Ligneam regulæ scriptoris hastulam, quam manu tenebat, in mare projecit." "Boll. AA. SS.," Jan. 16th p. 47, b.

[2] Desmay states that the ruler was long preserved as a relic.

The fame of such miracles drew many disciples to the school of Fursa, and a large congregation of monks grew up in his monastery. Religious men came to him from all quarters, among

Fig. 40.—DOORWAY OF ST. FURSA'S CHURCH, CO. GALWAY.

whom were his own brothers, Foillan and Ultan, all of whom he zealously strove to imbue with celestial grace. Even his grandfather, Aed Finn, his anger appeased, hearing of Fursa's greatness, came to him as an humble suppliant along with his brethren and chieftains. They cast themselves prostrate on the ground before him, and the king, folding his cloak around him, poured ashes upon his head, because that in his madness he had driven forth his noble daughter Gelgès. The saint, having sternly rebuked his pride, then spake holy words of comfort to him. The aged king sought and found pardon with Gelgès and her husband Fintan, and brought them back rejoicing to his house.

At this time Fursa, filled with the grace of God, abandoned his home and his family that he might devote himself to the study of Scripture in the monastery he had built on the shore of Lough Corrib. It was at this period and in this place and not in England, as supposed by the Venerable Bede, that "he fell into some infirmity of body, and was thought worthy to see the following visions from God, in which he was admonished diligently to proceed in the ministry of the Word which he had undertaken, and indefatigably to continue his usual watching and prayers."[1]

[1] See "Eccl. Hist.," bk. iii., c. 19.

Visions of St. Fursa.[1]

FROM "ACTA SANCTORUM HIBERNIÆ," IN CODEX SALMANTICENSI.[2]

Fol. 63*a*. 3.[3] It happened on a certain day, when he had gone forth to preach, that he fell ill, and his brethren asked him to return to his cell; this he did, leaning on the arm of a friend. As he approached, he bent his head in prayer, singing an evening hymn. Suddenly darkness fell upon him. In his infirmity he grew motionless, and was carried as if dead into the cell.

4. Then there appeared, through the darkness that surrounded him, four winged hands stretched downwards from above; these, lifting him beneath their snowy wings, bore him upwards. Gradually he discerned angelic bodies through the darkness, and as he ascended he saw the faces of two holy angels whose countenances shone with wondrous light. Then he beheld a third angel, armed with a bright shield and flashing sword, advance before him. A sound of wonderful sweetness filled the air at the motion of their wings. And the angels, surrounded by a great light, sang, one voice leading and the others following:

[1] "Acta Sanctorum Hiberniæ, ex codice Salmanticensi," folio 63*a*, edited by the Marquis of Bute. Blackwood and Sons, 1888.

[2] The version of these visions now given is from the first translation into English of the ancient copy in the Codex Salmanticensis, a manuscript of the twelfth century; and it would appear as if the account given by the Venerable Bede was abridged from an original life of the saint, of which this Salamanca manuscript is a copy. In the following treatment of the English translation of the story, condensation and paraphrase have been occasionally used where there was needless repetition in the original, and where such method seemed desirable for the sake of space and clearness.

[3] Paragraphs 1 and 2 contain an epitome of the same matter we have already related in full.

"The saints will go from strength to strength, the God of gods will appear in Zion."[1] There was in the song a rise, and, at the close, a fall. And then a chorus of many thousands of angels followed, singing as it were an unknown psalm, some words of which he could with effort hear, "They went forth to meet their Christ."

Fol. 63*b*. 5. Then a voice from out the heavenly host bade an angel, armed,[2] and going before, to lead the holy man back to his body, saying, "He may not yet put away his care (he may not shorten his probation)." The holy angels, in obedience, carried him back by the road which he had come. The saint, perceiving that he had been out of the body, inquired of his companions whither they were carrying him. The holy angel on his right hand said, "You must return to your body and take your life care again upon you." Then he, moved by regret at leaving the angelic company, entreated not to depart from them. The good angel of the Lord replied, "We shall return to you when you have completed your daily work." Here they chanted a little verse, "The God of gods will appear in Zion." But how his spirit re-entered into his body, charmed by the sweetness of that song, he failed to understand.[3]

6. It was at the sound of the crowing of the cock, when the rosy morning light illumined his face, that the angelic music suddenly ceased, and he heard voices of wailing and dismay. His friends, who stood around, beholding a motion of the mantle laid over him, uncovered his face. The man of God, now in the body, inquired of them, saying, "Why do ye, amazed, utter such disturbing sounds?" They, answering him, related the whole matter in due order; at what hour in the evening he had fallen into a trance, and how, until the crowing of the cock, they had watched around his lifeless body. But he, still dwelling on the angelic brightness and sweetness of his vision, thought with anxiety of the warning he had received, and he mourned to

[1] Psalm lxxxiv. 7.

[2] "D'un escu blanc et d'une glaive de fouldre" (J. MIELOT).

[3] Bede thus condenses this portion of the story. "Being restored to his body at that time, and again taken from it three days after, he not only saw the greater joys of the blest, but also extraordinary combats of evil spirits who, by frequent accusations, wickedly endeavoured to obstruct his journey to heaven." See "Eccl. Hist." bk. iii., c. 19.

think there was no wise man there with whom he could commune of the things that he had seen; and feared lest the angels should return and find him unprepared. He then sought for and received the Communion of the sacred Body and Blood, and lived in suffering on that day and another.

Fol. 63*c*. 7. At midnight, on the third day, when his parents, relations, and neighbours came to visit him, darkness again fell upon him, and his feet grew stiff with cold. Having been warned by like signs before the delight of his last vision, he now joyfully awaited death, with hands outstretched in prayer. But this time, when he had fallen back upon his couch, as if overcome by sleep, he heard the horrible sound of a great multitude shouting and urging him to go forth. Yet his eyes being opened he saw no one save the three aforesaid holy angels, one at either side, and the third standing armed at his head. Then finding himself suddenly deaf to earthly voices, and blind to earthly sights, he beheld the holy angels, and heard their songs of sweetness and delight. The angel who was on his right hand, comforting him, said, "Fear not, thou hast a shield and a defence round about thee."

8. Then as the angels bore him up past sight of house or home, the wailing and crying of demons reached his ear, and passing through the midst of them, he heard one saying, "Come, let us make war before his face." To his left he beheld a great army of demons, in warlike array, roll onward as a dark cloud curling before him. With long extended necks, and bronzed and swollen heads, their bodies were deformed and black and scranny, and as they fought, or as they flew, they seemed like hurrying shadows whose faces were lost in the dreadful darkness, even as before the faces of the angels had been hidden in the light.

Fol. 63*d*. 9. Now the burning darts of these warring demons fell powerless before the angel's shield, and the demons quailed at the sight of the warrior angel, for he spake to them, and said, "Hinder us not upon our way, this man is no son of perdition, as ye are." The adversary blaspheming argued with him, and said, that the saint was an unjust man, consenting with sinners, who ought not to go unpunished, since it is written, "Not only those who do such things, but also those who consent to them that do them, are worthy of death."[1]

[1] Romans i. 32.

While the angel thus contended with the demon, it seemed to the holy man that the noise and clamour of battle was heard over the whole world. And conquered Satan, the ancient Accuser, like a crushed snake, raised his envenomed head, and said, "Oft hath this man spoken idle words; why should he be happy? He hath been unforgiving, and it is written, 'If ye forgive not men their trespasses neither will your Father forgive ye your trespasses.'[1] He hath obeyed human laws, let him now receive punishment at a higher tribunal. If there be justice in God, this man shall not enter into the Kingdom of Heaven. This word he has by no means fulfilled." The angel of the Lord said, "Where did he avenge himself, or to whom did he do injury? Let us be judged before the Lord." The holy angel thus contending, the adversaries are crushed.

Fol. 64. 9. Then the angel on his right hand said, "Look upon the world;" and he looked and saw a dark valley in the depth beneath him, and four fires burnt therein at some distance one from another. The angel spake and said, "What are these four fires?" The man of the Lord replied that he could not tell: to whom the angel answered, "These are the four fires of Baptism. They burn for those whose sins are remitted, through confession and renunciation of the works and pomps of the devil. The first fire burns the souls of men who have loved falsehood; the second the souls of those who have been avaricious;[2] the third, the souls of those who have been stirrers up of strife and discord;[3] the fourth the souls of impious men who think it nothing to despoil the weak and to defraud the poor."[4] The flames, increasing as they approached, extended so as to meet one another, and being joined became one great flame.[5] When the flame drew near, the man of God was afraid, to whom the angel said, "That which you

[1] Mark xi. 26; Matt. xviii. 35.

[2] Dante, "Purg.," c. xix., l. 124, 129.

[3] *Ib.*, c. xv., l. 105.

[4] *Ib.*, "Inf.," c. xi., l. 52. This fire tries every man according to the merits of his works; for every man's sinful desire shall burn in the fire.—BEDE, p. 140 (Bohn ed.).

[5] Bede says of this passage: "But there is one thing among the rest which we have thought may be beneficial to many. When he [Fursa] had been lifted up on high, he was ordered by the angels that conducted him to look back upon the world. Upon which, casting his eye downward, he saw, as it were, a dark and obscure valley underneath him. He also saw four fires in

have not kindled will not burn in you; for although that fire is great and terrible, it searches and tries those souls alone that are inflamed by unlawful passion and have earned this just punishment." As they approached, the fire was cloven in two by the first angel, and it rose in high walls on either side; an angel standing before each to guard him from the flame.

10. In the fire Fursa saw devils flying about and fighting terribly,[1] and some approached to throw their darts at him, but were driven back by the angel at his side.[2] In all his passage through the fire-girt way, the saint and his angelic guide are assailed by the sharp tongues of demons, flying and struggling in the flames. They threatening cry, "The servant who doeth not according to his Lord's will shall be beaten with many stripes;[3] the Most High rejects the gifts of the unjust,[4] yet this man hath received them." To whom the angel answered, "What hath he not fulfilled of his Lord's will? If he hath received gifts from men, he believed in their repentance." The devil answered, "He ought to have proved them first, lest they should not persevere in penitence." The angel said, "Let us be judged before the Lord"

Fol. 64*b*. 11. The conquered demon blasphemed the Creator, saying, "God is not true. He hath not purged the earth, neither this man from sin; nor hath he punished it from heaven according to His word, which He spake by Elias the prophet, saying, 'If ye be unwilling and provoke me to anger, the sword will devour you.'"[5] The holy angel, chiding, said, "Do not blaspheme, when ye know not the secret counsels of God." The devil answered, "What secret counsel of God is there here? Here is no

the air, not far distant from each other. Then asking the angels what fires those were, he was told they were the fires which would kindle and consume the world." Then Bede adds, "*these fires, increasing by degrees, extended so as to meet one another, and being joined became an immense flame.*"

[1] "Raising conflagrations of wars against the just."—BEDE.

[2] "While the other two angels, flying about on both sides, defended him from the danger of that fire."—BEDE.

[3] Luke xii. 47.

[4] Ecclesiasticus xxxiv. 19; Deut. xvi. 19.

[5] Isaiah i. 19, 20. Satan here

"reflected back
The scripture image by distortion marr'd."
See DANTE, "Par.," c. xiii., l. 123; Cary (*trans.*).

place for repentance, a man's good works are of no avail unless he love his neighbour as himself;[1] this man hath not loved his neighbour thus, therefore he shall be damned." The angel answered, "Why do ye blaspheme, not knowing the secret counsels of God? So long as there is hope of repentance His mercy abideth; you know not the depths of the mysteries of God, nor where such penitence may lie. This man hath done good, and to do good is the fruit of love, and God will render to each according to his works."[2]

The horrid crowd contending, the holy angels were victorious.

Fol. 64*c*. 12. The devil, having been six times conquered, again broke out in blasphemy, and the angel answering said, "There is a time to speak and a time to be silent, concerning which it is written, 'Therefore the prudent shall keep silence in that time; for it is an evil time.'[3] And when hearers despise the word 'Hold thy tongue, for we may not make mention of the name of the Lord.'"

Fol. 64*d*. 13. But the contradiction of the Evil One continued, and the conflict was sharp until the Lord gave judgment against the adversary, who was conquered and laid low. Then the angels rejoiced, and a great light shone round about the holy man. He heard the choirs of heaven singing, and thought within himself that henceforth no labour can be too hard, no time too long, when the joy and sweetness and glory of eternity is the thing to be sought for. Looking forth again he beheld the heavenly host of angels and of saints;[4] and angels flew before him like great flocks of birds with gleaming wings, till, these surrounding him, all terror of the fire and of the demon host was driven away. Issuing forth from the band of saints he beheld Beoan[5] and Meldan, two holy men[6] that had come out of his

[1] Matt. xxii. 39. [2] Matt. xvi. 27; Rom. ii. 6. [3] Amos v. 13.

[4] "In fashion, as a snow-white rose, lay then
Before my view the saintly multitude.
* * * * * *
For through the universe,
Wherever merited, celestial life
Glides freely and no obstacle prevents."—*Par.* xxxi. 1, 21, 22.

[5] Mart. Ængus, Oct. 26th. Ed. Whitley Stokes, LL.D.

[6] Beoan and Meldan speak to him. Beoan, called præsul in the old and new Acts, and by Capgrave, bishop. "Tunc vidit duos sanctos episcopos," see "De S. Furseo. Legenda Angliæ," fol. cliv.

own country, and these advancing spake with him as with a friend, each telling him his name.

14. Then he beheld, and lo, there was a great calm in heaven, and two angels entered through the heavenly portals seeking its upper air and higher joy. A marvellous bright light shone round about them, and he heard the voices of four bands of singers with the multitude of angels saying, "Holy, holy, holy, Lord God of Sabaoth."[1] His soul filled with the sweetness of this heavenly melody, and upborne by these sounds of unspeakable joy, soared upwards to the point from beyond which the heavenly song came. Bands of angels encircled him there, and one on his right hand said, "Knowest thou where this joy and delight prevail?" He replying that he did not know, the angel answered, "At the heavenly congress whence we too have come." Then forgetful of all toil and trouble, the sound of the heavenly songs growing clearer and more melodious filled him with exceeding joy; it seemed that he alone was sung to, and, wondering thereat, he said, "These songs are a great joy to hear." The angel answered, "We may not often stay to hear them thus. We are the ministers of man, and we must toil and labour in his service, lest devils corrupting human hearts should make our labour vain." Again, as the saint is still wrapped in the heavenly melody, the angel of the Lord spake, saying, "There is no sorrow in heaven save one, no mourning here, but for the lost soul of man."

Fol. 65*a*. 15. Then he beheld the two forms of surpassing brightness he had seen before come forth from the innermost shrine of heaven. They seemed as it were two radiant angels who approached him. These were the venerable men Beoan and Meldan. Their message to him was that he should now return to earth. Silent, and overwhelmed with sorrow at these words, he straightway turned, the holy angels leading him. And the old

[1] Isaiah vi. 3.

"Hosanna Sanctus Deus Sabaoth,
Superillustrans claritate tuâ,
Felices ignes horum malahoth."

"Thus chanting saw I turn that substance bright
With fourfold lustre to its orb again
Revolving."—*Paradiso*, Canto vii., l. 1.

men asked for time that they might speak with him and say, "What dost thou fear? Thy journey is but for a day; go forth and preach to all that the day is at hand, that the judgment is nigh." Blessed Fursa inquired of them when the end of the world would be; and Meldan speaking said, "The end is not yet, but the day is at hand. During the past year the sun hid its beams, and his light shone as that of the moon. Pestilence and famine[1] will first come, and there will be famine of two kinds: the dearth of wisdom when men understand and do not fulfil the Lord's word; and the dearth of wealth, when men store riches in abundance and yet desire more, for money doth not satisfy the avaricious; the bitter fruit of avarice destroys the sweetness of good words. Unlawful desire bringeth malice and bitterness; for him who despiseth the signs and warnings of the Sacred Word, and doth not repent, death is at hand. But death may be held back by reason of the patience of God.

Fol. 65*b*. 16. Although the wrath of the Supreme Judge overhangs such men, yet doth His anger chiefly burn against the heads and teachers of the Church, through whose neglect and bad example so many faithful souls are lost; whose work is left half done; who are carnal and self-indulgent.[2] Some if chaste are avaricious, others if gentle are weak, others provoke anger, being themselves too easily provoked thereto, others are vain-glorious of God's gifts, as if they had earned them by the labour of their hands, others idle, cease to grow in virtue.[3]

[1] This refers to the famine and pestilence described in the annals of Ulster as happening in Ireland in the year 663-664, when "there was a great darkness in the ninth hour of the day, in the month of May, in the Calends, and the firmament seemed to burn, the same summer, with extreme heat. There was great mortality through the whole kingdom."—*Ann. Four Mast.* i. 274, note. Bede ("Eccl. Hist.," xxvii., p. 162) also mentions this plague which devastated the province of the Northumbrians, and depopulated the southern coasts of Britain no less than the island of Ireland, where many of the nobility and of the lower ranks of the English nation were at the time, either studying theology or leading monastic lives, the Scoti supplying them with food, and furnishing them with books and their teaching gratis.

[2] Dante, "Purg.," c. xvi., 126.

[3] Thus Dante, "Par.," xxix., 99, shows Beatrice censuring the vain unprofitable preaching prevalent among the clergy.

"The aim of all
Is how to shine: e'en they, whose office is

17. Some among them are beset by spiritual sin, thinking much of their visions of the night, and little of that pride through which the angels fell from heaven; or of avarice, through which paradise was lost; or of envy, through which Cain slew his brother Abel; or of false witness, through which our Saviour was condemned. But rather, nourished on these unlawful things and feeding on pride, avarice, envy, false witness, blasphemy, they eat as it were the flesh of their neighbour, and drink his blood.

Fol. 65*c*. 18. He who thinks lightly of these shortcomings is an enemy of souls rather than a teacher. Give him then these remedies. Humiliation in dust and ashes for his pride; the giving of gifts for avarice; benevolence for envy; confession of truth, for false witness; bridling the tongue, and being instant in prayer, for blasphemy; since it sufficeth not to afflict the body if the mind be not kept free from sin. And urge the teachers in the Church of Christ to provoke the souls of the faithful to the sorrow of repentance, and to bring them back to health by feeding on the sacred Body and Blood.[1] And warn them further to be slow to excommunicate, lest by this means they sustain the sinner in his sin, lest they plant an elm[2] tree instead of a vine,[3] an elder[4] tree instead of an olive.[5]

19. The anger of the Lord is kindled against such teachers; for king and priest alike do that which seemeth right in their own eyes,[6] pride is at the root of all evil, the people rise up against

To preach the gospel, let the gospel sleep,
And pass their own inventions off instead.

*   *   *   *   *   *

The sheep, meanwhile, poor witless ones, return
From pasture, fed with wind."

[1] Dante, "Par.," c. xviii., l. 123..

[2] Elm was commonly called the ear of Judas, the black fungus grows on it that grows on the vine. It is associated with the idea of death as providing wood for coffins. "Answer thou dead elm" (2 Henry IV., act ii. sc. 4.)

[3] *Vine.*—Christ.

[4] *Elder.*—Judas was hanged on an elder tree. Wood hard and heartless, both flowers and leaves have bad odour. It is used for funeral purposes.

"Now bringen bittre eldre branches seare."

[5] *Olive.*—Peace, abundance, use.

[6] Judges xvii. 6.

their rulers, the clergy against the priests, the monk against the abbot, sons against parents, youths against elders. Obedience not being taught, humility is lost, and each one acting in his pride all must suffer. Pride[1] is the great evil that overthrew the heavenly company of angels, and in its perversity destroys the present clergy."

20. When Meldan ceased to speak then also did the priest Beoan address the blessed Fursa in these words: "Preserve thy life by using the creatures of God; denying thyself, reject the evil; be a faithful steward, temperate in all things, for though the poor and the needy and the prisoner may beg, the rich should give to those that are in want.[2] Let there be no discord in the Church of God; let those that are in monasteries eat their own bread, working in silence.

Fol. 66*a*. 21. Some men there are who loving retirement, hide themselves and the light of their good example from the world, keeping secret the good that they do; others in the business and strife of the world let the poison of covetousness enter their hearts. Therefore be neither always in retirement nor yet always in the world, and, when alone, keep your heart with diligence, obeying the divine commandments, and, when in public, be intent on the salvation of souls. And though all may oppose and fight against you, give good for evil, and with a pure heart pray for your enemies. For he who hath resignation in his heart can change the fierceness of wild beasts to gentleness. No sacrifice of works is so acceptable to God as a patient and a gentle heart, to which, God helping it, adversity and loss is gain. Go forth, therefore, and tell the chieftains of this land of Ireland that if they abandon their iniquity and repent they may attain salvation. And announce these very tidings to the priests of holy Church, for our

1 "E ciò fa certo, che 'l primo superbo,
Che fu la somma d' ogni creatura,
Per non aspettar lume cadde acerbo."—*Par.*, c. xix., l. 44.

"In proof whereof,
He first through pride supplanted, who was sum
Of each created being, waited not
For light celestial, and abortive fell."

2 "Such cleansing from the taint of avarice
Do spirits, converted, need."—DANTE, *Purg.*, c. xix., l. 115.

God is a God jealous[1] lest the world should be loved before Him, and lest men, seeking the things of this world and delaying to repent till late in death, should receive their just reward and suffer fiery torment."

Fol. 66*b*. 22. Having thus spoken the holy Beoan and Meldan were received into heaven with the celestial company of angels.[2] Then Fursa prepared to return to the earth, when he saw a great fire approaching. But the angel smote it as before, and cleft it in two parts. Amid the flames were demons, who seized a man from out the fire and hurled his body over Fursa's shoulder, burning him.[3] And Fursa recognized the man as one whom he had visited in death, and who, when dying, had left to him his mantle. The angel of the Lord said, "Because thou didst receive the mantle of this man when dying in his sin, the fire consuming him has scarred thy body also. Nothing may be accepted of the sinner unless he repent, neither may his body be buried in a holy place." Then his angel said he did not receive the same through avarice, but in order to save the sinner's soul.

Fol. 66*c*. 23. And Fursa was then borne back by the angels through the flames, and he stood still over the roof of the church with the holy angels. His body lay beneath him and the angel desired him to resume it, but he, shrinking in horror, refused to approach it. But the angel bade him not to fear his body's weakness or temptation longer, since through his tribulation their power was destroyed. And he beheld his body open from its breast, and the angel ordered that water from the fountain should be poured upon it, and said, "Continue thy good course to the end, and so shall we receive you prosperous and blessed." Then the saint rising from the deep sleep of death, looked around amazed at the happy change, at the greatness of the recompense to those who enter the regions of the blessed. But when the living water was poured upon him he felt the scar between his shoulders burn,

[1] Exodus xxxiv. 14.

[2] Bede says, "When they had ended their discourse, and returned to heaven with the angelic spirits, the three angels remained with the blessed Fursey, of whom we have spoken before, and who were to bring him back to his body." (Bk. iii., c. 19). For notice of Beoan see Corblet, "Hagiographie, partie 2nde," "Béoden."

[3] He lived twelve years after this vision, and bore upon his shoulder and cheek the scar left by the burning touch of the lost soul.

and the mark was on his face of the blow he had received; and "thus the flesh shewed outwardly, in a wonderful manner, what the soul had suffered in private."

Here concludes the account of these visions in the "Codex Salmanticensis." Bede adds, referring to this period of St. Fursa's life:

"He always took care, as he had done before, to persuade all men to the practice of virtue, as well by his example, as by preaching. But as for the matter of his visions, he would only relate them to those who, from holy zeal and desire for reformation, wished to learn the same. An ancient brother of our monastery is still living, who is wont to declare that a very sincere and religious man told him, that he had seen Fursey himself in the province of the East Angles, and heard those visions from his mouth; adding, that though it was in most sharp winter weather, and a hard frost, and though the man was sitting in a thin garment when he related it, yet, so moved was he through fear or spiritual consolation, that his sweat was, as it were, great drops falling down to the ground."

When he had awakened from this vision Fursa went into Munster,[1] that he might there find some member of his own family to place at the head of his monastery, and it is held by some that it was on this occasion he was joined by his brothers, Ultan and Foillan, who returned with him to Lough Corrib.[2] He is said to have been present at a council held at Termon Molagga, convened by the King of Munster and St. Molagga, to discuss the grant of lands and immunities to be given to the saint.

When the chieftains conferred upon the church of St. Molagga in Cork the privilege of refuge and other immunities, then the men of Munster fasted to the saint, and Molagga stipulated for the freedom or perpetuity of his *termon*, for which he obtained security. The names of St. Fursa and four other ecclesiastics are recorded as present on this occasion. They all subscribed to

[1] It appears from lives of St. Barr, cap. 24; of St. Molagga, cap. 19, 20, and of St. Cronan (Cron-Cronanus, an alias of Cuan or Mochua), cap. 16, that the saint visited Munster before leaving Ireland. See Colgan, "AA. SS.," p. 94.

[2] Here also he studied with Beoan, the dear Master who appeared to him in his vision of heaven, and whose relics he carried with him on his mission. The beautiful oratory of this bishop still stands in marvellous preservation in Bishop's Mountain Valley (Coomaneaspuig), in West Kerry. See "Brendaniana," by the Rev. D. O'Donoghue, p. 287.

the charter, and stood as sureties for carrying out the necessary conditions. The scene is thus described in the life of Molagga:

"Then the king bowed to Molagga and he gave him alms, namely, his two steeds, his robe, and a chalice of silver, and a paten of gold with a *leisreach* every year. The king agreed that Molagga should be his soul-friend for ever, and that this privilege should belong to his descendants in office, and added that the saint's bell should take precedence of all other bells except the bell of St. Patrick; and Molagga promised that these agreements should be fulfilled towards every king who reigned in Cashel hereafter, so that not one should ever die without a soul-friend through his blessing."

On this occasion it would seem as if Molagga had visions as well as his friend Fursa, for it is said that Victor, the angel, and Patrick descended from heaven to bind and confirm the treaty, and Patrick ordained that Molagga should come every Thursday to hold converse with him in heaven.

Leaving Munster, Fursa then travelled for the space of one year among the people in the islands of Ireland, preaching to them until the day came round which was the anniversary of that on which, when out of the body, he had seen the vision. That same night, while many wise and religious men were with him, his life scarce beating in his breast, he was caught away from the trouble of the body, and he beheld the angel of the Lord, who announced to him the day on which he must go forth to preach, instructing him in doctrine, and telling him that twelve years were to be spent in such labours. The time named by the angel being accomplished, Fursa having preached the word of God to all, without respect of persons, and not being able to bear the multitude of people crowding to him, proposed to retire to a certain little island in the sea. About this time Fursa had ordained three brothers as priests, Algeis, Etto, and Goban.[1] They beheld the Lord Jesus Christ appear to them in a vision, in the sixth hour of the night, and say unto them, "Come unto me, all ye who labour and are heavy laden, and I will refresh you.[2] Come, ye blessed of my Father, inherit the kingdom

[1] These three missionaries, in the end, became respectively the patron saints of the towns of St. Algise, St. Gobain, and Avesnes in France.
[2] Matt. xi. 28.

prepared for you from the beginning of the world." The next day being Sunday, they sought out their master Fursa, and told him what had occurred, and how they had all seen the same vision and heard the same words, and that having taken counsel together, and remembering the words of Christ when He said, "Unless a man forsake father and mother, and even his own life, he cannot be my disciple,"[1] that they had resolved to set forth and preach on foreign shores. Fursa, on hearing these words gave thanks to God; but, smiling, said to them, "Certainly ye shall not leave unless I go with you."

He then called his brethren Ultan and Foillan, and said, "Do ye desire to serve Christ with me?" And they said, "Whither you go, we will follow." In like manner spake Corbican and his servant Rodalgus. And Fursa said, "Let us follow Christ, and offer ourselves a holocaust to Him." So Fursa went and carried with him the relics of Meldan and Beoan, whom he had seen in his vision.

They seem to have travelled to Dublin from Lough Corrib, for Fursa is said to have visited St. Maignenn, of Kilmainham, with whom, says the Martyrologist of Donegal, "he agreed to exchange tribulations in token of their union." The existence of an ancient dedication to the saint, near Dundalk, may give us a clue to the direction now taken by these missionaries. The ruins of Killfursa serve as a landmark on their way. Here, when they reached the seashore, and awaited their embarkation, a great tempest arose, and the waves swelled mightily. Fearing to venture forth in the storm they fasted there for three days; then celebrating the Holy Sacrifice "*ad secretæ Missæ orationem*," the storm suddenly ceased, and they sailed forth. Landing upon foreign shores, Fursa and his companions are borne through Britain to Saxony, *i.e.*, East Anglia, where, being honourably received by King Sigebert at Burghcastle, he softened the hearts of the barbarians.

Bede describes his advent in the following passage, Bk. iii. c. 19:

"There came out of Ireland a holy man called Fursey, renowned both for his words and actions, and remarkable for singular virtues, being desirous to live a pilgrim for our Lord, wherever an opportunity should

[1] Matt. xix. 29.

offer. On coming into the province of the East Saxons, he was honourably received by the aforesaid king, and following out his usual employment of evangelist, by the example of his virtue and the efficacy of his discourse, he converted many unbelievers to Christ, and confirmed in his faith and love those that already believed."

"Sigebert," adds the same writer, "was a good and religious man, who long before had been baptized in France, while he lived in banishment, flying from the enmity of Redwald." When at last Sigebert succeeded to the government of East Anglia, "he proved," says William of Malmesbury, "a worthy servant of the Lord, polished from all barbarism by his education among the Franks. On his coming into power he graciously communicated to the whole of his kingdom those rites of Christianity which he had seen abroad. The promoter of his studies, and the stimulator of his religion, was Felix, the bishop, a Burgundian by birth, who had become very intimate with Sigebert while he was an exile in France, and who encouraged his designs. He accompanied him to England on his return, and was at length appointed bishop of the East Anglians."

It seems not improbable that it was this meeting with the Burgundian bishop at Burghcastle that decided the course of the further missionary labours of Fursa and his companions, and made them select north-eastern Gaul as their ultimate field of action. When Fursa stopped at Burg (Cnobheresburg in Suffolk), some of his Irish companions stayed with him, and others seem to have gone on to France before him. Algéis, Corbican and Rodalgus went on to Corbei, and thence to Laon; while Foillan and Ultan, Goban, Dicuil, and Etto, and another follower, Madelgisilus, remained behind with Fursa.

For some time Fursa preached the gospel successfully at Burghcastle, and here he had another vision, which lasted three days, and he heard a voice saying, "Watch and pray, for ye know not the hour neither the day;" urged on by this he laboured earnestly to found a monastery in that place, and chose a spot near the shore, within the area of a certain camp or castle, made pleasant by the woods and the sea, which monastery was afterwards adorned and enriched by King Anna. King Sigebert gave evidence of his piety by casting away his purple, his sceptre, and his crown, and becoming a monk. Not ungrateful to the saint, and feeling that Fursa was indeed a great solace to him, and knowing the good that he brought to the whole island, and above all to the Picts and to the Saxons, the remnants of whom he converted from idolatry to the true faith, he gladly helped to build him a monastery, where those who wished could embrace a religious life.

When Fursa had completed his monastery the only thing that seemed wanting was a bell. Just at that time a widow's only son died, and the body was carried to the church for burial. As Fursa met the funeral train, an angel descended from the sky and gave him a bell. At the first sound of this bell the boy awoke to life, and lived a holy monk long after in this monastery.[1]

A great famine prevailed soon after in this part of England, when Fursa, followed by his friend and usual travelling companion, Lactan,[2] went into a certain field adjoining the monastery. They both began at once with spade and rake to till the ground. Fursa then sowed it with seed, which in three days sprang to maturity, corn ripe for the sickle and ready to be drawn into the granary.

Fursa, now desiring to withdraw himself from all the care of the world, conferred with his brethren, for he had still with him many wise and very reverend and spiritually minded men, who, through his high example, both in government of the monastery, and in various labours, had attained to the grace of humility and

[1] "Cette cloche est de si grande auctorité qu'elle garde et a gardé le pays où elle est jusques orres (maintenant) de tonoire, de tempeste et de fouldre et d'embrasement, aussi loingz comme le son en peut estre ouy."—Latin Legend translated by Mielot.

Another bell, belonging to St. Fursa, is spoken of in the life of St. Cuanna (Colgan, "AA. SS." February 4th), his friend, whom he had left on the shores of Lough Corrib. On one occasion, when Cuanna was presiding over a conference of 1,746 holy men, a bell was seen in the air, moving as a bird, and suspended over their heads and the congregation, astonished, inquired of Cuanna why came this bell, and how came it moving through the air, as though it could not touch the earth, and Cuanna answered, "This bell, which you behold in wonder, flying through the air, belongs to St. Fursa. He hath sent to us this bell as a token that he longs to be present with us here." Then he told them that St. Fursa was dwelling at Péronne in Gaul.

[2] Lactan (Lactanus, Lactantius), disciple of St. Fursa, abbot of Lagny, and companion of his missionary labours in Gaul. Colgan, "AA. SS.," 96, c. vi., 291, c. xii., 299 n. 12. Lanigan, "Eccl. Hist. Ir.," xii., 462. O'Hanlon, i., 262, 285. Lanigan says Lactan was with Fursa at Lagny.

Fig. 41.—ROMAN FORT AT BURGHCASTLE.

love: among these were his own brothers, Foillan and Ultan. Fursa forthwith consigned the care of the monastery and souls to Foillan, along with the holy presbyters, Goban and Dicuil.[1]

His brother Ultan had already, after a long monastic probation, adopted the life of an anchorite. Repairing alone to him, Fursa lived a whole year in abstinence, contemplation, and prayer, labouring daily with his own hands.

Then after the lapse of a year Fursa was summoned, yea, even compelled, by the king and the people to give counsel, he being a person of great talent; therefore he had to abandon the hermitage he had chosen. Regarding all things of the time with a very watchful mind, and seeing the province in confusion, through the irruption of the pagans, and foreseeing that this monastery would also be in danger, leaving all things duly arranged,[2] he sailed over to France, having first bequeathed his girdle to his monks,[3] which they afterwards lovingly covered with gold; but he still carried with him the relics of his Irish masters Meldan and Beoan.

When Fursa first started on his mission to the north-east of Gaul, his companions Rodalgus, Algéis, and Corbican had gone before him. These missionaries kept along the banks of the rivers Authie, Somme, Seine, Oise, Marne, Aisne, and Meuse. Madelgisilus having joined Fursa worked with him at St. Riquier, and Péronne on the Somme, and at Lagny, in the department of Seine-et-Marne. When the friends they had left behind at Burghcastle followed them into Gaul, they laboured with them at Lagny and St. Gobain, near Laon, and Péronne, and afterwards carried the work into Belgium, to Soignes, Hainault, Nivelles, and Fosse, while Algéis and Corbican, who had first arrived in France, worked near Amiens, Celle, Corbei, Vervins, and Laon.

Having crossed to the shores of France, Fursa, entering the bay of the Somme, and landing at Mayoc, near Le Crotoy, went inland up the river to St. Riquier, a monastery in which he

[1] French, Gobain and Desle.

[2] Bede says, "dimissis ordinatis omnibus navigavit Galliam."

[3] The monks are said to have folded some locks of his hair in this girdle, and then to have enshrined it in gold and precious stones, and applied it for the healing of certain diseases.

must have found traditions of his native church.[1] The history of its origin has already been briefly noticed here. In the course of years, when Mauguille had closed his master's eyes in death, he returned to St. Riquier, and submitted to its Rule.

But now the travellers pursued their course along the Roman causeway, through Picardy, to Frohens-le-Grand, a village near Mézerolles[2] between Doullens and Auxi, two leagues from Doullens. When he reached this village the saint heard a great wailing in the house of a certain Duke Haymon, who lived in the neighbourhood, because his only son was dead. The man of God asked permission to watch the body through the night, and ordered that it should be placed beside him in a quiet little cell, the door being closed. This done, Fursa bowed his knees and made supplication to the Lord with tears; they soon arise together, the holy man from the dust, the child from the bier. Early in the morning, Haymon, coming to the house with his wife, and with a great crowd of men and women, making lamentation as they came, on their arrival found their son, whom they supposed to be dead, singing and praising God, together with the man of God. Then Haymon, thus blessed, along with all his people glorified God, who was made glorious in His saints. For this act he offered to give Fursa in possession the place called Mézerolles, and he implored that he should never leave him. But the man of God, refusing, continued his journey to Austrasia. The people followed after him, kissed his footsteps, and sought his benediction, and he healed many of various infirmities. Among them was Haymon, who, casting himself at his feet, said, "I pray thee, man of God, that, though we are unworthy thou shouldest remain here, yet thou wilt reveal to us the time of thy departure from the world." The man of the Lord answered, "When you see me re-appear with three bright lights in one night, then will you know

[1] Fursa reached France in the time of Clovis II. Mayoc, at which place Fursa landed, was a Merovingian villa on the seashore, at the mouth of the Somme, near Crotoy, where Haymon, Count of this province, lived. Le Crotoy, is identified by Valois and Cluvier with the Carocotinum of the "Itin. Anton."

[2] Mézerolles in Ponthieu. In the village close by the memory of St. Fursa is still honoured. It is now called Frohens-le-Grand, formerly Fors-hem—meaning the house of Fursa; Ham or Hem signifying house or dwelling.

I am about to depart." The place where this miracle was wrought, was thence named Fors-hem, or house of Fursa.

When Fursa came to the district of the Ambiani he entered a village called Autolium (Auteuil), near the river Corbeia.[1] Here he was met by a certain evil-minded man, who stripped him of his cloak, threatening his followers with his stick, then turning to his own house, he took the cloak of the man of God and threw it to his wife, when immediately he, and his wife, and daughter were possessed by an evil spirit, and the daughter became both blind and dumb. The man of the Lord, who had followed him to the house, on asking leave to enter, and no reply being given, was moved with pity. He prayed that they might be pardoned. They believing then in the merits of the saint were converted, and consecrated their lives to the Lord.

On another occasion Fursa coming into a large city, called Grandis Curtis,[2] in the district of the Atrebati—the sun was setting and he was weary—he asked a lady named Hermelinda to give him lodging, as she appeared to be wealthy, and in possession of a large property; but she refused his request. When the man of the Lord, seeing her unkindness, departed, she became possessed of a devil; and, being tormented, she sent a messenger after the saint, saying, "O servant of God, behold our mistress calls thee, come deliver her from torment, for she knows that it is on account of thee that she suffers such great evils." At first the man of God was reluctant to return to her dwelling. However, moved with pity, he gave his staff to one of his disciples, who, entering her house, drove the demon from the woman, and she was made whole.

Thus the power of the saint was not only manifested by his own hand, but even lay in the staff which he carried. Whenever this staff was sent to the sick they were immediately made whole, and such miracles were daily spoken of throughout Gaul.

At this time there dwelt at Péronne a man of the Lord, named Erchenwald, who came forth to meet St. Fursa at Grandcourt. He was mayor of the palace under Clovis II., and the king had endowed him with his fortress at Péronne. Erchenwald has

[1] In Canton Albert, near Doullens, Picardy.
[2] Grandcourt in Canton Albert.

been described as a man of peace, full of goodness and prudence, a well-wisher to the clergy, neither haughty nor avaricious, but courteous to all. Such a lover was he of peace and unity, that he seemed as if sent by God to maintain them. He was learned, yet he was simple in his actions. He had amassed riches, yet with moderation. He was dear to all.

Some years before the advent of Fursa to Picardy, Erchenwald had sheltered the young Princess of Saxony, who afterwards as Queen Bathilde became the friend of the Irish missionary, and with her husband, Clovis II., did much to further his work. She had been carried off by pirates, who sold her for a small sum as a slave to Erchenwald. Concealing her rank, she waited on him, and she was accustomed to fill his drinking-cup at table. But Erchenwald soon perceived the value of the jewel he had purchased for so small a sum. Seeing with what grace she fulfilled the humblest duty, and that her whole appearance bore traces of high birth and queenly dignity, he, on his side, became her slave, and turned to serving her with reverence. His passion, always lawful, was for some time borne in silence; but when at length he sought her hand in marriage, she fled into concealment. Her royal soul must wed with royalty, and in due time she gave her hand to Clovis II., King of Neustria, who finding none other in his kingdom so worthy, made her his wife and the companion of his throne.

Meanwhile Erchenwald had married, and his wife having borne him a son, he, hearing the fame of the Irish saint, and the miracle he had wrought on the Duke Haymon's son, went forth to meet him at Grandcourt (*Grandis Curtis*), and brought him to Péronne. There the saint, loving the father as himself, received the infant Leudisc to holy baptism, and taking the child in his arms he held him at the font; and there was great joy in the household of the mayor. It was in the old church of St. Quentin en l'Eau that this ceremony was performed. Another church was then commenced by Erchenwald which he intended for St. Fursa's use, but this was thirty years in progress, and the saint had died before its completion.

It is said that six men, who had been some time imprisoned in the town, when they heard of Fursa's arrival, cried aloud, "Pray for us, thou servant of God! we believe we may be saved by thy coming." The holy man, moved with pity, asked that they might be released from prison, but his petition was then refused. Yet the man of God said that when the hour of midday meal approached, he would see the prisoners before his repast. And lo! the Lord having heard His servant's prayer, they who had been confined, came forth unhurt, none helping them. Standing before the duke they asked his pardon and glorified God, because that virtue, salvation, and help had come to them.

The fame of the visions and revelations of St. Fursa now spread through the villages and towns of the district, till it reached the ear of King Clovis II. and Queen Bathilde, who conceived a strong desire to entice Fursa to their court, while Erchenwald was hoping to detain him at Péronne. Obliged in the end to submit to the command of the king and queen, Erchenwald desired three of his household to lead the man of God from place to place until he could find a spot that might be given him to inhabit, which also they did, and out of all the places that he saw, the holy man chose Lagny[1] (Latiniacum). This place is so called because of its great seclusion, as if indeed God had meant it to be hidden from our gaze. It was overgrown by a thick wood, and the beautiful waters of the river Marne are drawn from this source. Fair wide meadows stretch around; here thick and fruitful vineyards grow, bright and sparkling; it seemed a pleasant place in the eyes of the man of God.[2]

Fursa, on coming here, struck his staff on the ground, and immediately there issued forth a great fountain, which to this day irrigates the place and affords healing for many infirmities. Here Fursa drove out devils from many who were possessed, restoring them to health. And when tidings of such things reached Erchenwald, he gave thanks to God that He had sent so great a man to him, and one by whom such miracles were wrought. Coming to St. Fursa, the king said, "I am thankful to God that He has enabled me to grant you such a dwelling as this which you have made your own. Now build at [Lagny] and arrange all things carefully so that it may be suitable to

[1] Lagny-sur-Marne, in the neighbourhood of Chelles, and dependent on the diocese of Paris. Latiniacum in Bricio of the Gesta Dagoberti.

[2] Colg., lib. 1, cap. xxxvi., p. 82.

Fig. 42.—VIEW OF PÉRONNE.

thee and thine for all time. Meanwhile, I shall hasten to Cigne [Mons Cygnorum], which is at Péronne, so that, if it should also prove acceptable to thee, thou mayest have it besides, and, by God's providence, our bodies may rest together there." A hymn being sung, the holy Fursa began to build Lagny with his own hands, and the happy Erchenwald hastened on the work at Péronne.

Lagny was close to Chelles, about six miles from Paris, where Clovis and Bathilde had their *villa regia*, and where this good queen founded her long famed nunnery. Aided by these sovereigns, Fursa was enabled to build a monastery and three chapels, one of which was named after him. While here he was given to hospitality, and on one occasion being warned in a dream of the approach of a youthful pilgrim from Rome, he went forth to meet him and bid him welcome. They recited psalms of goodwill and greeted one another by name, though they had never met before. Twenty years after this youth was known as Bishop Hildebert of Meaux.

At this time Algéis, who with his companions Corbican, Rodalgus, and Caribert had parted from Fursa in England, and had preceded him into France, was dwelling in a retired place in Picardy, near Cellula, Mont St. Julian, on the Oise, in the woods of Thiérasche, now called St. Algise. When Algéis arrived there, he, choosing a piece of ground for his habitation near a well, which sprang forth at the planting of his staff, spent the night in prayer, before his work commenced. But at the hour of dawn two of his disciples went out to a wooded hill, without knowledge of their master, and began to cut down trees thinking to erect the building in that place. However, a dove, carrying a leafy branch in its bill, appeared to them and flew before them towards the place chosen by the Almighty for their foundation. The disciples ceased their work, and, coming down from the mountain, they followed in the direction the dove had taken, till they reached the spot where the master still knelt in prayer and they beheld the dove standing beside him. The saint then rising from his knees took an axe in his hand and began to build, assisted by his disciples. The place was called Cellula, and here he and Corbican, Rodalgus, and Caribert settled down.

When tidings reached Ireland that this settlement had been made at Cellula, Enna and several other Irish pilgrims sailed over to France to join them. They were received with joy; the saint, embracing them, said, "How good and pleasant a thing it is

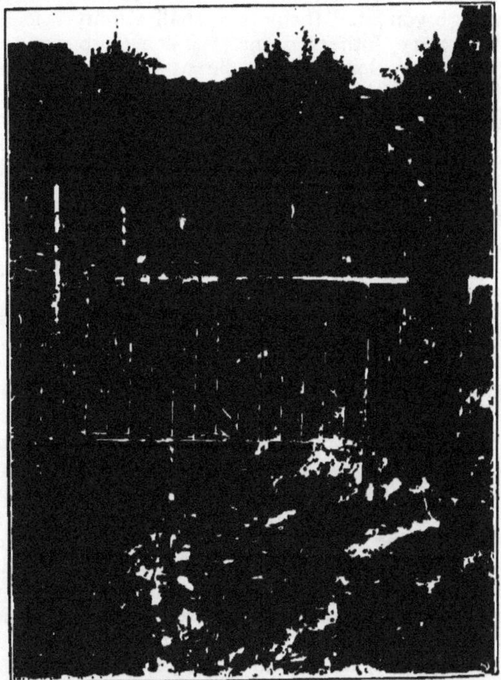

Fig. 43.—HOLY WELL OF ST. ALGISE.

for brethren to dwell together in unity." Then, having eaten, the travellers rested for that night, and next morning they joined Algéis and the brethren in their labours. Here all these holy men, working together, raised a church in honour of St. Peter, and when it was finished Algéis said to Corbican, "My son, it behoves you now to cross the sea and go into my country, and tell my father and mother, my brethren and sisters, the things that we have done here. Say to them that my portion of the inheritance must be sold, and the proceeds thereof sent here to me through you; tell them they shall see my face no more unless they come hither to me." Then Corbican answered, "Should it happen that I were to die, what would become of the treasure?" And his master answered, "If death overtake thee, tell my father and mother to cover you with a waxed linen cloth, and place the treasure by thy side; then let them set thy body on two hides of animals sewed up on every side, and afterward commit it to the deep, and the Lord will guide it hither." Corbican, having received his blessing, humbly obeyed his master, and started on his journey. Crossing the sea, he bore the saint's message to his parents. They, greatly rejoiced to hear tidings of their son, immediately sold his portion of the inheritance and gave the proceeds to Corbican. He, when making preparation to return, felt his strength begin to wane, and the chill of death approach. After his soul had departed, the parents of his master covered his body with a waxed cloth, placed the treasure by his side, and set all in two hides of animals sewn up on every side. They carried the body down to the sea and committed it to the waves, and angels came and steered its course across the ocean till it reached the mouth of the river Seine, up which they travelled till they entered the river Oise, and kept moving onward against the current of the stream. The shepherds standing on the bank saw the floating object, and left their flocks that they might follow and secure it; but their efforts were in vain, they could not draw it towards them. Eluding their grasp, it glided on, at which they wondered greatly. Algéis, hearing of this thing, came down and stood upon the river's bank. Instantly the coracle bearing the body of Corbican floated up to him. On opening the covering of skins the treasure was found. Algéis bore the relics of his faithful disciple into his oratory. Then the body was religiously interred with hymns and psalms of praise.

Having now established his church at Cellula, Algéis carried the Gospel through Hainault, working in the district between the rivers Oise and Helpra[1] until he had banished all traces of still lingering idolatry.[2]

While these events were occurring at Cellula, another Irishman arrived at the monastery of Fursa in Lagny. He was named Æmilian, and in his youth had been the saint's disciple in the monastery on Lough Corrib. When the fame of his master's labours reached him there, and he heard a report of the great monastery he had founded abroad, he journeyed forth to assist him in his work along with some companions, ready to follow their master's footsteps, in contempt for human things, in mortifying of the flesh, and zeal for pilgrimage.

After long journeyings in foreign lands, and many wanderings backwards and forwards, seeking St. Fursa from place to place, the holy band of Irishmen found their master even greater and more saintly than they hoped when they reached him at length in his monastery at Lagny. On their arrival the brethren of the Caritas[3] of the monastery were filled with delight, and rejoiced with one another, because of their advent.

Few facts of Æmilian's life have been preserved from oblivion, for his *acta* have disappeared, and the record of his deeds in imitation of his master has long since perished. In the "Life of St. Fursa" he is spoken of as singularly simple and pure of heart, and we are told that Fursa, acknowledging his long and faithful service, chose him as the fitting person to name as his successor. For now our saint had had forewarnings of his approaching end, and before his death he longed to return to East Anglia to revisit his brothers Ultan and Foillan, and the monastery of Cnobheresburg, made famous through his efforts there, desiring

[1] Helpra. See Molanus, "Natales SS. Belgii," June 2nd, pp. 108, 109.

[2] Adalgisus died on June 2nd, and was buried at Laon, whence his relics were translated, by desire of St. Forannan, April 30th, in the year 970, to the church of St. Michael, Thiérache, on the road from Hirson to Mezières. See Migne, Paris, 1856. MM. Maxime de Montrone, "Dict. des Abbayes," col. 527.

[3] *Caritas*, Publicum, ni fallor, valetudinarium. Gall., Hôtel-Dieu, hôpital (Du Cange). *Caritarius*. Monachus qui harumce caritatum prædiorumque ad eas pertinentium curam habebat.

to strengthen and confirm his brother Foillan, and its inmates won by his efforts and his faith.[1]

Therefore, placing in his abbacy the holy Æmilian to watch over his flock, Fursa, with his faithful companion Mauguille,[2] hastened on his journey. Coming to the land of Count Haymon at Mézerolles, near Doullens, this saint of the Lord was seized with sickness, and being warned by an angelic vision that his end had come, he bade farewell to present things, and passed into the region of eternity.

It will be remembered that St. Fursa, on his first visit to that town, had promised Haymon, the duke of the district, that he should receive a sign when Fursa's last hour arrived, the man of the Lord having said, "When in one night you see me reappear with three bright lights, then you will know I am about to depart." Now it happened that Haymon, coming one day in to his noonday meal, just at the hour of Fursa's departure, saw three figures bearing three tapers, which they placed, standing, on his table in his room, and then vanished from before his eyes, and he knew them to be the holy Fursa and his two deacons. Then Haymon, in amazement, asked those standing by, "Do ye see the wonder that I see?" They replied that they saw nothing. But he, remembering Fursa's promise, believed that the man of God was dead. Rising from his table, and followed by his household, he rode back to Mézerolles, where he found the clergy, monks, and inhabitants of the village singing the requiem around St. Fursa's bier. He ordered his soldiers to guard the body, and joined in their devotions.[3]

When news of St. Fursa's death reached Peronne, Erchenwald,

[1] During the years that St. Fursa presided over the monastery at Lagny, he worked in conjunction with Audobert, Bishop of Paris, and perhaps, also with his successor, Landry, who held the see of Paris a little before the death of Fursa. He held the office of *chorévêque* to the Bishop of Paris, an office equivalent to that of vicar-general. It was in this capacity that he, with the aid of Bobolenus, built a church at Compans which was consecrated by Audobert. Compans lies between Lagny and Gournay-sur-Marne.

[2] St. Mauguille has been identified with Mauger, who held the office of Prior of Lagny under St. Fursa. See Abbé Henoque, "St. Riquier," tom. i., p. 77.

[3] In memory of these events three wax tapers are still lighted on the altar of St. Fursa at Péronne.

divining Duke Haymon's design of enshrining his relics at Mézerolles, marched with a royal guard to secure them. The duke refused to resign the relics, saying, "He restored to me my first-born; but what is this matter between us? Let two wild bulls be ordered to be yoked to-morrow, that they may take up the bier and go whithersoever they will, God ordering them." Then Erchenwald, the man of the Lord, moved with joy, said, "Let it be so." Now it happened, while each party was guarding the body of the blessed man, that a girl, blind from her birth, approached, who, falling down, touched the pall with which the bier was covered, and immediately her sight was restored. Next morning they proceeded to try the matter. They yoked the bulls to the bier on which the holy body rested.[1] The bulls moved straight on until they reached the village called Péronne. Erchenwald followed the body with a great crowd, singing psalms, and glorifying God.[2] These things being done, Bercharius, Count of Laon, came with a great army, that he might carry off the body, and Erchenwald spake and said, "Why hast thou come hither armed in this manner?" And Bercharius answered, "He whom you are taking away is mine by right, and while he was alive I was duke above all others in this land, and whatever power I had I gave up for the sake of his love and that of his companions. In life he desired to come to me, which you prevented; now since I could not have him in life, give him to me that at least I may have him in death, his relics to preserve. Let us here place two boys who are ignorant of the matter, and let them choose between us in this very hour." Erchenwald replied, "As thou hast said, so let it be." Erchenwald sent one boy, aged seven years, to the side of Bercharius, and Bercharius sent his boy to the side of Erchenwald, and the children, raising the bier, carried it to Mont des Cignes, near Péronne.[3] They were met by Erchenwald in front of the still unfinished porch of the church that he was building. A tent was prepared to shelter the precious relics until the works were concluded. And all this time the body,

[1] The town of Les Bœufs takes its name from these oxen. It was granted to the collegiate church of St. Fursa by Bercharius.
[2] Boll., "AA. SS.," Jan. 16th, lib. ii., cap. v.
[3] Colg., "Vita S. Fursæi," lib. ii., xii., xiv.

being watched by night and day, saw no corruption. The rivals, now at peace with one another, gladly followed after the body, and buried it amid sweet perfumes in the place where the saint himself had formerly laid the relics of Patrick,[1] Beoan, and Meldan, which he had brought with him from Ireland. Meanwhile, within thirty days, a church was prepared and built in honour of the twelve apostles.

A shrine was then prepared to which these relics should be transferred by the three men, Eligius, Autbertus, and Medardus, and when his body was laid therein it was as uninjured as on the day of his departure.[2] This concludes the life and virtues of the holy Fursa.

The Venerable Bede adds, "Four years after, a more decent chapel or tabernacle being built for the same body to the east of the altar, it was still found free from corruption, and translated thither with due honour; where it is well known that his merits, through the divine operation, have been declared by many miracles. These things and the incorruption of his body, we have taken notice of, that the sublimeness of this man may be the better known to all readers. All which whosoever will read it, will find more fully described, as also about his fellow labourers, in the book of his life before mentioned."

[1] Colg., "Vita S. Fursæi," lib. ii., xvi.

[2] In the life of St. Eligius we read that he returned some time afterwards with a shrine that he had wrought meanwhile, in which the relics of St. Fursa were reverently laid and placed upon the altar.

LEGEND OF MAUGUILLE.

A.D. 650.

May 30th.

AUTHORITIES.

Hariulfus in "Vita Magdegisili." "Patrologie," tome clxxiv. Boll., "AA. SS.," Maii 30.

MAUGUILLE having fulfilled all the last duties to the master he mourned so truly, doubted, in his affliction, whether he should return to Lagny, or, continuing his journey back to England, merely seek some quiet retreat more close at hand. In his perplexity he thought of Centule (St. Riquier). He was already familiar with this now celebrated monastery. He came to the gate of this sacred place. Humbly and with earnest prayer he craved admission, and was eagerly welcomed by the monks. "He found," says the old legend, "that which he sought, true Israelites, willing fugitives from a faithless Egypt, eager to gather that heavenly manna which will support them in solitude, monks pure as the angels, bearing their shield of humility and abstinence." One day an angel appeared to him in a dream and said, "Follow me; take note of the place that I will show thee; since it is there that God has appointed for thee to serve Him." Then the angel led him through devious ways to the place ordained. When they stopped the angel spake again. "Behold, here is the spot where thou must live and die." The vision disappeared, and Mauguille awoke. He knew that God had revealed Himself to him, and rising he prostrated himself on the ground in gratitude for this signal favour.

Next day, after the holy office, the servant of God told some of the brethren of St. Riquier this mysterious dream, in which the place of his blessed solitude had been revealed to him. Then the bishop ordered all things to be made ready for his installation in the desert, and selected the monks who were to accompany him, and assist in building his cell. When all was ready this athlete of Christ bade farewell to his brethren. He passed along the divers ways he had trodden in the dream with his divine messenger, and recognized with secret joy the place the Lord had chosen for him.

The monks of St. Riquier stayed with him until they had built an oratory and a cell. This hermitage was named Monstrelet. It stood on the banks of the Authie, three hundred metres from the river. Here stood the parish church of Monstrelet for a thousand years, which is now destroyed.

The hermitage of Mauguille was surrounded by the impenetrable forests of Boisle and La Broie. The saint's happiness would have been perfect, but that he was prevented from drawing water by the miry marsh which lay between the river and his cell. The long walk round was beyond his strength, therefore he prayed to the Lord that he might be spared this labour. Secure that his prayer was heard, he made the sign of the cross on the turf of a dry hillock, and a clear thread of water sprang up through a cleft in the stone, forming a well from which the waters flow into the Authie. "This miraculous fount," says Hariulfus, an old chronicler of the ninth century,[1] "was full of heaven's blessing, and they who drank of its waters in faith, were cured of divers infirmities."

Here the saint continued to live till his health gave way. The Abbot of St. Riquier, warned of his state by an angel, came with some of his brethren to visit the holy anchorite, to support him in his trial, and to offer him the consolations of his ministry. Mauguille was restored by his gentle words, and for the time forgot his suffering, and the abbot returned, leaving him under the care of one of his servants.

However, Providence designed a better way by leading a fellow-countryman of his own to his side, who was willing to share his solitude. Wulgan, then bishop-elect of Canterbury, shrinking from so responsible a post, chose to serve God in the

[1] "Chron. Cent.," Liber iii., cap. xxix.

poverty and obscurity of an unknown solitude. He prayed for deliverance from so great an honour, and an angel announced to him that his prayer was granted. "Cross the sea," said this heavenly messenger, "and go into the kingdom of the Franks. Thou shalt land upon the banks of the river Authie, where a servant of the Lord lies sick in his hermitage. Cure him of his ailment, and remain with him to share his life of penitence and prayer to the close of thine own earthly pilgrimage."

Wulgan joyfully quitted the town and went down to the sea-side. He stepped into a boat, which he found lying on the shore, and let it drift as God willed. Guided by an invisible angel, it advanced, without the aid of any oar, till it reached the bay of the Authie, then passed up the river and stopped before the hermitage of Mauguille.

Wulgan entered the humble cell of the anchorite, and with a prayer for heavenly medicine he laid his hands upon him. At that blessed touch Mauguille revived; all his pain had vanished. Lifting himself up he fell into Wulgan's arms, and they held one another in a long embrace. Inspired by a like faith and a like devotion, they strengthened and sustained one another in their life of piety, until, after many years, Wulgan fell ill. Mauguille watched his friend's suffering with the deepest sorrow, and sobbing, cried, "Wilt thou leave me, brother, in this life of sorrow, when thou hast passed into eternal joy? I hoped it might have been for you to recommend my soul to God, and lay my body in the earth; and behold! you seek to go before me and leave to me this mournful office." And Wulgan answered, "Be patient, dear brother; humbly bow to the divine will. What profit would it be that our lives were passed in the rugged paths of the divine law, if, in our last hour, the tempter, who has followed us step by step that he may wound us at some unforeseen moment, caused us to murmur and rebel? I do but leave you for awhile; I shall soon see God face to face, then shall I pray without ceasing for you, that you may be delivered out of exile."

Strengthened by these words Mauguille sent the servant, given him by the abbot, back to the monastery of St. Riquier to tell the brethren of his friend's state, and pray them to bring him the Holy Viaticum and Sacrament of the Dying. The monks hurried to the hermitage of Monstrelet. Wulgan, having received the Communion of the Divine Mystery, slept in the Lord on the 2nd of November. The monks of St. Riquier buried him near his hermitage with psalms and hymns, reciting verses from the Holy Scripture.

Mauguille survived him but a short time. He died in the year following on the 30th of May, A.D. 685; and his body was laid by that of his friend in the hermitage of Monstrelet, where it remained until the year 1003, when it was translated to St. Riquier. Then on the 13th of July, 1113, Abbot Anschar caused a new shrine to be made for his body, very precious, and adorned with plates of silver, sculptures, and bas-reliefs, representing events in the saint's life.[1] The old biographer of St. Mauguille remarks that the envelope of deerskin, by which the skeleton was covered, was found to be too short to hold all the bones, and they were obliged to procure a fresh covering. This translation took place in the year 1513, the fifth of the reign of Louis the son of Philip, and sixteenth of the prelacy of Anschar.

The following inscription was placed upon the shrine:

"Ossa Madelgisile tenet hæc lectica Beati;
Quem confessorem sibi Christus rite beavit,
Ancharusque novam sibi capsam jure paravit."

We have now to learn the fate of the other disciples who followed Fursa from Ireland; and our next legend will be that of the patron of St. Gobain, in the forest in the diocese of Laon, department of Aisne, in France.

[1] On opening the old shrine he found a parchment containing these words: "*Corpus sancti* Magdelgesili confessoris hic positum, III Kalendas junii."

LEGEND OF ST. GOBAIN.[1]

Circa 648.

June 20th.

AUTHORITIES.

See Boll., "AA. SS.," tom. iv., Junii 20. A. Butler, "Lives of the Fathers," vol. vi., June 20th. Baring Gould, "Lives of Saints," vol. vi., June 20th, p. 280.

IT is related in the old life of St. Fursa, p. 121, that St. Gobain, with two others of the brethren, saw a vision and heard a voice in their Irish monastery on Lough Corrib, bidding them go forth and preach the Gospel, and that he also induced Fursa to start on his mission. Born on the shores of Lough Corrib, Gobain was noble looking and of noble family, and from his childhood his life was dedicated to the service of God. He was ordained a priest by St. Fursa, and coming with his master to England, remained for some time behind him at Burghcastle when Fursa went on to France.

Before leaving Ireland he is said to have met a blind man by the way, and, moved with compassion, he prostrated himself upon the ground, and earnestly besought the Lord in his favour; then rose, and signing the blind man's eyes with the sign of the cross, he restored his sight.

Gobain followed Fursa to France in a short time, and travelled to Corbeny in the department of Aisne, canton of Craonne, about sixteen miles south-east of Laon on the way to Rheims. Here he and a band of brethren who had accompanied him from England, parted from one another with the kiss of peace, each choosing his

[1] In Irish, Gobhan; French, Gobain, Gobin.

own field of work in the district. Gobain then repaired to Laon, and spent some time with the brethren in the church of St. Vincent, which had been founded a few years before by Queen Brunehilde, after the death of Sigisbert in 580. Anxious to found a new monastery, the saint, followed by one disciple, penetrated to a place in the ancient forest of Voës or Vosage (*Vosagus sylva*, *Vosagum foreste*), a southern portion of the *Sylvanectes*, where its woods are met by those of the Forêt Charbonnière to the south of Laon, which was haunted by wild beasts, and where he found an ancient fortification on the summit of a steep rock called Le Mont d'Hermitage.

Being weary with his journey he lay down; folding his cape under his head for a pillow, and fixing his staff in the ground, he bade his disciple watch while he slept. Singing in his sleep he chanted the psalm "Lord remember David," down to the eighth verse.

"Lord, remember David, and all his afflictions:
How he sware unto the Lord,
And vowed unto the mighty one of Jacob:
Surely I will not come into the tabernacle of my house,
Nor go up into my bed;
I will not give sleep to mine eyes,
Or slumber to mine eyelids,
Until I find out a place for the Lord,
A tabernacle for the mighty one of Jacob.
Lo, we heard of it in Ephratah,
We found it in the field of the wood."

On awaking he found a clear fountain had sprung up where he planted his staff; a sign, as he told his disciple, that he should build his hermitage in this spot. He then sought the king at Laon, that he might gain his permission to do so. The king, then resident at Laon, was Clothair II. He granted Gobain the land on which to found his monastery: he was the son of Chilperic, and having lost his father while he was still an infant he had been brought up by his uncle Gontran, the same who, many years before, had granted the lands of Annegrai to St. Columban. The portion of the forest to the west of Laon in which he permitted Gobain to settle was that where its woods are met by those of Forêt Charbonnière. The most important part of this forest was henceforward named, from Fursa's follower, Forêt de Saint Gobain. It is watered by the river Oise.

He reached the mountain called Bibrax,[1] and passing the fortifications of Laon, he approached the church of the Blessed Virgin and saw two men, one blind the other dumb, sitting in the porch. He offered prayers for them and forthwith they were restored, and the fame of this miracle reached the king's ears, who sent for the stranger and said, "Whence have you come, and to what race do you belong?" He answered, "I am a Scot who for the love of Christ, leaving the Island of Hibernia, have now journeyed hither, and entreat you to grant to me a certain small piece of ground in the wilderness near your city." The king, on hearing this, directed one of his household to go with the saint, who led him to the spot he had chosen in the forest on the banks of the Oise, and finally confirmed the gift of this land by royal charter to the holy man.

Here St. Gobain built his cell, and with the assistance of the king and the people a church was founded in honour of St. Peter, which was afterwards named, from the saint himself, St. Gobain. He seems to have remained in this place teaching and preaching, waging war against the wild pagan traditions and barbarous customs of the inhabitants, for whom he interceded in prayer, saying, "Take away, O Lord, their guilt from them, or else take away my life." At last, in a vision of the night, the voice of the Lord came to him, saying that barbarous men, more fierce than the Vandals, were coming out of the north, through whose onslaught his labours would be crowned with the martyr's crown. These words brought consolation to the servant of Christ, who had left father and mother, household and brethren, for the love of his divine Master. In a short time the wild horde of invaders prophesied of came out of northern Germany, laid waste the country, and penetrating the forest even to Le Mont d'Hermitage attacked and beheaded the holy man, whom they found reading the Bible at the door of his cell. He was buried in the church afterwards called from his name, and his head, inclosed in a silver shrine, was long preserved in the sacristy. A large stone

[1] Laon, anciently Bibrax Laudunum. Lugdunum clausum.

sarcophagus was also there, in which the saint's relics were deposited for many years; but all these vestiges disappeared during the wars of the Calvinists in the sixteenth century.

The church of St. Gobain is a very interesting building, in the crypt of which the well may still be seen which sprang up miraculously beneath the staff of St. Gobain. At some height in the wall a Latin inscription in Gothic characters was also found,

"O Gobane gratiam impetres et gloriam his qui tibi serviant."

"Oh! Gobain, mayest thou obtain by prayer, grace and glory for those who serve thee."

These being the closing lines of a sequence to an ancient mass which gives a summary of the holy martyr's career in Latin verse.[1]

[1] See O'Hanlon, "Lives of Irish Saints," June 20th, p. 749, note 12.

N.B. Camerarius in his work, "De pietate Scotorum," lib. iii., says that St. Gobain's festival was observed on the 3rd of November, according to some tablets preserved at Péronne.

ST. ETTO.

(*In French, St. Zé.*)

DIED CIRCA 670.

July 10th.

ANOTHER Irish follower of St. Fursa, who is said to have spent some time with his master in Lagny, was Etto. He was warned of God in a dream that he should preach the Gospel in the Low Countries, and his companions on this mission were Eloquius, Amandus, Humbert, Mombolus, Fredegand, Bertuin, and Waldetrude. He became the patron saint of cowherds, and one of the first miracles recorded of him is, that while walking in a field one day he came upon a dumb man sleeping, who was a cowherd. Touching him gently with his staff the man arose, and immediately his tongue was loosened and he spake like other men.

Etto built an oratory at a place called Maloigne, near Liège, upon the Sambre. He also lived as a recluse in a solitary place on the little river Corbriol, in the forest of Thiérache, near Avesnes, where he cleared away the brambles and built himself a cell. While at his work he was much interrupted and harassed by a native of the place named Jovinus, whose opposition the saint could only overcome by the aid of a miracle.[1]

Maelceadar and Bertuin were among his friends and associates when he entered on this mission to the Low Countries. Towards the close of his life he dwelt at Fiscau, near Avesnes, where he founded an oratory, which afterwards became a monastery; and when it was revealed to him that the close of his life was

[1] See Boll., "AA. SS."

approaching, he called his disciples to him, admonishing them to observe charity and peace one with another. The night before his death he had a vision of the place of his sepulchre; and on awaking he desired one of his friends to repair to a certain wood, where he would find a man making a coffin. This he was to seize and bring away with him on a waggon drawn by a bullock. His friend having done as he desired, the saint, gazing upon his coffin before him, partook of the Body and Blood of our Lord in the holy Sacrament, and then yielded up his spirit in the sixty-fifth year of his age, A.D. 670.

The body of St. Etto is now preserved in the church of Dompierre, and there is a tomb on which he is represented wearing a mitre, and clothed in episcopal vestments, with a cross in his hand. Close to the church there is a fountain named the Well of St. Zé.

In art he is represented as restoring speech to the dumb by the touch of his staff, or surrounded by oxen and calves. He is invoked in Hainault against the disease of epizootis.

SS. FOILLAN[1] AND ULTAN.[2]

(*In French, SS. Feuillan et Outain.*)

OCT. 31ST-MAY 1ST.

AFTER the death of Fursa in 650, his brothers Foillan and Ultan were invited by St. Gertrude of Nivelles to come and assist her in her labours in South Brabant. St. Gertrude was the daughter of a prince of that country, Pepin of Landen, and his sainted wife, Itta, or Iduberga. Her father was minister of the king, and mayor of his palace. His daughter Gertrude, was born at Landen in the year 626; when she had grown to maidenhood her father invited King Dagobert to visit him, along with his son, who then ruled over Upper Austrasia, and who sought the princess's hand in marriage. The young prince thought it a favourable moment to speak of his love when the king was seated at table, and he asked her father for her hand in the royal presence. The king approved, and Pepin, the father, was ready to consent, so he invited the princess and her mother to the table. When they had entered the hall, the king asked the young Gertrude whether she would not rejoice to have the young prince for her lover, one so beautiful and strong, clad in rich silks, all shining with gold; but, to the amazement of all, the child seemed indifferent, despising those things which in the eyes of the others seemed most precious, and showing that her heart could not be won by the delights of the world.

[1] French, Feuillan, Foignan, Foiland, Féland, Fillan.

[2] Feast of St. Ultan in an ancient MS. copy of St. Ado's "Martyrology," preserved in the monastery of St. Laurence, at Liège. See Bede, "Hist. Eccl.," lib. iii., cap. xix. Boll., "AA. SS.," tom. i., "Maii 1, de S. Ultano, Abbate Fossis et Peronæ."

Educated in rigid seclusion and virtue, she did not soften her refusal by any studied terms, but simply told the king, before her father and mother, that she did not care for this or any other youth, and that she would have no spouse save Christ. Alarmed that any man should thus desire to win her, she strengthened this protest by a vow, therefore the king declared that she should be pressed no further. Her father died when she was fourteen, and her mother chose St. Amand as her spiritual director. This godly man exhorted her to found a monastery to which she might retire with her daughter; she took the veil and built the Abbey of Nivelles in Brabant between Mons and Brussels, endowing it with all her wealth.[1]

Alarmed by the attacks of her enemies and persecutors, and fearing lest Gertrude should be carried away from beneath her care, she cut her child's hair in the form of a crown. Gertrude rejoiced to feel that she was thus marked as the spouse of Him who wore the crown of thorns. Having taken the veil she was invested by her mother with the government of the nunnery of Nivelles when she was yet but twenty-one years of age; here she soon became known as the friend of the poor, of the stranger, and the pilgrim. She was careful for the decoration of her church and altar, offering on them relics of the holy martyrs, and books of prayer; while she persuaded men of fame and learning to visit her from distant lands and parts beyond the sea. Her institution was a double one, one part being allotted to monks and the other to nuns, as was a common practice in those early times. St. Foillan had apparently become known to her when she was still under the instruction of St. Amand, for he is said to have embarked for Flanders about the year 633, and to have reached the monastery of Ghent, then newly founded by St. Amand. Along with him came Ultan, who had hitherto lived in a hermitage in Suffolk. Gertrude had long known that these two Irish saints united a strong mental capacity to their piety and virtue, and therefore she resolved to secure their services in explaining the Holy Scripture to her nuns, and preaching among the inhabitants of the farms and villages on her estate.

[1] "Ste. Gertrude, Abbesse de Nivelles en Brabant." Anon. ap. Boll., p. 504. "AA. SS.," Ben. p. 464. Balt., l. iii., c. 40. Le Cointe, "Ann. Eccl. Fr."

After the death of her mother, the blessed Itta, which happened in 652, she gave St. Ultan the land of Fosse, between the rivers Meuse and Sambre, formerly in the diocese of Maestricht, now of Liège, along with all things necessary for the erection of an hospital for pilgrims, and a monastery of which he was to be the first abbot; but she still kept St. Foillan at her side, that she might profit by his advice and instruction, and she appointed him the spiritual director of her nuns. Two years afterwards Foillan, desiring to visit his brother, the Abbot Ultan, and to see the economy of his new monastery at Fosse, started with three companions on this expedition. One day they entered the forest called Sonef, otherwise Charbonnière; the saint lost his way amongst its winding paths and fell in with robbers. Their leader, on the pretence of offering hospitality, invited the man of God and his disciples into his den, but the saint, inspired by the Holy Spirit, when he found himself therein, foresaw that the hour of his passion was at hand. He passed the time in watching and prayer, and warned his disciples not to fear, but bravely to meet a sudden death that might be the gate to eternal life. While he was thus speaking the robber entered with his accomplices. He attacked and beheaded the holy abbot, and then his followers smote the disciples in their faces with their swords. Then these ministers of crime, taking the bodies of the saints, hid them away in the dark lairs of wild beasts and divided the spoils amongst themselves. In the meantime, St. Gertrude, warned by many dreams, and waiting in suspense for the saint's return, sent to St. Ultan at Fosse to inquire after him: this abbot, also surprised at hearing nothing of his brother, answered, "Last night, while praying in the church, there appeared to me a dove of snowy whiteness whose wings were stained with blood." From this he knew what had happened to his brother, and he sent answer to St. Gertrude of what he feared. But she had already gone in search of the body in the forest, and an angel of the Lord pointed out the scene of the passion of the holy abbot. Then beholding a column of fire arising to heaven, and moving onwards till it stopped at a certain spot, she, following it, knew that here the saint's body was hidden. So long as it burned steadily in the one spot, the virgin knew that here the saint must lie, therefore she summoned her holy confessor, and he accompanied her to the ground beneath the fiery pillar. The virgin quickly entered the path overgrown with brushwood, and followed by a wondering crowd she arrived at the place of martyrdom thus illumined by heaven. As the virgin had loved St. Foillan greatly, she reverently lifted the covering and found that which she sought, and the venerated bodies of the saint and his followers were placed in coffins. At that moment the Bishop Dodo, of Poitou, together with the patrician Grimoaldus were passing through this country on a pilgrimage to the holy places, and while the body of Foillan was on its way in the watches of the night they fell asleep. An angel appeared to them in a dream directing them to go and meet the holy prophet. They were then aroused by the voices of the singers and hastened out to meet the funeral. The bishop and Grimoaldus took the dear burthen from those who were carrying it, and bore it on their shoulders for the glory of the Lord. The body was thus carried into Nivelles, where St. Gertrude rendered it all the honours of burial.

In later years a monastery was erected in the forest of Charbonnière at the place of martyrdom, as well as the Abbey of Premontré in the town of Rœux, in Hainault, where Foillan and his three companions are still commemorated. St. Foillan's principal feast day is October 31st; his invention, January 16th; his translation, December 3rd.

In the year 659 St. Gertrude felt her end approaching, and sent a monk to the Abbey of Fosse to tell St. Ultan of her condition, and inquire whether God had revealed to him at what time she should die, for the thought of death, ever present with her, filled her heart at once with fear and joy. The saint told her that on the next day she should die, but that she need have no fear and suffer no distress, because St. Patrick and the angels chosen of God were ready to receive her into glory. Consoled by this answer, Gertrude passed the night in prayer with her sisters, and the next day she departed.

Ultan subsequently governed the monastery at Mont St. Quentin without resigning the administration of that of Fosse. Little more is known of the life of St. Ultan; it is said that when St. Amatus (called in French Amé) was banished from his See of Sion in Le Vallais by Theodoric III., son of Clovis II., King of Austrasia, he fled for protection to St. Ultan, at Péronne, where the holy abbot received him with every token of respect and veneration.

The year of St. Ultan's death is uncertain, but it was close upon 680, as he is said to have survived his brother Foillan nearly thirty years. He was buried at Fosse in the church he had founded under the invocation of St. Agatha.

After the death of Fursa, St. Eligius, Bishop of Noyon and Tournai, lost no time in appointing a *conducteur* for the monks of Mont St. Quentin. He could make no better choice than that of St. Ultan, who under his brother Fursa had already acquitted himself so well. It was under Abbot Ultan that this great Bishop of Noyon had consecrated the church of this monastery, dedicating it to St. Quentin, apostle and martyr of the Vermandois.

St. Ultan is patron of Courcelette, in the deanery of Albert. The statue of St. Ultan, with that of his two brothers, formerly stood at the porch of the church St. Furcy, Péronne. He is represented with a crown at his feet, to show his contempt for worldly splendour.

LETTERS

WRITTEN ON A JOURNEY IN SEARCH OF THE EXISTING MEMORIALS OF ST. FURSA AND HIS COMPANIONS.

The Neale,
Co. Mayo,
Sept. '94.

DEAR H.,

I SAW the birthplace of St. Fursa yesterday on the island of Inisquin in Lough Corrib, and the foundations of the little monastery of his uncle St. Brendan, the traveller. It was my first expedition in search of any traces of Fursa's footsteps in this part of the world. I started with my kind friends, Mr. and Mrs. Burke, at eleven o'clock, and had a delightful drive for about two hours till we reached the ferry from the shore of the lake to the island. The road winds down from the ruins of St. Fursa's church near Headford for about two miles in a south-westerly direction, till it reaches the little creek from which we were to embark for the island. We passed through a wild plain filled with stone and brushwood, and carpeted with harebells and purple heather, with here and there patches of soft velvety grass, till we reached a bog in which every conceivable bog plant seemed to grow luxuriantly. Groups of peasantry were scattered here and there, men in brown corduroys, women in red petticoats, busily employed digging and shaping their turf, as they do in cases of great moisture, by trampling it with their bare feet.

At last we reached the creek where we found the boatman's

cottage, where Pat Kelly dwells, who ferries passengers to and from the island. I shall never forget that delightful ferry, the first sight of the long low island to which St. Brendan retired for rest, after his voyages in search of the new world in the western ocean, after his visit to St. Gildas, in Wales, who named him the *Pater laboriosus.* On this island he retired to die, and close by, at his sister's nunnery in Annadown, he breathed his last, within sight of this island.

The rising ground encircling the creek is covered with wild wood, the grassy island lies in the middle distance. From its highest point the eye roams over the wide reaches of the lake to the islands of Inchagoill, the wooded Ardilaun, Inismacatreer, and numberless other islands,

" Like precious stones set in a silver sea,"

to the fine amphitheatre of mountains at whose feet Lough Mask and Lough Corrib extend. It was strange to travel back in thought to the time when thirteen hundred years ago this ferry was crossed by students from far and near, seeking the knowledge of letters and religion from Brendan, and Meldan, and Fursa; and it is recorded that Fursa, after he had left the island for his own monastery on the mainland, was wont to recross this ferry, after his dear master Meldan's death, that he might spend the night in prayer beside his tomb. The island is now inhabited by a poor widow and her young daughters, with two or three herdsmen, whose sheep enjoy its rich pasture. All traces of the monastery are fast disappearing; the abbey is a shapeless heap of ruin among whose fallen stones I found the remains of one capital carved and broken. The size of these foundations is fifty-three feet in length by twenty wide. Another oratory, now a mere heap of stones, twenty feet long, and a portion of a wall, rising from a plinth, are still shown as vestiges of the ruins.

In 1845, when the island was examined by the officers of the

Ordnance Survey, a monument was still in existence called *Lebayd in Tollceand*, the bed of the wounded head, the legend of which is given in the life of St. Brendan.

Fig. 44.—CAPITAL FOUND IN INISQUIN ABBEY.

It is said that a monk was buried here who died of a wound in his head, and who had been restored to life by St. Brendan; and the legend says that when the saint saw him lying lifeless on the ground, he called him to his side, and the dead man arose and approached the saint, carrying the iron weapon with which he had been wounded still sticking in his head. The saint asked the wounded man whether he desired to remain alive or pass away to heaven, and the monk at once replied that he desired the latter. I was sorry to find that this monk's grave had been only lately destroyed, and some farm buildings erected over its site. Other legends are told of St. Brendan's life here, but of Meldan the abbot, and the teacher of Fursa, I could find no trace. His relics were carried to Gaul and buried with those of the patron saint at Péronne, and so nothing was left here to keep his memory alive.

The Neale,
Co. Mayo,
September, 1894.

DEAR H.,

We started from The Neale at half past ten o'clock to drive to the ruins of St. Fursa's monastery on the mainland, near the shore of Lough Corrib, and passing through the picturesque little village of Cross, I stopped to ask for the second church of which I had heard. This is now named Kill-arsagh, formerly Killfursa. The farmer of whom I inquired, told me I should find the ruin a little to the west of the cross near Ballymagibbon. However, I now refrained from turning aside, as there was work enough before us at the larger monastery, and I looked forward to exploring this second ruin in a few days with the greatest interest. Leaving Cross by the road which passes Houndswood, we branched off from the main road by another leading down directly to the shore of the lake through Finshona, and here the scenery grew more charming at every turn. The mountains of Lacamra, Kirkaun and Benlevi came into view, and the undulating ground in the middle distance revealed the lake and its tiny islands stretching far to the west. After passing Ballycurrin we reached the Owenduff river, which forms the boundary

Fig. 45.—BRIDGE OF SHRULE, CO. MAYO.

line between Mayo and Galway, on whose banks we saw the fine ruin of Ross Abbey, and which is spanned by the Bridge of Shrule a few miles higher up.

When we had reached the wooded grounds of Ower, I stopped again to ask at a carpenter's house for more information as to the ruins I was in search of. And glad I was that I did so, for this poor man proved to be one of the few left in the country who took a genuine interest in its old monuments, and preserved the memory of their traditions. He told me that near the church of Fursa I should also find a cromlech, or, as he called it, *leaba Dermod agus Grania*, and a high pillar stone, marked by a cross within a circle, that has a great name for curing rheumatism, and the people come from distant parts of Mayo to lay their backs against it and to ease their pain. He also told me that there was a weir up the Owenduff river called Corra Fursa, or the weir of Fursa, the legend of which proves that for centuries after the saint's death his protection was felt throughout the district.

It was during the plague that swept across Europe in 1348, when twenty-five millions of the human race were said to have been carried off, and Connaught was devastated by the scourge, that Aed, Bishop of Tuam, grew sick at heart when he saw the dead and dying around him. One night, as he was praying in the Church of the Shrine at Tuam, he saw a great light, and heard a voice telling him that he should build an abbey for poor friars, and that the plague would cease when the foundations were laid, adding that he should go forthwith to Corra Fursa, and that there a sign would be given him. The bishop awoke and went straightway to Corra Fursa, and when he arrived at the spot three swans flew up from the river side, and each swan had his bill filled with flax seed. The bishop followed the swans as they flew in a straight line to a certain point higher up the river, but when he reached the place where they had alighted, he found they had vanished, and in their place three bunches of flax were growing, and though the season was the month of February, the flax was in full blossom. Here, then, was the sign he sought for, and here he determined to plant the monastery. He went across to St. Fursa's church and proclaimed a fast for three days and three nights, and on the third day the people assembled at the river side, and on the night of the third day the

Fig. 46.—CORRA FURSA.

foundation was dug, and the plague ceased throughout the land. The three swans stood for the three hundred years that the abbey was to flourish, and so it happened that three hundred years after its foundation the sanctuary was profaned, the cross was cast from off the altar, and it is said that on the day the friars were expelled, as they passed through the great gate at early dawn, before one man could know another, the three white swans reappeared over the abbey; they flew away towards Fursa's weir, screaming, and wheeling to look backwards, and finally their dead bodies were found at Corra Fursa, on the spot whence they had risen three hundred years before.[1]

At a distance of a mile or two from this bridge we entered the grounds of Mr. Burke, of Ower, in which the ruins I was in search of are still standing. The group is a remarkable one, commencing with a small cromlech which the people call *leabha Dearmod agus Grania*—the bed of Dermot and Grania. Several raths remain on the townland to the north-east, which is still named after St. Fursa's father, Ard Fintan, or Caher Fintan. Then just outside the churchyard there is the pillar stone, with a very rude cross and circle incised upon it, which is said to be good for rheumatism. The only holy well near the church is dedicated to a St. Ciaran ; and the people still drink its waters for medicine out of little wooden cups, very beautiful in form, made at Headford.

The best point of view for a sketch of St. Fursa's old church is from a high field on the road to Headford. Here you can see the double light east window, which is an insertion of a later date, and whose lancet apertures, so thickly draped with ivy as to hide their mouldings, are visible from this point ; and the south wall of the church, seventy feet in length, may also be seen. It is singularly irregular, as it follows the uneven curves of the rock on which it is built. It stands in a large burial ground on a slight eminence, the trees of Ower Park behind it to the north, and the long range of mountains rising over Lough Mask to the north-west.

Although the east window and south door of St. Fursa's church are of a later date than the rest of the building, yet we could find nothing to prove that the walls were not all original and of very great antiquity. The west doorway is a good example of the primitive Irish style, with horizontal lintel and inclined jambs.

[1] This legend appears, with some slight differences, in Mr. Oliver Burke's "History of the Abbey of Ross," p. 5.

The lintel is of rough calcareous limestone, and measures three feet in length by two feet wide (see fig. 40, p. 85, *supra*). There are slit windows in the south wall, one over the other, both showing a very wide internal splay. At the east end there are four recesses, one at each side of the altar, and one in the north, and another in the south wall. A round-arched recess, now falling into

Fig. 47.—KILLFURSA, INTERIOR, WEST END.

ruin, beside the altar is another feature in the north wall. This was once probably filled by a tomb which has now disappeared.

The interior of the church proper, not including the western chamber, is fifty-five feet in length by twenty and a half feet wide in the middle, but it narrows gradually towards the west door, in fact there is no regularity in the ground-plan, nor is there a single right angle in any part of the church. It seems to have been built so as to suit the irregularities of the foundation on which it stands.

The most interesting feature of this building is that it was divided into nave and a western chamber, which may be termed a Galilee, while there is no transept or chancel. This external chamber measures nine feet across by nineteen wide, and is entered from the church by a door on a line with the west door in the outer wall. It appears that this was a two-storey chamber, which accounts for the occurrence of two slit windows in the south wall, one above another. Such a chamber exists in the church on Aranmore dedicated to the four beautiful saints, Fursa, Brendan, Berchann and Conall, and we know that St. Fursa visited the islands of Aran before founding the church of Killfursa. Both these churches are built with grouting and with undressed stone, and may well be coeval with the life of our saint.

When Professor Mahaffy was travelling in Brunswick he noticed a similar peculiarity in some early German churches, and his observations may be quoted here.[1]

"At Hildesheim the three Romanesque churches seem all to have had a western apse with small windows, precluding any western door, a most extraordinary feature to anyone accustomed to English or French churches. . . . A further study of these churches shows us that the western apse was at one time their usual plan, which seems to have been copied from the famous old Benedictine settlement at St. Gallen, of which a complete plan is still preserved The main church of that convent, built about the year 800, combined in it two older churches dedicated to SS. Peter and Paul, who were both accommodated with altars and chapels in the new church in this way. Under each apse there was generally a crypt, in which the founder was buried. . . . Boniface was buried under the western apse of the cathedral at Fulda. As a consequence of this fashion the entrances to these churches consisted either of two little doors beside the western apse, or more frequently of doors

---

[1] "Sketches from a tour in Holland and Germany." J. P. Mahaffy and J. E. Rogers, p. 117.

in the north and south walls of the nave. . . . This occurrence of western apses with an altar and special consecration seems to be peculiar, and therefore worth describing to those who study early churches in England, where examples must be rare, if they occur at all."

Fig. 48.—KILLARSA, EAST WINDOW.

The western chamber in the primitive Irish church being invariably rectangular cannot be termed an apse, which word implies a semicircular termination, *Rond* in German. It seems to correspond rather to the Galilee, though even this was rather a porch than an integral part of the building under the one roof. At Ely and Durham the Galilee appears however to be a division at the west end of the church rather than an appendant to it, and traces of such a western division are very frequently found in the larger Norman churches, comprising the first and part of the second arches at the west end of the nave. It is quite possible that in these primitive two-storied west chambers of the seventh century Irish church, the origin of a distinct feature of the Romanesque style of Great Britain may be traced, a feature which corresponded to the western apse of Germany, and that the purposes were similar

Fig. 49.—KILLARSA, NEAR CONG.

in all, the chamber being allotted to penitents, and also used as a place in which bodies were deposited previous to their interment, while the upper room became a muniment room. In the early ages of the Christian Church it was customary to bury persons of rank or of eminent sanctity in the church porch, none being allowed to be buried in the church itself (see Appendix, "Erdam").

Although this church of Fursa in the barony of Ower was the site of the principal monastery founded by the saint in Galway, yet an earlier and smaller building in Mayo was probably the first cell to which he retired on leaving the island of Inisquin, before his fame had attracted those crowds of foreign students which made the larger building necessary. The ruins of this earlier hermitage yet remain to be described, and I spent the greater part of yesterday drawing the little building, from a rising ground above it. It stands in the townland of Ballymagibbon, near the village of Cross, two miles from Cong, and a little boreen leads from the Cong road down to the wooded dell in which the ruin stands; the building has been much injured since it was visited by Mr. Kinahan and Sir William Wilde. The west end wall and door have disappeared, accidentally undermined by an ash tree growing where the west door must have stood; nor could I find the three stone corbels spoken of by Mr. Kinahan. The carved figure mentioned by Sir William Wilde is still to be seen in the stable wall of the deserted house of Ballymagibbon, but has been used by the boys as a target or cock-shot. However, the greater portion of the east wall and the window with the south wall are still standing. The east gable now measures twelve feet in height, and the walls are two feet thick; the foundations of the church are twenty-two feet long by fifteen feet wide.

Shocked by the utter neglect of this interesting ruin, I could not help remonstrating with the poor man upon whose farm it stood. "How can you look for the blessing of your patron saint," I said, "the first that ever taught you Christianity, if you will not take the trouble to cut the nettles that grow where his altar stood?" "Oh, he's all forgot now; sure, that was long ago." 'Long ago," said I, growing hot with indignation; "why, you may say the same of Christ. He was hundreds of years before your saint; are you going to forget Him, too?" The poor man looked at me with gentle remonstrance as he quietly said, "Sure, Christ is never long ago. He's always with us here."

I was very much interested to learn from Miss Knox, who lives in this neighbourhood, that the peasantry here still keep up a funeral custom which is also practised near the mouth of the Somme, where St. Fursa first landed in France.

When the coffin is supplied, the pieces of wood which remain over are cut into small crosses measuring two feet eight inches in height by eleven inches wide across the arms. These crosses are painted in various colours—green, blue, red, and yellow. They have pointed shafts; and one, which is meant to be planted in the soil at the head of the grave, is laid on the coffin, while the others are carried by the chief mourners behind. At the cross-roads nearest to the cemetery there is always a tree, either hawthorn or ash, at the foot of which the procession pauses, and the cross-bearers lift their crosses to its branches, where they fix them and leave them. In some places the tree has fallen from age or other causes, but its root remains, or at all events the memory of the place where it grew; and so the practice is continued, and the crosses are thrust in a heap, lying one upon another, till a mound often eight or ten feet high may be seen (see Appendix).

Fig. 50.—FUNERAL CUSTOM, CONG.

I went yesterday to see the spot on the roadside where Miss Knox told me I should find a heap of these little crosses, and I now send you a sketch of it. I could find no trace of cross-roads here, but still the funeral processions going to the old abbey of Cong pause here to deposit their crosses at the foot of

Fig. 51.—FUNERAL CUSTOM AT TENACRE.

an ash tree, and Lord Ardilaun, to whom the ground belongs, says that here the cemetery is first visible from the road.

The only other part of Ireland where I have found this practice is in the baronies of Bargy and Forth in the county of Wexford. Fig. 51 is from a drawing I made more than twenty years ago at Tenacre, assisted by a photograph taken two years ago, when, however, half of the tree had fallen. M. Du

Fig. 52.—FUNERAL CUSTOM AT BANNOW.

Noyer also has left us a sketch of another instance of the same custom at Bannow, where the tree has altogether disappeared, and the crosses are still set up where it stood.

The Neale,
September, 1894.

DEAR H.,

I have been eight days here, and these are all the traces I have succeeded in finding of St. Fursa, viz., the foundations of the monastery on Inchiquin, the large church and pillar stone, and holy well at Ower, the stone oratory at Cross, and the weir at Corra Fursa, on the Owenduff river. But even had there been

Fig. 53.—ON THE BRINK OF A SUBTERRANEAN RIVER, CONG.

nothing left save the scenes in which he passed his early youth; save the shores on which he walked with holy men who came to him from every side, and whom he assembled round him; save the caves and subterranean rivers, the mountains, islands, and lakes where the imagination of this early seer might well have fed on the daily and hourly changes of sky, and cloud, and mist, there would still have been ample reward for lingering on here.

The character of all this Galway country has been painted by Emily Lawless with such wonderful fidelity that one has but to open her Irish stories to see these scenes again: the wild expanse of grey stone and marshy land, and "the long winding stretch of lake, wasting away southward into a mist of dimness;" the lake that "might have been some great untravelled ocean, where never sail had fluttered, never boatman plied an oar;" the "shadowy shore that seemed to stretch away to all infinity, lost, formless, void," form the background to the first scenes of her tragic tale of "Maelcho."

I can never forget the walk I took one afternoon on leaving Fursa's hermitage near the village of Cross. I went along a little by-road, which at first follows the windings of the river as it threads its way to the lake's margin, through low, marshy land, and finally ascends the hill of Cordoon, till I reached the high ground near the top. From this point the view was magical. The silvery lake, streaked with placid blue, lay south of me; while, to the west, arose the mystic mountain range, upon whose heights the seer may have watched the morning vapour rise, fold by fold, and detach itself in floating forms, like the veiled figures of his heavenly vision, while

"Far withdrawn
Beyond the darkness and the cataract
God made Himself an awful rose of dawn."

Meanwhile the evening was drawing on; the low marshy lands were slowly changing beneath the pomp of radiant light that flowed upon them as the sun cast down its slanting rays, before it sank along the edges of the hills. Pool after pool was touched with golden light, and the rushes that fringed their borders cast long reflections upon the illumined waters, like eye-

Fig. 54.—LOUGH CORRIB, MOUTH OF CROSS RIVER (J. MARQUIS).

lashes veiling the liquid depths of some soft human eye. Beyond the low ground the grand masses of the mountains rose in dark violet depths of colour against the crimson and the gold of heaven. From high Benlevi and the gloomy range above Lough Mask, along Lacamra and Kirkaun to where the distant hill of Doon melted into the summer sky, the eye travelled on to the low ranges of Iar Connaught. In the middle distance the lake changed from blue and silver into liquid gold, save where it made a twofold image of the sweet wooded islands on its bosom, or the dark lines of the tall reeds beneath which it slept its golden sleep upon the shore.

But the hour came to our Irish seer when all these scenes were to be left for ever, and Fursa with his newly-ordained disciples, Algisus, Etto, and Gobain, and eight other of the brethren, were bade to go forth and teach in foreign lands. It must have been about the year 600 that they started, and the next place for our pilgrimage in search of their traces will be in the country of the East Angles in Suffolk.

One cannot but ask oneself why they chose Suffolk as the first scene of their labours, and I have sometimes fancied that the thought of this mission to the East Angles may have been inspired by St. Fursa's visit to Munster. He may there have met with some of the students spoken of by Bede: "Multi nobilium simul et mediocrium de gente anglorum," who had retired there for the sake of divine study, "going about from one master's cell to another." The Bishop of Limerick, Dr. Graves, has drawn attention to the fact that there seems to have been a school frequented by students in that part of Munster which was the country of Fintan or Finlog, St. Fursa's father. Two Ogham inscriptions have been found near a group of ancient cells in Corkaguiny in Kerry, ruins of this monastic school. On one stone he reads the name Finlog, on the other the Anglo-Saxon Eadfrith.[1]

[1] Trans. Royal Irish Academy, vol. xxvii., p. 31, and vol. xxx., part ii.

LETTERS

WRITTEN ON AN EXPEDITION IN SEARCH OF VESTIGES OF ST. FURSA IN SUFFOLK.

Yarmouth,
June 15th, '93.

DEAR E.,

WE shall now have to follow the footsteps of St. Fursa and his brethren from the shores of Lough Corrib to East Anglia. They probably travelled along an ancient causeway which seems to have extended in a straight line from Galway to Dublin. Its course is still marked by a line of eskers, or low embankments, which crop up at intervals along the great midland plain of Moynalty. The company of missionaries may have then crossed direct to Wales, or may have gone northward and embarked at a place where the channel is narrowest, and the existence of the ancient church of Killfursa, near Dundalk, seems to favour this latter view. They may have crossed to the monastery founded by St. Ninian on the Mull of Galloway, and thence proceeded east and south by Melrose and Lindisfarne to Suffolk. The Life only says, that "landing upon foreign shores, Fursa and his companions were borne through Britain to Saxony" —*i.e.* East Anglia—and speaks of the good he brought to the whole island, and, above all, to the Picts and Saxons. Here they were hospitably received by King Sigisbert at Cnobheresburgh, now called Burghcastle; and it is added, that "desiring to found a monastery there, St. Fursa chose a spot near the shore, within the area of a certain camp or castle made pleasant by the woods and the sea." This camp is still standing, and my next expedition must be to visit it, which I can easily do from Yarmouth or from Beccles.

We learn from the description of this remarkable place, given by Dr. Raven,[1] that the remains of these great fortified walls may be identified with a Roman camp named Garianonum in *Notitia Imperii*, or the Survey of the Empire,—and on the other hand called Cnobheresburgh by the Venerable Bede; the earliest literary evidence of the existence of which place is to be found in Ptolemy.[2] A gap of some 240 years occurs between this period and that in which the survey of the Roman Empire was made under Arcadius and Honorius, when Garianonum is classed in the *Notitia Imperii* as one of the stations of the Count of the Saxon Shore, whose jurisdiction extended from Brancaster to the middle of Sussex. And we find also in the *Notitia*, where the forces under the command of Ursicinus the Roman *comes* are enumerated, that the African Horse called Stablesian, were posted at this Garianonum, or Burghcastle, as well as in other parts of the Roman Empire, such as Pelusium in the Delta of the Nile, Scythia, etc. The doings of the Counts of the Saxon Shore in the neighbourhood of this Roman camp are again mentioned in the year 368, by Ammianus Marcellinus (xxvii. 8), where the story is told of the rising of a body of barbarous pirates, and their treacherous massacre by Severus. Here the Roman record comes to an end, and there is a long hiatus which separates the Count of the Saxon Shore from the blessed Fursa, whose settlement at Burghcastle, *i.e.*, Garianonum or

[1] "Garianonum," by the Rev. James Raven, D.D., Proc. Suffolk Institute of Archæology, vol. vi., part 3, 1888.

[2] "Geog.," lib. 2, cap. 3.

Cnobheresburgh, is thus described by Richard of Cirencester, "Speculum Historiale," ii., c. 38:

"Where [in the province of the East Angles], being seized with some bodily infirmity, he [Fursa] obtained the joy of a heavenly vision, in which he was bidden sedulously to devote himself to the ministering of the word which he had begun, and to give himself unweariedly to the wonted vigils and prayers; because his end was certain, but the hour of that end would be uncertain; as the Lord said, 'Watch, therefore, for ye know not the day nor the hour.' Being strengthened by this vision he turned his cares to the site of a monastery, which he received from the aforesaid King Sigisbert, to the speedy building of it, and to establishing it with disciplinary rules. The monastery, indeed pleasant in its neighbourhood to woods and the sea, was built in a certain camp which in the English tongue is called Cnobheresburgh, that is, the town of Cnobheric; which monastery, however, the king of that province, Anna, and each of his nobles adorned thereafter with handsomer buildings and sanctuaries."[1]

And again:

"Anna . . . . . provided the monastery built in his kingdom by the blessed Furseus, the man of God, with more august buildings and sanctuaries, and ceased not to enrich those serving Christ there with possessions and supplies of temporal things."[2]

The Roman name is derived from the name of the estuary, Garianensis, which the Roman Præpositus or General of the African Horse was placed here to guard.

The camp is situated near the confluence of the Waveney and the Yare, on a height, and the walls now standing form three sides of a quadrangle, 642 feet in length, and 321 feet in breadth, occupying an area of 5 acres, 2 roods, and 3 perches, including

[1] Rolls Series, vol. i., p. 157.

[2] *Ibid.*, ii., cap. 64 (Rolls Series, vol. i., p. 263).

the walls, which are about 9 feet thick, and the average height is from 14 to 15 feet, according to measurements made by Dr. Raven in the year 1886. They are built of grouting, faced in triple bands, at regular distances, by red Roman bricks separated by layers of cut flints. The walls are strengthened by six cylindrical bastions which have all the external aspect of towers, but are solid circular masses of masonry. Down the middle of each is a round hollow space, apparently for the insertion of the central timber of a temporary wooden turret to be raised in case of an attack on the camp. Dr. Raven discusses with great care the question as to whether the fortress had originally four walls, or only three as now visible, and whether the side to W.N.W. was protected by what was then an arm of the sea. He considers that the existence of a fourth wall has been sufficiently proved by the results of Mr. Harrod's excavations in 1850. The ragged ends of both north and south walls, and the broken bonding courses, convince him that both the north and south walls had been extended beyond their present terminations. Then, in the course of the excavations, foundations of walls were discovered, and four feet below the surface a fragment of wall was reached which had fallen in an unbroken mass. Below this a number of oak piles were discovered, on which the wall had originally rested. These piles were about a foot apart, and had clay, chalk, stones, and mortar very firmly rammed in between them to the depth of eighteen inches, after penetrating which space, black mud was thrown out, speedily followed by the water, which then rose a little above the top of the piling. The lost fragments of this west wall may, perhaps, now underlie this oozy bed of the Waveney, or be dispersed in the neighbourhood of the camp, in the farm buildings or cottages, or in the walls of the parish church close by.

Roman cinerary urns have been found here: they are generally of coarse blue clay, ill-formed, brittle, and porous; many in fragments as if broken by the plough. One was taken up in several pieces, which had contained a quantity of bones and ashes, among which was a coin of Constantine and the head of a Roman spear. Ashes in great abundance have been also found, along with a stratum of wheat, black as if it had been burned, and mostly reduced to a coarse powder. Near these were a Roman spoon, with a long sharp-pointed handle, rings, buckles, fibulæ, silver and copper coins of the Lower Empire; and many skeletons were dug up within the area of the camp in 1842. A gold coin of Gallienus was a few years ago put into the offertory at Gorleston, which was probably picked up by some peasant in the neighbourhood. Horses' teeth abound to an extraordinary extent, and one really fine ceramic relic of Burgh-castle is a Durobrivian vessel, now belonging to Mr. Nash, of Great Yarmouth. The castrum has been in possession of Sir John Boileau since 1845.

It is said that within the entrenchments of the station foundations of buildings may be traced at certain times by the colour of the growing crops. Excavations carefully conducted might lead to important results in relation to the history of the site, but they have never been undertaken.[1] I sometimes think that the English antiquaries of the present day, with some rare exceptions, devote their energies too exclusively to the Roman remains found in England, ignoring the far deeper interest of their own native traces of early history.

To-morrow I hope to pay my first visit to this old place.

* * * * * * *

[1] See "Archæological Journal," vol. xlvi., p. 344. "Roman Suffolk," "Archæologia," vol. xxiii., 1831, p. 358.

Burghcastle, Suffolk,
June 16th, 1893.

DEAR E.,

I hired a boy at Belton to guide me to Burghcastle, and we walked for about half an hour along a flat road between hedges, the monotonous character of the landscape and wide cornfields only broken here and there by occasional clumps of trees and neat farmsteads with pretty gardens. At last we saw the old round tower of Burghcastle Church, its red brick summit telling brightly in the sunshine against the background of fine trees surrounding it. I opened the churchyard gate, and went round to examine the tower, mentally resolving that after I had done my work at the Roman encampment I should return to photograph it. A shady walk leads to the quiet rectory among the trees, and, seeing a gardener there, I asked the way to the old Roman castle. He told me to follow a lane leading south-west from the church till the old walls came in view in a field to the right. Five minutes after, I beheld this wonderful ruin. It was much more imposing than I had been led to expect. The kindly old farmer to whom the cornfield belongs in which this great monument stands, let me in on condition that I did not tread on his crops, and afterwards brought me a lunch in a basket from his farmhouse.

The path ran along a hawthorn hedge, up a gentle incline, and when we came close underneath the old wall and turned to the right, away from the fence, I was astonished at the view that suddenly revealed itself. The river, which is indeed a winding inlet of the sea, threads its quiet way on to the horizon through a flat marshy country intersected with canals, and the long horizontal lines of plain are only broken by windmills, or the sail of an

Fig. 55.—VIEW FROM ROMAN CAMP, BURGHCASTLE.

occasional fishing-boat which proves that the sea, though concealed from view, is still near,

> "Tells that the wide Atlantic rolls behind."

The whole character of the scene, looking westward, is curiously foreign, and suggestive of the plains in Picardy and Flanders to which these Irish missionaries emigrated after spending five years here. Yet here we had the happy song of English birds, the scent of the wild rose and woodbine, and that peculiar flavour in the air, that seems only to be found in the pastoral districts of England, that reminds one of the odour of new milk and fresh-mown hay, and brings back to us the first impressions of childhood, and the memory of our first conceptions of English fields and farmsteads and quaint old parish churches, with which stories like "Simple Susan," and "Hope on, hope ever," filled our minds at seven years old.

The great walls of the Roman encampment inclose three sides of a platform, the fourth side of which falls perpendicularly to the bend of the river. I first climbed to the top to see the interior, since there is so much evidence to prove that it was within the area of this fort that Fursa erected the huts and oratory of his primitive monastery which have long since disappeared. Then I walked all along the base of the three sides of the exterior of the wall, and then back along the top of the wall, making my way with much difficulty in some places through the thick ivy. I found a hole in the centre of the top of one bastion, such as Dr. Raven has drawn attention to in the description referred to above. The masonry is of the flints of the country, with triple bands of narrow red Roman bricks alternating in regular layers. The farmer confirmed the statement that many Roman remains, including pottery, have been found here, and the landlord of the little inn at Burghcastle showed me a chromo-lithograph of the fine Durobrivian vase found here, with a woman's head painted on one side, which he said was now preserved in a private house at Yarmouth. As the photographs already made of this ruin which one can buy at Yarmouth are excellent, I did not waste my time taking fresh ones, but tried a pencil sketch of the land-

Fig. 56.—TOWER, BURGHCASTLE CHURCH.

scape, so as to help you to realize the character of the scene (see fig. 55). It must be much the same in all its main features as when Fursa and his brethren saw it in the year 630, but perhaps the windmills were missing and the boats were coracles.

On returning to the church [1] I was glad to find that, owing to the care of the Rector, Canon George Venables, the name of the Irish founder was not likely to be forgotten. A beautiful stained glass window has been placed in the south wall with a picture of the saint, copied from an old miniature in a manuscript in the British Museum (Royal 20 D. vi., f. 17). Also a short account of the saint's history is given on a framed leaflet hung in the porch.

The round tower rises on the arched roof of a recess in the west end, and it is mainly built of the small flint stones of the district; the top of the tower, evidently an addition of a later date, is all of red brick. The fact that the whole country round is full of ecclesiastical round towers, and these of great antiquity, is interesting and apt to be misleading, for it may appear, at first sight that these towers derive their origin from the still older church towers of Ireland. But, though round, they are not Irish round towers. They do not taper as they ascend, but are almost uniform throughout in outline. The wall also is of uniform thickness, does not thin off as ours do towards the top; the doors are on the ground, not at a considerable height from the plinth, as are ours. The apertures, also, are quite different in character.

I wish search could be made for some earlier vestiges of the first Christian settlement here. When, for instance, was the girdle left by St. Fursa, and afterwards enshrined, last heard of? When did his bell disappear? Where is his holy well? Are they all forgotten? The want of poetry in our Protestant movement, which failed to see the pathos of the past, has a great deal to answer for! I shall cross to France before writing my next letter, and perhaps be more successful in my search there for traces of Fursa and his companions.

[1] This church is said to have been built of material taken from the Roman station. (See Harrod in "Norfolk Archæology," vol. v., p. 146-147.)

LETTERS FROM FRANCE.

Hôtel de la Gare,
Abbeville, Picardy, Dept. Somme,
April 10th, '93.

*   *   *   *   *   *

DEAR B.,

AND now for my adventures! I wrote to M—— before I started, telling her my intention of starting in search of the places where Columban and Fursa landed, when they first reached the continent, at the mouths of the Somme and the Canche, the next *embouchure* you will find in the map, north of that of the Somme, on which river this town of Abbeville stands. I found this out in a book to which I treated myself, by the Abbé Hénocque, published by the Society of Antiquaries, Picardy, and also that our saints travelled by a great Roman road leading from the sea across France, one to Burgundy, the other to Lagny. Well, I started by the 10.32 train (which did not stir itself till eleven o'clock!) for Etaples, which in Columban's time was called Quentovic. A very refined-looking man, with a cheery, good-natured-looking wife got into the carriage, and he proceeded to open a Gladstone bag; the first thing he drew forth seemed to amuse him immensely—it was a bunch of radishes! He then lifted a carefully tied up paper parcel, which I at once suspected to be a ham, thinking they were going to lunch on ham and radishes! However, it proved to be pig in another form; for when he uncovered it, with tender care, it turned out to be a statuette of

St. Anthony with his *cochon.* I recognized at once a sympathetic soul in this man, and went into the best raptures I could, in my poor French, over this really interesting figure, till I found its owner could speak English. Then I told him of my quest, and he wrote in my note-book the name of a gentleman in Abbeville who would give me the whole history of this Roman road. When I arrived at Etaples I went into a nice little wayside inn, where I lunched. An intelligent-looking man came in and sat opposite me, and, after the usual observations about the wonderful weather, I told him I had come in search of an old Roman road. He turned out to be an engineer, or county surveyor, whose business it was to know everything about every road in Picardy! Well, he told me that the road did exist still, and in parts was still in use, but at Etaples it had been effaced, while, about an hour's drive from this, it is found at Montreuil, and again at Abbeville, and again at Laon, and so on, probably the route Columban took to Burgundy. So I ordered a *voiture*, and a battered old coach appeared, with an aged horse and driver. I sat, by preference, on the coach box, and, to my indignation, a fat Frenchwoman and her husband jumped inside, though I was paying twelve francs for this expedition. However, good-nature proved the best policy. Walking up a hill, the woman came to my side, and told me that she was a native of Montreuil, that the *Chaussée* I was searching for was behind a certain Carthusian monastery a mile or so from that town, and that her brother was gardener in the monastery. So we drove to the monastery gate; I explained my mission to the porter. No woman, of course, may enter the Chartreuse, but the white-robed porter threw the gates wide open so that I saw the beautiful façade and garden in front of the building. I wish you could have seen how this porter rushed at me when I carelessly put my foot inside the threshold. However, he took my card, with my request written on it, and then I had to wait what seemed an interminable time. At last he reappeared with a sheet of paper in his hand, on which one of the Carthusian monks had drawn a plan of the roads in the neighbourhood leading to the famous *Chaussée*. Did you ever hear of anything so kind?

With this help I found the road quite easily, and got a poor man to carry my photographic bag. At the village below the hill, along which the road runs, I made two photographs, and got back to Abbeville by the express which leaves Etaples at a quarter past seven.

Will you send this letter on to W——, and when you get it back, will you keep it. You must know though the antiquaries call it a Roman road, yet the tradition is that Queen Brunehilde (who seems to have been a rather fine character in her early years, deteriorating into something tremendously wicked in after life), was really the author of this, as of many other great works in France, and the road is only spoken of as Chaussée Brunehaut.

Abbeville,
April 11th, '93.

DEAR E.,

One of the first places I determined to explore in Picardy was St. Riquier, the site of the Irish monastery which Fursa rested in on his arrival in France, near the mouth of the river Somme. This is the first station on the line, on reaching which I crossed a field, and then a stream of clear running water, which proved to be the historic Scardon. A long, delightful pathway under an arch of lofty trees, whose banks were lined with celandine and wild violets, led to the little town, and in a few moments I reached the square in front of the façade of the Abbey of St. Riquier, one of the most perfect examples of Gothic architecture, not only in Picardy, but even in all France (see frontispiece). In the delicate sculpture that covers its great façade, like a veil of exquisite tracery, we have an epitome of religion under the law of nature, the written law, and the law of grace. From the summit of the tower, which is 150 feet high at the opening of the pent-house to the left, the statue of Adam on one side and of Eve on the other may be seen. In the face of the first man we read the repentance he feels for the fruit of his sin. These two statues symbolize the condition of the world under the law of nature. To the right of the pent-house we see the statues of Moses and Aaron. Moses carries the Tables of the Old Law upon his breast. Aaron is clothed in the robes of the High Priest of the ancient covenant. The written law is represented by these two statues. Above these are four figures, which symbolize the Old Testament, and then a colossal figure rises, ruling over all. This is the Lord Jesus Christ, who was from the beginning, Lord over all, who came, preordained through all eternity, for the redemption of mankind. The Saviour holds the cross in His hands, with which He pierces the demon, the enemy of all mankind. A vast triangle, being the symbol of the Trinity as the basis and foundation of the Old and New Covenant, is traced below these statues, which represent the natural and the written law. In the midst of this great triangle we see the three persons of the Godhead, the Father as an old man, His head crowned by a tiara; on His right hand the Second Person offering himself to the Father as a victim for our salvation; while the Holy Spirit, in the form of a dove, symbol of purity and fertility, hovers above these two divine persons; then in the very centre of the Trinity is seen the form of Mary, crowned by two angels. Beneath this great triangle the New Testament is represented on the richly sculptured frontal. We may perceive God as Saviour of the world, surrounded by other divine forms. The Father seated on his throne as the Ancient of Days, offers His crucified Son to man; the Son, hanging on the cross for our salvation; and the Holy Spirit, which has inspired the victim of

Fig. 57.—ST. RIQUIER.

Calvary, is again seen, in the form of a dove, above the cross. Two kneeling bishops, with their crosiers, offer salutation to the Saviour in the name of the abbey. To the right and left are ranged the twelve colossal statues of the Apostles, who, after Christ, were the founders of the New Covenant. They are each represented with his individual attribute. Then come the pontiffs, bearing mitres on their heads, and the doctors carrying the book of the law in their hands. In the tympanum above the great porch may be seen the tree of Jesse, giving the descent of Christ from the kings of Judah. These twelve kings are seen amid the branches of the tree, on the summit of which rests the statue of the Holy Virgin with her Infant Son. Among the statues which decorate the sides of the porch are those of SS. Riquier, Angilbert, Louis, Vigor, Firminius, Nicholas, Wulfram, Eligius, Mauguille, Roch, Anthony, Sebastian, Clotilda, Anna, Mary Magdalen, and Martha.

The figure of Francis I., in whose reign the church was rebuilt, in his costume as knight, may be seen to the right hand of the central door. A delicately cut trefoil runs like lace-work along the arch of the porch. The face of the pointed arch of the great door is enriched by a double row of groups of medallions representing the most remarkable events in the lives of St. Riquier and St. Angilbert. All these ornaments were formerly gilded.

On entering the great doorway of the church I was astonished at the noble proportions of the interior (see fig. 57). At either side of the nave five great arches spring from ten columns, whose varied capitals are so designed as to reveal the wonders of the vegetable kingdom. Amid the foliate designs and blossoms, dragons and grotesque figures are seen entwined. A gallery of open-work carved stone and interlaced design forms a horizontal band, like a rich girdle, running the whole length of the nave and choir. Passing the colossal statue of St. Christopher on the right, and St. James Major, who was patron of pilgrims, on the left, the eye rests on the epitaph of Eustace Lequieux, fifty-fourth Abbot of St. Riquier, to whose genius and devotion we owe the restoration of this mighty temple. Then reaching the choir, we find the tomb of Angilbert, son-in-law of Charlemagne, he who in the ninth century wrought the golden and jewelled shrine to contain the relics of our Irish Caidoc and Fricor.[1] The visit of

Fig. 58.—RELICS OF IRISH SAINTS, ST. RIQUIER.

Charlemagne to this very Angilbert is the subject of one of the scenes represented in the carved medallions of the stalls. In the south transept is placed the statue of St. Riquier, a fine figure, full of devotional feeling, work of the thirteenth century. On the high altar stands a shrine, on the face of which we read the names of our three Irish saints, Mauguille, Caidoc, and Adrian

[1] See p. 76, *supra*.

(Fricor). Mauguille, follower of Fursa, as you may remember, died at Monstrelet, but Ingelard had his relics transported to this church, where they have ever since been honoured on May 30th, along with those of Caidoc and Fricor.

I then entered the chapel of the Trésorerie, so called because the treasures of the abbey are here preserved. The walls are covered with frescoes of the life of the saint. But I looked in vain for the scene in which he meets the two Irishmen to whom he owed his conversion. The subjects of these pictures were connected with the death of the founder, and the miracles wrought by his relics after his death, rather than with the actual events of his life.

1st and 2nd.—The apparition of St. Valery to Hugh Capet, desiring him to reclaim the relics of St. Riquier.

3rd.—Hugh Capet sends envoy to Count Arnulph to request that the saint's body be restored.

4th.—Count Arnulph orders that the body should be carried back to the abbey.

5th.—Count Arnulph carries the body of the saint on his own shoulders.

6th.—Count Arnulph restores the body to Hugh Capet, kneeling before the shrine.

7th.—Hugh Capet carries the shrine on his shoulders into the monastery.

8th.—St. Riquier miraculously delivers pilgrims from Jerusalem who are pursued by Turks.

9th.—St. Riquier restores a man and woman who had been drowned in a well.

10th.—St. Riquier restores a monk to life.

I was intensely interested to see in two arches above these frescoes two fine illustrations of *Le Dit des Trois Morts et des Trois Vifs*, the best-known version of which is that of Orcagna in the Campo Santo at Pisa. This poem first appears in the thirteenth century as one of the collections of moralities painted on the walls of cemeteries to remind the world of the vanity of human things. In the first picture, three young noblemen on horseback are revelling in the enjoyment of hawking when they are confronted by three skeletons issuing from the forest before them. The first carries a winged arrow, which he presents or aims at the first young horseman, while he says these words:

> "Nous vous dénonçons tous pour voir
> Qu'il vous convient Mort recevoir;
> Tels comme vous en temps nous fûmes,
> Et tels serez comme nous sommes."

The second carries a pickaxe, with which he prepares to dig the graves of these three worldlings, while he says:

> "Vous qui êtes outrecuidiés
> Plus brièvement que ne craignez
> La Mort en tout temps vous épie
> Pour vous ôter du corps la vie."

The third says:

> "Il n'y a point de réconfort,
> Obéir il nous faut à la mort,
> Pourquoi nous tous jeunes et vieux,
> Ayons la mort devant les yeux."

These young riders, richly clad, and devotees to falconry, are struck with terror at the aspect of the skeletons who thus suddenly appear before them. They collect themselves, however, and form the resolution henceforth to change their course of life.

The first says:

> "Mon pauvre cœur de peur tremble,
> Quand trois morts ainsi voir ensemble
> Défigurés, hideux, divers,
> Tout pourris et mangés de vers."

The second says:

"Otons du monde les plaisirs,
Mauvais vouloirs et faux désirs,
Car de la mort tous les détroits
Nous passerons comme ces trois."

The third says:

"Il n'y a point de réconfort,
Obéir il nous faut à la mort,
Pourquoi nous tous jeunes et vieux,
Ayons la mort devant les yeux."

In the glass press of this chamber I noted a shrine of the eleventh century, a crucifix with angels represented on its face, made of enamel and bronze; also two reliquaries of the same date, a triple cross of ivory, said to be of the tenth century, and a Christian reliquary of the twelfth century. But the most interesting thing to me there was a very curious and apparently ancient bell of bronze, much worn, somewhat the shape of a sea-urchin shell, about six inches in diameter. I could not get the glass case opened to examine this, as also a fine missal and gospel therein which I longed to see more closely. After lunch I walked up the hill in search of a point of view for the exterior of this church, and found it would make a delightful subject for a landscape painter as seen from a ruined tower in a garden on the hill. I then went on to the chapel of the great Séminaire, and I saw a stained glass window there in which our three Irish saints are again represented. St. Mauguille is also said to be intended by the statue opposite that of St. Riquier with his dog, on one of the side doors of the façade.

On all my expeditions through this part of Picardy I was forcibly reminded of the landscape painting of Browning in the beginning of his poem, "Turf and Towers." First, at Etaples, I seemed to see "the unpretending beach below the little village," a sea-coast nook where the continent meets the vast ocean, and in its semicircular sweep the "earth shell scallops out the ocean," while the tiny white cottages dotting the shore seem to his eye "the milk-white incrustations" with which the border of the shell is studded as the sea "sleeps and sets to slumber that broad blue." Then comes the little road that seems a pathway leading up from the beach, passing the weeders stooping in the field. His loving eye delights in the aspect of this land, which to many would seem monotonous and dull.

To me the description of French scenery in this poem is as happy as anything Browning ever wrote. The old French house, once a priory, with its grey roof and tower crowning the landscape, from whose summit the solitary mourner sees that stretch of sea and land throughout the season's change, and feels the winds advance with welcome wafts of sea-smell, and watches the first white bird that flaps thus far to taste the land again. It is well thus to feel this strong wise spirit near us in the opening of our journey through a land he has so truly painted, and, even in our special aims, he seems to stimulate our energy; when he, too, stands within a ruin, fane, or bath, or circus famed in story, or confronts some work of art gnawn hollow by Time's tooth, he shows that even Time does not work for death in the end.

"Since little life begins where great life ends,
And vegetation soon amalgamates,
Smooths novel shape from out the shapeless old,
Till broken column, battered cornice block
The centre with a bulk half weeds and flowers,
Half relics you devoutly recognize."

April 13th, 1893.

I started this morning for Mézerolles, the place where Fursa worked his first miracle on Duke Haymon's son, and also the place where he died years afterwards, on his way home. On the way we passed by the little towns of St. Riquier and Auxi, and leaving the train at Frevent took a carriage and drove for an hour across a vast extent of undulating ground, now and then entering groves of wood, generally of beech-trees, filled with picturesque groups of wood-cutters, and women in reddish-brown costumes, tying faggots. Then through villages almost always buried in trees, where the houses, beautifully clean, were often painted in two colours, bright green picked out with a shade of lavender grey. However, this is not the best season for seeing this country to advantage. The long brown tracts of newly-broken earth, which in autumn will bear rich crops, along with the patches of white chalk that break the soil in every direction, do not form as pleasant a combination of colour in the foreground as the same patches on the rich fields and downs at Dover. The English grass is something we cannot be too grateful for; but, nevertheless, under a brilliant sky such as I enjoyed to-day there is a certain charm in the vast expanse of earth and heaven, the peculiarly delicate tints on the distant plains and heights, the lavender and greyish greens of the fields of luzerne, varied here and there by long level lines of white chalk which, when seen far away, seem to suggest the sandy reaches of a distant river slowly passing westward; while all through the country there is a cheering sense of steady industry and quiet pastoral life in the aspect of the homesteads, farms, and hamlets on the roadside. Everything that met the eye was pleasant, the length and breadth of grain crop, the meadow ground, the orchards, the stalwart strider by the side of the green-hooded waggons, the comely women-folk, so rosy, and healthy, and tall, at work tying faggots in the woods, or sitting at their cottage doors. Everything was a picture; everywhere the same cheerful atmosphere prevailed.

The village of Mézerolles rises in a wooded dell. The little church standing on the bank of the river Authie, the same stream on which our saints, Mauguille and Wulgan, had their hermitage.

The sacristan here told me that I should find the Chapelle de St. Furcy about a quarter of a mile further on, at Frohens-le-Grand—the ancient Forshem, or house of Fursa—as also his well and his statue.

Fig. 59.—CHAPELLE FONTAINE DE ST. FURCY.

So I went along this delightful valley of the Authie, revelling in the fresh green of the trees, now first bursting into leaf, and the dancing shadows on the green sward, till I came to a tiny chapel on the roadside, built over the Holy Well of St. Fursa, and my eye was caught by the name of Furcy over the door. I at once stopped the carriage and got down to read the inscription, which is as follows:

"Hommage des Habitants de Frohens le G. à St. Furcy."

This is an interesting example of the Chapelles-Fontaines, or Holy Well Chapels, often built at the side of these springs throughout France, for the convenience of pilgrims coming to the healing waters. It is probably owing to the existence of such chapels that the evils which have arisen from the practices of well worship in Ireland have been prevented in France. While in Ireland the patron-day was allowed to be spent in dancing, and otherwise profaned,[1] the pilgrim here had his oratory for quiet prayer. I found the slab in the centre of the floor of this little chapel, which, when raised, reveals the deep spring first opened by St. Furcy. The ground-plan of the chapel is that of a rounded apse where stands the altar of St. Furcy, on which his statue is placed, while his medal hangs at the foot of the figure. The well extends beneath the south wall of the chapel, and forms a pond outside, the water running in a bright clear stream into the wood behind. This was evidently the favourite resort of some turbulent ducks, which seemed bent upon destroying my photograph by frantic flapping of their wings, as they rushed forward to disport themselves in the wider sheet of water near the well, destroying all its quiet reflections in their wild career.

[1] Yet these very dances would seem to be the survival of some ancient ceremony. "La danse propre aux fontaines" is still held at Font Roumeou in the Eastern Pyrenees, and though, as practised now among the young people there, it is hard to draw the line between these performances and the ordinary amusement of the dance, yet the elders in the company still retain the memory of old associations, and connect them with the religious ideas of their ancestors.

To drink of this cool, sparkling fountain is still held to be a cure for fever; and the people wash their hands in it to preserve them from scurvy; children also are bathed in its running water when suffering from skin disease.

Fig. 60.—HOLY WELL OF ST. FURSA.

After photographing this well I went on to the parish church, in which there is another altar and statue of St. Fursa, and having photographed these, I walked to a very beautiful Calvary on the cross roads outside the town. But now the evening began to cast its long shadows, and I had to remember the drive before me ere I could catch the night train to Abbeville. I was sorry to leave this humble village so soon, feeling that could I have stayed longer I might perhaps have found still more traces of our saint's life here. I might have succeeded in discovering some indication of the foundation of Duke Haymon's dwelling, or of the Forshem, the house of Fursa, the little cell in which the duke's son was restored from death. But I hope to revisit this place, which has the additional interest of being that in which St. Fursa died on his journey from Lagny back to England.

We must now follow the road taken by our saint to Péronne, the next place of importance visited by him, and the place to which his remains were carried for interment. If you will take your map of Picardy, and mark every holy well dedicated to St. Fursa in this district, you will seem to have his line of progress clearly indicated from St. Riquier to Péronne, and these wells lie close along the Roman road reaching from Abbeville to Doullens ; thence to Yvrench, about six miles from St. Riquier, where there is a Fontaine de St. Furcy, still visited by pilgrims suffering from diseases of the eye. Again, at Maison Ponthieu, in the Canton of Crécy, at Frohens, Outrebois, le Meillard, Authieule, Mailly in the Canton d'Acheux, to Grandcourt and Pys, in the Canton d'Albert, on to Les Bœufs, a village that takes its name from the oxen that drew the bier of St. Fursa at his funeral, when his body was borne from Frohens to Péronne.

LETTERS FROM PÉRONNE.[1]

DEAR A.,

I HAVE been here some twenty-four hours, and delighted with my rambles through this most curious and ancient city of Picardy. It is larger than I expected, containing upwards of 4,000 inhabitants, and I have already seen the old castle described in "Quentin Durward," the fifteenth-century church of St. Jean, where St. Fursa's relics are *now* laid, with its beautiful porch and tower, and mural paintings and old pictures; the Hôtel de Ville, and the old-fashioned wooden houses, in one of which I saw a carved figure of St. Fursa kneeling on his bullocks so as to support a wooden balcony on his back! You drive across a wide expanse of water to approach the town from the station, and the town reminds one of a little Venice, surrounded as it is by lagunes and marshy lands (see fig. 42).

The first inhabitants of Péronne appear to have been the fishermen, who, having in course of time been ousted from the mainland, ultimately took refuge in the little island of Sobotécluse, attracted, no doubt, by the abundance of fish and waterfowl.[2] The Swan Hill, or Mons Cygnorum, Cygnopolis, was the name by which Péronne was known before the sixth century. The gentle incline of the valley of the Somme forced the waters of this great river to wind from one side to another, forming alluvial deposits in its course, till it touched the base of this

[1] See p. 108, *supra*. [2] De Sachy, "Hist. de Péronne."

height. Multitudes of water birds, swans, geese, and wild ducks, found a refuge in the reeds growing on the river banks, which, being half domesticated in the Middle Ages, offered to the nobles and esquires of the district the delights of the chase then reserved for them alone.

This town, the ancient capital of Santerre, grew into a place of considerable importance after the interment of St. Fursa within its walls, so great was the throng of pilgrims to the shrine wrought for his relics by St. Eloi.[1]

Cæsar does not mention this place in his "Commentaries." However, the people of Péronne hold the tradition that they owe to the Roman conqueror of Gaul that long pier-mole by which the Somme is crossed at its wider part, from the end of Mont-des-Cygnes to the point then called Samarobriva, *i.e.*, the starting-point of this road to Amiens.[2]

When St. Fursa reached this place, this Hill of Swans was overgrown by forest trees, it being one of the outlying portions of the great forest of Thiérache Nouvion, and, even at the present day, huge roots of oak, and other trees, have been unearthed at various depths in the soil, while vestiges of this forest may still be seen in St. Fursa's wood at Combles, in the woods of Anderlu, Faffemont, Grandsart, le Forêt, Marière, Cléry, and another wood, named after St. Fursa, at the extremity of Bouchavesnes and Cléry, close to the gates of the town. A royal residence or Villa Regia existed, before the time of Erchenwald, in the neighbourhood of Péronne, and was occasionally occupied by Clothair I.[3] It is mentioned by Fortunatus in his life of Radegonda. He tells us, "Radegonda was only eleven years old, when, in the year 530, she witnessed the tragic scene in which her father Bertarius, King of Thuringia was robbed of his crown and his life by Ermenfrid."

[1] M. G. Vallois, "Péronne, son Origin et ses Développements," 1880.
[2] Amiens, Samarobriva (Cæsar, "Bell. Gall.").
[3] See "Mémoires de la Société de Picardie," vol. iv., p. 226.

She found an avenger in Clothair. He had taken her captive in the victory he won over Bertarius, and, enchanted by her beauty, had sent her to be educated at a place two leagues from Péronne, called Athies.

One day, having dined at the castle of Péronne, she was walking in the garden, and her heart was much moved by hearing cries and sobs from the prisoners in the stronghold. She ordered their delivery on the instant, which gave great displeasure to her ministers. The next time she heard the same cries she could only send the prisoners alms, but she prayed for their release, and suddenly, at dead of night, their chains fell from them, and they went forth free men.

It is very difficult to trace any remains of primitive structures at Péronne. The royal residence then occupied by Radegonda was probably of very modest proportions ; indeed, we learn from Viollet-le-Duc[1] that such dwellings of the Merovingian rulers were generally of wood, and the transitory nature of such erections easily explains the poverty of Péronne as regards monuments contemporary with her foundation.

When the mayor, Erchenwald, was endowed by King Clovis II. with the government of Péronne, he proceeded to build himself a palace on the summit of the Hill of Swans, the outworks of which appear to have inclosed a considerable portion of the woods with which the hillside was clothed, and traces of its foundations have been found by the local antiquaries. Here the primitive wooden structure, if it ever existed, seems to have been replaced at a very early date. Two lofty walls which flank the northern and southern sides of the summit of this Hill of Swans extended east and west so as to form a complete inclosure. These walls appear to have been strengthened with towers such as the one still traceable in the Tour Millant at the corner of the Rue

[1] See "Dictionary of Architecture," pp. 208, 365 375, 454.

St. Furcy, forming an irregular square, and which is held by tradition to have been at different times either the habitation of the retainers of Erchenwald, the prison of the savage Herbert, the castle of Albert the Pious, or the residence of Robert le Barbu. It is at all events certain that here we have a portion of the structure distinguished in ancient documents by the titles of palatium, villa regia, vicus, and castrum. It was quite in accordance with the practice we are familiar with at home, that Erchenwald should found the first church he built for St. Fursa's use within the precincts of his castrum. This church, by means of which he hoped to entice Fursa to return and end his days beside him at Péronne, was commenced on the site of a small chapel dedicated to the apostles SS. Peter and Paul. "This basilica, containing the shrine of St. Fursa, represented all the magnificence of the age," says Dom Michel Germain ("De re diplom.," lib. 4), and, after the death of the saint, a convent of Irish monks was established here, January 16th, 650; it became the collegiate church of St. Furcy when Erchenwald endowed the chapter with the forest lands in the neighbourhood. This property was enjoyed by them until the beginning of the tenth century, when the church was despoiled by Herbert II.

We have seen that at the time of Fursa's visit to Péronne, a chapel dedicated to SS. Peter and Paul stood on the Mont des Cygnes. This either formed part of a church begun by Erchenwald, or was close to it and had existed long before. Desmay asserts that it was here that St. Fursa buried the precious relics of SS. Beoan and Meldan which he had carried with him from Ireland, and that in the corner where he laid them, the holy man used to pass days and nights in prayer. The spot was well fitted for contemplation, surrounded as it was by the forest trees of which we have spoken. It is quite possible that the name of the street now called Beaubois, which is the first street to the left on entering the town by the Faubourg de Bretagne, is derived from the woods which once covered not only the Hill of Swans itself, but the suburbs around the town. Although St. Fursa's church was the only sanctuary within the castrum, and the one which ultimately became the chief glory of Péronne, yet we are not to suppose that it was the only Christian church of the district; that of St. Quentin en l'Eau in the parish of Sobotécluse, and that of St. Radegonda, near the pathway leading to St. Nicholas' gate, were both in existence at this early period.

So little is known of the primitive history of Péronne that I have only been able to collect the following bald extracts, two of which, relative to Irish missionaries, Moenan and Cadroc, are important to our subject, as showing the connection between the Irish settlement and its native land to have lasted, at all events, for three centuries. Fursa's entombment by St. Eloi took place in the year 654. Shortly after this time we find the chronicler Fredegarius speaking of the monastery at Péronne as if it had grown to be a very strong place; and he describes how, at the approach of King Pepin and his army, crowds of the inhabitants in the neighbourhood took refuge in that monastery in which the body of St. Fursa rested; and the Irish name for Péronne given in our annals, as we shall see hereafter, Cathair, or Cahir Fursa, is also suggestive of a fortress or strong place, which is owing to its position within the castrum of Erchenwald.

The next mention we have is when the historian Molanus,[1] speaking of the royal town of Péronne, tells how, in the year 660, St. Amé, Bishop of Sens, was sent into exile by the cruel Ebroin "*ad Peronam urbem regiam in pago Vermandensi.*"

Mabillon[2] quotes a bull of Pope Leo II. which dates before the year 682, in which he speaks of "*Abbatiam in pago Viromendensi supra fluvium Somonam cui Perona nomen est,*" which

[1] See Mabillon, "De re dip.," 4, cxi., p. 312.
[2] *Ibid.*, p. 313.

Erchenwald, patrician of that kingdom, had constructed for the repose of his soul.

In the "Annals of Metz,"[1] A.D. 687, it is stated that some fugitives from the army of Bertarius took refuge "ad Peronam Scotorum monasterium in quo beatus Furseus corpore requiescit."[2] M. Vallois states that these are the only texts containing information on the local topography of Péronne during the Merovingian dynasty.

In the "Irish Annals of the Four Masters" we read, "A.D. 774, Moenan, son of Cormac, Abbot of Cathair Fursa in France, died."[3]

Colgan, in his "AA. SS. Hib.," t. I, p. 787, mentions the Irish St. Moenachus, son of Cormac, abbot of the monastery of St. Fursy in France in the eighth century. He also fixes his death at the year 774. My inquiries with respect to this personage have proved rather barren of result, since no such name is known of any abbot of St. Fursa's Abbey here in the eighth and ninth centuries. It is possible that Moenach, having been sometime Abbot at Péronne, returned to Ireland and died there, having given proof of such sanctity as won for him the rank of saint.

The name Moenach, or Mainach, is a derivative from Máin, Móin, "treasure," which was given to ecclesiastics and laymen indiscriminately. It appears to have been a name in the O'Conor family in Connaught, who possessed a burial-ground at Clonmacnois. The name Mainach is inscribed on a tombstone found there, and were it that of the Abbot of Péronne it would be another proof of the continued intercourse between Galway, or

[1] See Mabillon, "De re dip.," p. 312, "Ann. de Metz." D. Bouquet, "Rec. des Hist.," t. ii., p. 69.

[2] Had. de Vallois, "Not. Gall.," p. 442.

[3] St. Moenan, Abbot of St. Fursa of Péronne A.D. 774 (called also Moenachus).

Mayo, and the French monastery. The same name is found repeated in an inscription on a tombstone in the churchyard of St. Senan's monastery on Scattery Island, where our prayers are invoked for Moinach, and again, for Moenach, tutor of Mogron.

The next entry we find is in the year 880, when the Northmen first invaded Péronne, as recorded in the "Chronicle of Mont St. Quentin;" and in 890 we read that Herbert I. of Vermandois repaired the ravages of the Northmen. In the year 942 the church of St. Fursa at Péronne was visited by an Irish saint, Cadroc, with his company of twelve disciples. Cadroc prayed to the saint for guidance as to his future sphere of work, and his biographer records that St. Fursa appeared to him in a vision of the night, and told him that his mission did not lie at Péronne, but that if he would pursue his journey his pathway would soon be indicated. Then Cadroc, travelling westward, was met by the Countess Hersinda, who, in concert with her husband, Eilbert, pointed out the site of Rupes Fortis, now Roche Fort, in the forest of Thiérache, as the site for a monastery, and furnished him with means to carry out the building. This was the origin of the celebrated Abbey of St. Michael in Thiérache. This Cadroc ultimately became Abbot of St. Clement's at Metz, and died on March 6th, A.D. 978. The author of this life, which is quoted by Colgan and the Bollandists, was a monk of Vassor, and appears to have been a contemporary of St. Cadroc, though not a countryman of his. But there is much in the legend, as he relates it, to lead us to suppose that this missionary may have come from the same place in Ireland which, three centuries before, sent forth Fursa and his disciples. He is said to have had a brother named Madadhan, and this is the name of an ancient family in South Connaught, now spelt O'Madden (Ua Madadhain). Cadroc and his brethren, having rested some time in Armagh, crossed to Wales, and travelled thence by Leeds, York, London, to Winchester, where they visited King Edmund, and were conducted by St. Odo to the port of Hythe, whence he and his companions embarked for Boulogne, and so found their way to Péronne. After this date I have not been able to find any evidence of connection between Péronne and the parent country.

Four years after this event we read of the entombment, in this very church of St. Fursa, of the unfortunate King of France, Charles the Simple, who had been imprisoned in the Castle of Péronne by Herbert of Vermandois, and there abandoned by his wife, Ogwina, sister of Athelstane, King of the Anglo-Saxons. Charles was interred in the middle of the choir of the church, without any royal ceremony, and the grave into which he was laid was only a little tomb of rough oblong stone set up on end. Behind the high altar the following words were inscribed:

"Ici gît Charles III., roi de France, décédé au château de Péronne le 7 Octobre, 929."

This church of St. Fursa was first consumed by fire in 1130, and a second building, raised upon its ruins, was partially destroyed by lightning, when its archives perished also. However, the body of the edifice, built in the twelfth century, escaped destruction. Important additions were afterwards made to this building, and travellers of later centuries have referred to its magnificence and splendour when restored. Thus it has been described for us in an old German work of great interest as "a marvel of Gothic architecture." The author, Zeiler, writing of Péronne, remarks: "Among buildings the Basilica of the B. Virgin is eminent among the few that are in Gaul. Its choir is radiant with gold, beyond all in Picardy. It has Irish canons."

Le Coulon also, in his work on the "Rivers of France," published in 1644, describes it as an admirable example of architecture, adding that there are no buildings similar to it in France; and as to the decoration of the choir, he speaks of it as: "Enrichi d'or depuis quinze ans, une des plus rares pièces de Picardie."

Standing on a site now occupied by prisons and some private buildings, this church was cruciform and oriented, as were most twelfth century churches. It had no apse, properly so called. It ended abruptly at the east wall, against which the Maitrise—Lady's Chapel—was built, says Abbé Gosselin, breaking "ses belles lignes architecturales, ne permettant pas à la perspective de développer ses illusions, si imposantes et si gracieuses tout à la fois dans toutes nos grandes cathédrales." But, he adds, this unfavourable impression was soon modified by the vigorous and noble character of the architecture displayed throughout the building. The great tower placed at the extreme end of the left side, and without any external portal, which its position rendered unnecessary, was not the richest or most striking part of the structure. Its cone-shaped roof was not of height proportioned to the massive building which supported it. The peal of bells used for the offices of the Community of Chaplains was kept in this tower. A magnificent flight of steps led from the base of St. Fursa's Hill to the main entrance at the end of the nave. A side door was placed at each end of the transept, which was surmounted by a rose window, breaking the line of the clerestory by the beautiful detail of its outlines. The north porch was higher than that opening on the Rue des Minimes, and formed the principal entrance into the collegiate church.

The statue of St. Fursa in his episcopal robes, with those of his brothers, Foillan and Ultan, at either side, stood on the pier which divided the doors, under a beautiful Romanesque *voussoir*, and all was surmounted by an elegant embossed turret of Renaissance style, in which hung a peal of bells, the most harmonious in the country. It was under this portal that, in the middle of the seventh century, the body of St. Fursa, followed by an immense crowd, arrived miraculously, to take possession of the yet unfinished sanctuary, and Erchenwald had to place a watch over it for thirty days, beneath a tent of precious tapestry; and it was held that the sweet odour of the spices from the embalmed body lingered for many generations around the spot.

The tomb of St. Fursa, and the miraculous virtue supposed to exhale from it, attracted an enormous crowd of pilgrims to Péronne in a short time, and the church, which was the depository of these sacred relics, found in the expression of the people's gratitude a fertile source of wealth, which, in return, caused an increase in the largesses of the chatelaine. Gold and silver were used profusely in every ornament that could contribute to the splendour of the service, and most of all, its reliquaries and shrines were of such magnificence, that, century after century, the church proved a temptation to the despoiler. The relics of St. Fursa, when taken out of the original shrine of St. Eloi, in 1056, were deposited in another shrine, quite as rich, but more modern, in which they remained until the Revolution.

Among the treasures of this sanctuary there was a fine painting by Perugino, representing the marriage of the Virgin, which afterwards found its way to the museum at Caen, having been stolen from the church at the time of the Revolution. The High Priest is here represented in the centre, the Virgin and a group of women to the left, while on the right Joseph, assisted by various companions, passes the sacred ring on her finger. In the background a temple may be seen, and other buildings. The aspect of this picture is bright and luminous, and Perugino's exquisite drawing and modelling of faces in full light are manifested here.[1]

[1] Baignères, "Les Beaux Arts en provinces; les musées du Calvados;" "Journal Officiel," Oct. 21st, 1879, p. 9766. Kugler, "Handbook of Painting," gives illustration of this work, ed. Layard.

FIG. 61.—CHURCH OF ST. JEAN, PÉRONNE.

It is indeed to be lamented that a building so clothed in beauty, so rich in association with our past, should have perished, but so it is. It was razed to the ground in the time of the

Fig. 62.—CHAPEL OF ST. FURSA, ST. JEAN, PÉRONNE.

French Revolution, and only the relics of the saint appear to have been saved from the ruin. They are now enshrined in the church of St. Jean.

This church stands upon the site of an older parochial church dedicated to St. Jean. The new building was commenced in 1509, as we learn from the inscriptions on the vaults. It was finished in 1525. The porch opens on a narrow, winding street named

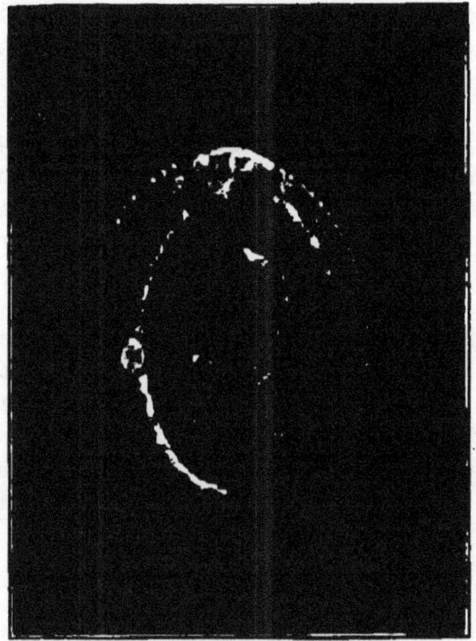

Fig. 63.—RELICS OF ST. FURSA.

after the church. This portal consists of three Gothic arches, surmounted by a Flamboyant rose window.

The interior of the church measures 36 metres in length, by 23 metres, 70 centimetres in breadth. There are no transepts. The building consists of three naves of unequal length. The vaults spring from two rows of round pillars, resting on octagonal bases. These pillars have no capitals, but spread out at the top into multiplied groins over the roof. The tower of this church, situated to the south side, is remarkable for its lightness and delicacy of ornament. It is quadrangular, and flanked at one angle by a *tourelle*, or stair turret, divided into six stages, the three upper stories being richly decorated. A fine chapel, built to the memory of St. Fursa, stands to the left of the high altar at the end of the side aisle. Here, on the altar of this chapel, repose the relics of the saint, and three statues are placed above it, the central one representing St. Fursa, that to the right his brother Foillan, with his crosier, and his brother Ultan to the left. A lofty stained-glass window, rising to the roof, is decorated with the following scenes in Fursa's life. First, his consecration; secondly, Fursa healing the possessed of devils; thirdly, the body of St. Fursa being conveyed to Péronne by bullocks; fourthly, King Clovis giving the bishopric to Fursa; fifthly, the ascension of Fursa to heaven. An ancient picture of the translation of his relics on a second occasion, when this ceremony was presided over by St. Louis of France, hangs on the east wall of this chapel. Another old picture represents Fursa, after death, being carried to his hearse. The skull of the saint is preserved in a shrine which was shown me by the kind curé, M. Leroy. It bears the following inscription:

> "Sacrae Reliquiae Sanct. Fursaei
> Urbis Peronensis Patron."

In the old lives of St. Fursa we find it stated that when he and his brother Ultan appeared at Péronne, they were often visited by people from their own country, and that this concourse of Irishmen increased to such a degree after their death, that there was an unceasing flux and reflux of Irish and Britons to and from the monastery. Some remained there as monks, others settled elsewhere in France, but the abbey at Péronne was long known as the monastery of the Irish, the Scots, or the Britons, the three words being used irrespectively for the inhabitants of

Fig. 64.—PORTE DE BRÉTAGNE.

the three islands. Hence it is that one of the gates of Péronne and a suburb in the neighbourhood are named Porte de Brétagne and Faubourg Brétagne. Thus our islands were so often included under the name of Britain, that the portion of the town in the neighbourhood of Fursa's monastery was gradually termed the British Quarter.

As may be supposed, after the ravages of the French Revolution, the treasury of Péronne is not now particularly rich in specimens of antiquity; but M. Leroy showed me a beautifully illuminated manuscript copy of a work to which I have already alluded, "La Vie et les Miracles de Saint Furcy." It is a volume of 200 pages, on vellum, written at Lille, in 1468, by Jean Mielot, priest and secretary of Philip, Duke of Burgundy and Brabant. At the close of this fine manuscript there is a curious treatise on pathology, in which empiricism is more conspicuous than science, yet, nevertheless, which is of great interest in the history of medicine. It opens with these rhymes:

"Les seigneurs d'église a peronne
Afferment que toute personne
Qui a fieures ou pamoison
Ou paralisie a foison
Ou une pierre en la vesie
Ou lenfleure didropisie
Ou dentrailles decompisons (coliques)
Ou de boyaux avalisons (descente)
Et Bricmet tout quaquez physique
Ne peut saner par sa pratique
En priant à Saint fourssy
Est tost guarie et saine aussy."

Among the finest memorials of St. Fursa in France is the great painting in the town hall of Péronne, executed in the seventeenth century, where the saint is represented as Patron of the city (see fig. 65). Ten of the principal miracles of his life are represented in miniature paintings, which form a kind of frame around the figure, connected by scrolls, on which the

Fig. 65.—ST. FURSA, PATRON OF PÉRONNE.

(*Painting in the Hôtel de Ville, Péronne.*)

explanations of the subjects are given. They are as follows:—(1st) The mother of the saint saved from the flames, is inscribed, *Fontes ex oculis matris extinguñt ignes, i.e.*, "The fountains of the mother's tears put out the flames." (2nd) The descent of the Holy Spirit on the roof of Brendan's house, *Lumen refulsit supra Domum*, "A light shone above the house." (3rd) The restoration of the children, who walk on the waters to their home, *Pueros suscitatos remittit supra mare.* (4th) Fursa rapt in visions, *Ex tollitur mente audit arcana divina*, "His spirit is exalted, he hears the heavenly mysteries." (5th) He receives a bell from heaven, *Campanū affertur ei ab Angelo*, "A bell is borne to him by an angel." (6th) *Fugat demones*, "He putteth the evil spirits to flight." (7th) *Sacratur Episcopus a Sto. Martino*, "He is ordained bishop by St. Martin." (8th) *Excipitur in Gallia a rege Clodoveo*, "He is received in Gaul by King Clovis." (9th) *Exitum suum indicat Haymoni*, "He shows Haymon the manner of his death." (10th) *Trahunt boves hunc Peronam*, "He is drawn by oxen to Péronne." On the ray of light descending from the clouds on the city in the background we read, *Dissipentur inimici ejus*, "Let his enemies be scattered."

The devotion to St. Fursa generally manifested during the *neuvaine* of January 16th was very fervent in former times. The sick laid their linen on his tomb, and never failed to drink the water of his holy well.

This holy well still exists, and is one of the most interesting of the authentic monuments in Péronne. It is of peculiar form, being square; and this, says M. Desachy, is probably a sign of great antiquity. It is built of limestone, and is three or four yards below the level of the present Rue St. Furcy, near the very ancient wall which is supposed to have formed part of the castrum of Erchenwald, and near the site of the church of St. Furcy. Close to this well there once stood a high cross, called Croix Vert, which was placed opposite the church, the shaft of which was formed of one block of limestone, and it measured twenty feet in height with the base. This base was ornamented with bas-reliefs and Gothic characters.

Péronne bore the epithet La Pucelle, because it was said in the Middle Ages that it had never been captured. In the year 1536

Fig. 66.—ENTRANCE TO CASTLE OF PÉRONNE.

it was besieged by Henry of Nassau, one of the officers of Charles V., but without success. But now it is no longer of importance as a fortress, though still very strongly fortified by a brick rampart and a deep fosse. It was captured at last by the Duke of Wellington, in 1815, whose troops took by storm the hornwork which covers the suburb on the left of the Somme. The whole town is surrounded by the ruins of its ancient fortifications, and we all remember the episode in Sir Walter Scott's "Quentin Durward" (vol. ii., pp. 170, 172, ed. 1839) when after parting from the Countess Isabella, he approached "the famous and strong town of Péronne, La Pucelle," in company with the Count of Crèvecœur, and they passed the rich level banks of the Somme and the deep green meadows adjoining the ancient walls of the little town. And again, the scene in which King Louis was escorted into the citadel, so soon to become his prison-house. The whole scene came vividly before me as I stood before the gate of the castle.

"As he descended from his horse to cross the drawbridge, over a moat of unusual width and depth, he looked on the sentinels, and observed to Comines, who accompanied him, with other Burgundian nobles, 'They wear St. Andrew's crosses—but not those of my Scottish archers.'"

It was the first expression of suspicion he allowed himself to use. And then again the scene when the lords of Burgundy retired, and the king was left with only one or two of his own personal followers under the archway of the base court of the Castle of Péronne, looking upon the huge tower which occupied one of the angles, being, in fact, the donjon or principal keep of the palace. This tall, dark, massive building was seen clearly by the moon, which that night shone with peculiar lustre.

"The great keep was in form nearly resembling the White Tower in the citadel of London, but still more ancient in its architecture, deriving its date, as was affirmed, from the days of Charlemagne. The walls were of a tremendous thickness, the windows very small, and grated with bars of iron, and the huge clumsy bulk of the building cast a dark and portentous shadow over the whole of the courtyard."

I leave Péronne this evening with great regret, feeling how

much there is still left unexplored here. But it would take months of research among its ancient walls to find all the traces that may still remain of buildings coeval with St. Fursa and the Mayor Erchenwald. Besides, you must remember, that although our Irish annalists only mention him as the Patron of Péronne, yet he was also Patron of Lagny, on the Marne, and most of his time, while in France, was spent in the neighbourhood of Lagny and Paris. My next letter will therefore be written after I have sought out his vestiges on the banks of the Marne.

LETTERS FROM LAGNY.

June, 1893.

DEAR M.,

I STARTED from Paris for Lagny at 12.35 p.m., and in a short time came in sight of the wooded banks of the river Marne. The town is small, and wonderfully primitive for a village so near Paris. I walked up its steep, narrow street to the church now in use, but was told by the sacristan there that this was not the original church of the patron saint, Furcy; that it had long fallen into ruin. He then led me across the square and down two streets, when, on turning a corner, I came in view of the noble façade of the Gothic church of St. Furcy. This abbey was founded in the year 645 on the piece of land granted by Erchenwald, mayor of the palace of King Clovis II. There remains nothing but a fragment, which is a doorway of the beginning of the sixteenth century, and the details of which are very beautiful and perfect in execution, a pointed arch springing from engaged pilasters, with double pinnacles, with carved niches for statues and fine wrought canopies. Three concave mouldings lead up from the splay of the arch to its apex. The third of of these is filled by mouldings of foliage intermingled with monsters, chimeras, vine branches, and birds, among which I observed the pelican tearing its breast. Above the arch is a festooned and moulded cornice, and at the top, a low gable, almost a pediment, completes this ruin. Crockets may be

Fig. 67.—CHURCH OF ST. FURSA, LAGNY.

seen cut into the shape of cabbage leaves. There are also gargoyles formed of winged dragons alternating with monsters' heads.

Although this was the church at Lagny named after the patron saint, Fursa, yet it is the church now in use which is really built on the site of Fursa's original foundation. Among several oratories upon the hill of Lagny, St. Fursa founded a church to St. Peter, as also another to the Holy Saviour, and the aforesaid ruin which bears his name. The monastery of St. Peter was governed by abbots from Ireland, after the departure of St. Fursa for his intended return to Britain, and it became a nursery of saints, which the *chorévêques* of the diocese of Paris and Meaux selected as their retreat when they went to exercise their functions in the distant parts of their dioceses. Hence it arises that we may not only count among the saints of this place Aemilian, who presided over the monastery after St. Fursa, and Eloquius and Mummolinus, who were, at all events, monks, if not abbots, but also a St. Deodatus, a St. Landry, St. Mauguille, St. Fulbert, St. Ansilion.[1]

This is all that we can tell of the general history of this first period of the Abbey of Lagny, the monuments of which were all destroyed by the Northmen, when they ascended the Marne about the middle of the ninth century. Herbert de Vermandois, Count of Champagne and of Brie, touched by the sight of these ruins of the monastery of Lagny, which he passed on his route to Paris, obtained a grant of the place from King Robert, and he then restored the monastery, and placed Herbert, a disciple of the famous Gerbert, as abbot, who endeavoured, along with the count, to restore its ancient demesnes to the monastery. And the Count Stephen obtained, from the same King Robert, letters which confirmed this restoration.

[1] Ansilio, Mon. Latiniacum, Oct. 11th; Fulbert, July 5th; Landry April 17th.

An interesting memorial of this church is described by Guilhermy in his work on the inscriptions of France from the fifth to the eighteenth century.[1] It was the great bell of St. Peter's which bore the following inscription :

"✠ J'ai ete benite et nommee Furcy.'

Its date was 1669.

Among the relics mentioned in the act of dedication in 1018, was a bone of St. Eloi, "disciple de St. Furcy." Its shrine was repaired in 1307, after injuries inflicted upon it then, when the English broke into the monastery, and committed "des dégâts infinis."

The fountain in the middle of the town is said to have been the original holy well of St. Fursa. The water now flows into a great stone basin of simple and massive design. It issues from a vessel held by a figure like an ancient caryatide, standing at one side of a column, with a capital formed of grotesque figures of Romanesque style of the eleventh century. Having explored the little town, I then walked about to look for a point of view for a sketch of the scenery round Lagny. I recrossed the river Marne, walking over the iron bridge, and, passing the station on my right, climbed a very steep hill by a lane leading from the Route de Clay.

I was reminded of a passage in an old history of the diocese of Paris, which I had looked up in the Bibliothèque Nationale the day before,[2] where the writer says that one of the oldest historians of St. Furcy has painted the scenery of Lagny in the most expressive language that can be found. He points out that, in his day, a dark forest overspread the heights around, while the lowlands were clothed in verdure. The Marne wound through

[1] "Inscriptions de la France du Ve Siècle au XVIIIe," M. F. Guilhermy, tome iv., p. 517.

[2] "Hist. du Diocèse de Paris," tome xv., Paris, 1758.

rich fields, and the slopes were clad with vines. "On one side it is covered by a dark forest; on another it is adorned by the waters of the Matrona; on another there is a varied and delightful plain of meadow-land; on another a number of very fertile vineyards flourish," and all the gladness and the beauty of this fertilizing stream is attributed to the virtue of the saint. The description, written more than a thousand years ago, is not so far astray even now. As I climbed the steep hill, on each side of the narrow road were gardens filled with roses in full blossom, cherry-trees laden with their blood-red fruit, vines just bursting into fresh green leaf, the air heavy with the scent of flowers and fruit. At last I reached the top of the hill, and the scene grew wilder as the road ascended. I sat down on the face of the hill and looked back down the valley of the Marne. The town of Lagny rises in tier above tier of houses from the banks of the river up the hills on either side. The loveliest portion of this beautiful valley lies to the east, where the river appears outside the walls of the city, "that shall be made glad" by its silver stream as it flows along on its western course. Looking towards Paris, lying far in the west, the rays of the afternoon sun threw the rich woods of the undulating plain into masses of broad shadow, and veiled the uplands in the misty light. It reminded me of one of Turner's river scenes; the shining surface of the water, now broadening to receive in its bosom the reflection of the magnificent trees that line its banks; now narrowing and winding in serpent-like curves as it threads its way through the forest to the horizon.

It was through that forest 1,250 years ago that Algise and Gobain must have traced their way when, leaving their master at Lagny, they sought other fields of labour in the diocese of Laon, and thither I must ask you now to follow on with me, for we have yet to trace their footsteps through the outlying portions of the forest of Ardennes.

Fig. 68.—CATHEDRAL OF LAON.

LETTERS FROM LAON.

I WISH I could convey to you some faint idea of this most striking place. A lofty, precipitous rock, rising from the centre of a vast plain, engirdled by ramparts, crowned by the numerous towers of its ancient cathedral, is planted like a city in the clouds; and when you have climbed along the winding road and the avenues of lime trees to its summit, the view from thence is most delightful. I have seen it at early dawn, by sunset, and by moonlight, and can hardly tell which was most inspiring. The eye is led across the great sea of verdure by those straight roads, bordered by poplars, which we learn to love in France, till it loses sight of them in the horizon; looking out from the southern walls of the city a little grey belfry rises above the trees and shrubs surrounding Verdun. It is the tower of Bruyère,[1] a village on the site of the ancient city of Bibrax, now a tiny group of red-roofed houses, whose old walls, painted green or blue, seem to melt into the landscape and disappear beneath the pinkish veil of mist that envelops them at early dawn. So that we might question whether indeed there were human dwellings among them until we see faint wreaths of smoke arising in succession from their little chimneys. And the pictures are quite as charming formed by the rich and lovely fields in the

[1] Antiquaries still continue to find in the environs of this village of Bruyère a vast number of tombs enclosing human bones, medals, arms, rings, bronze armlets, etc., that the plough has brought forth from the soil; all vestiges of the ancient city of Bibrax. Cæsar, "Bell. Gall.," ii. 6.

foreground as in the distance, on this spring morning, when the banks are white with cherry blossom seen against their floor of deep green sward. Poplars, elms, and nut trees swing their branches by the streams and pools, at one side of which the woods extend, while, at the other, lie the flowery gardens of some happy homestead.

Last night I went to this terrace again to see the view by moonlight, and I thought of the legend of the lovely Marguerite de Noailles, whose ghost still haunts these walls by night, and whose story forms the subject of an old ballad still chanted here.

"Quand minuit sonnera,
La folle toute blanche
Ira sur la muraille,
Et chacun tremblera.
* * * *
Son âme est comme un four
Que l'on chauffe à toute heure,
Le démon y demeure,
Ce démon c'est l'amour."

She had loved her confessor, and the sense of her sin in so loving drove her mad. The priests, believing her to be possessed, were making ready to exorcise her evil spirit, when she fled from before them and disappeared from view. Thirteen days afterwards she was seen at dead of night walking on the walls of Bruyère, and speaking in an unknown tongue. She was thus seen again the next night, when she flung herself off the wall. Her body was found in the fosse beneath, and her ghost still haunts the cliff.

So much for the surroundings of Laon, but, of course, the centre of interest lies in the towered, fortress-like cathedral that crowns this mighty rock round which the town is built. I dare-say it strikes many as inferior in beauty to most of the other great French cathedrals, but it must always appeal to the imagination

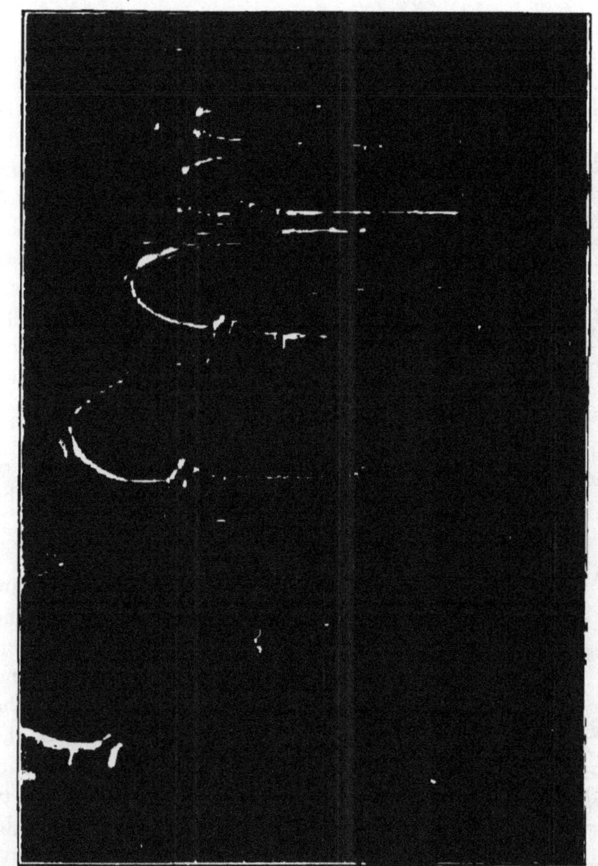

Fig. 69.—CATHEDRAL OF LAON (INTERIOR).

of those who delight in originality, individual character, and wild barbaric grandeur.

Animal life is there in all its force and vigour; and in the colossal statues of the two oxen, standing out against the sky above, the beasts who of their own will ascended to the summit of the rock, drawing the vast blocks of stone for the completion of the tower, we have the glorification of patient labour, and the noblest expression of man's gratitude to the faithful animals that served him.

Fig. 70.—GALLERY OF TRIBUNE, LAON.

If we, too, are patient, and will study the sculptured details of this building, we shall find our reward. In the symbolic figures of the liberal arts, of the virtues and the vices of human nature, in the divine calm of the loving Creator as He first plans His work—then rests, seeing it is good—we learn that behind this rough exterior there breathes a spirit, pure and tender as a child's.

When St. Fursa's companion, Gobain,[1] came to Laon, having

[1] See page 122 *supra*.

found that his mission lay in the diocese of that city, we are told that he sought permission from Clothair II., King of Neustria and Burgundy, who was then residing at Laon, to found a church in the forest of Voës; and we read that on his entry into the town he restored sight to the blind, as he had done on a former occasion in Ireland. This miracle was wrought in the porch of the church of Notre Dame, now the famous cathedral of Laon, *circa* 648. The building must have been that sixth century church on whose ruins a portion of the magnificent cathedral now to be seen at Laon was erected in the twelfth century, and another portion in the thirteenth. How interesting it would be could we find a clue to the real aspect of the building when seen by St. Gobain. It was the church endowed by St. Remi, about the year 500, with a portion of the grant he had received from King Clovis I. after his conversion, and it had been therefore about 150 years in existence when St. Gobain entered its porch. But even this was not the first or oldest Christian sanctuary upon this site. It was preceded by the church in which St. Remi, in his boyhood, was placed by his parents, with a number of clerks, to be initiated into the knowledge of sacred literature.

"Ecclesia Laudunensis . . . . Dei Matris nomine, primitùs antè tempora Sancti Remigii fuerat ædificata, et in eâ idem Sanctus Remigius à parentibus fuit reclusus inter clericos ejusdem ecclesiæ litteris sacris erudiendus."[1]

"The church of Laon, by name Notre Dame, was founded before the time of the holy Remigius, and the holy Remigius was placed here (*reclusus*) by his parents, among the clerks of this same church to be educated in sacred learning."

And, according to tradition, the foundation of the church

[1] See "La Cathédrale Notre Dame de Laon," p. 6, par l'Abbé Bouxin, Laon, 1890.

of Notre Dame de Laon may be traced to the very origin of Christianity in Gaul. However, there is no proof that a church of any architectural pretensions existed there at that early date. The first oratory mentioned is that of St. Beatus, which would rather seem to have resembled that of St. Walbert, in the forest of Luxeuil (see p. 32 *supra*), where a natural cave was converted into a subterranean chapel by the assistance of some rude masonry. In the life of the saint we read, "the apostle of the Laonnois, St. Beatus, constructed a chapel in a subterranean grotto in the mountain, under the invocation of the blessed Virgin Mary, where the faithful assembled to celebrate the holy mysteries, to sing psalms, and to pray in safety." It is the opinion of Fleury that the primitive church, built by St. Remigius early in the sixth century, was replaced in the twelfth by a building on a vaster scale, when the town had grown in importance under the later Merovingian kings ; but, if this be the case, it would appear that very important modifications and very considerable additions must have been made to this church in the course of ages. Thus, in the ninth century, the custom of summoning the faithful by the sound of bells necessitated the construction of towers and belfries ; and we know, besides, from the epitaph of Adalberon, who was bishop of Laon for fifty years, from the year 977 to 1030, that very important works were carried on in the church by him, repairing what had fallen into decay, and adding numerous rich ornaments.

The church of Laon was destroyed by fire in 1112, and the present church—in which the square apse is a marked feature—was rebuilt about 1114, with its cupola, transepts, and six towers, two rising from the west end, and two from the terminations of the east and west transepts.

It is curious to learn the means by which funds were raised for the building of such cathedrals, and to find that Britain contributes her share in the rebuilding of Laon after the

Fig. 71.—SIDE CHAPEL, CATHEDRAL OF LAON.

fire.[1] The clergy and people agreed to make a *quête* through the provinces of France, carrying with them a shrine containing relics saved from the fire. Seven canons and six laymen, noted for good works, were chosen to carry and convoy them. These persons started on the 7th of June, 1112, crossed a portion of France, and returned to Laon, bearing many presents with them; nevertheless, this journey not proving sufficiently fruitful, nine other canons started on the 23rd of March for England, and, after having visited successively Canterbury, Salisbury, Dartmouth, Bristol, with several shrines, the relics in which worked miracles, they returned to Laon the 6th of September following. As the acquisition of 120 marks silver,[2] and also many ornaments, was the result of this voyage, they began to build the cathedral.

The great cathedral of Laon, although mentioned in the life of Gobain, is not so closely associated with his memory as was the old church of St. Vincent, where he had lived for some time before he penetrated to his hermitage in the forest. This church, founded by Queen Brunehilde, was built on a strikingly picturesque site, and was regarded as the second church of the bishops of Laon. It is stated that for six centuries the prelates of this city were interred here; and it was the custom on the election of a new bishop that he should hold his vigil through the night before the tombs of his predecessors in the church of St. Vincent. It was long connected with Irish missionaries. The first bishop buried here was Cagnoald, who died in 656. Maelcalain, a pilgrim from Ireland, first bishop of St. Michael in Thiérache, was called to restore the monastic discipline of St. Vincent, in consequence of the great reputation he had earned for wisdom when in Thiérache. Another Irish hermit

[1] "Mém. Antiq. Picardie," vol. v., p. 331.

[2] The silver mark was then worth two livres. One mark is now about equivalent to twenty-seven.

Fig. 72.—CATHEDRAL OF LAON (INTERIOR).

in the seventh century, Boëtien, was also connected with this church.[1]

There was a fine building here of the twelfth century, but this was destroyed in 1794; no part escaped the fury of the democrats, except the abbot's house, a building of the seventeenth century, and the outer walls, part of which belong to the thirteenth century. From the road approaching it, Chemin des Creuttes, near the Calvary, one of the finest views of Laon may be seen. The abbacy is now the property of the Jesuits, and is situated on the south side of the town.

The Library of Laon contains one manuscript which cannot but possess very great interest to the searcher for traces of Irish learning on the continent. It was written by an Irish scribe between the years 850 and 900, and contains two glossaries of the Greek and Latin languages, containing occasional passages in the Irish language, and also a Greek Grammar. It is said to have formed part of the library of Charles the Bald.

M. D'Arbois de Jubainville, referring to this MS., says:[2]

"What surprises us most about these Irish emigrants on the continent in the ninth century, is that they knew Greek, and that they appear to have been the only people then in Western Europe who did know it. They have Græco-Latin glossaries, Greek Grammars, the books of the Bible in Greek accompanied by Latin translations; one of them, Johannes Scotus Erigena, has translated the apocryphal works of Dionysius the Areopagite from Greek into Latin. He was a disciple of Plato, whose Timæus he appears to have read in the original text; and he has founded a system of philosophy, as astonishing for its time as it is dangerous for its temerity, on the doctrines of this celebrated Greek writer. It was considered good taste amongst the Irish, and a few other people also at this period, to scatter Greek words throughout the Latin text

[1] See "Antiquités de Laon," J. F. M. Lequeux, tom. 1, p. 124.

[2] "Introduction à l'étude de la Littérature Celtique," livre iii., p. 379.

which they composed. J. Scotus was bolder than this: he wrote verses entirely in Greek. M. Ernest Renan[1] is the first French writer of this century who has described these Greek studies in Ireland, in his 'Memoir on the Study of the Greek Language in the Middle Ages.'"[2]

St. Gobain,
Laon.

DEAR H.,

On Tuesday I went into the forest in search of any vestiges I could find of St. Fursa's friend Gobhan, called by the French, Gobain. I started from Laon at eleven o'clock, in an open carriage, and drove for three hours through the woods of St. Gobain. The view of the plain as we descended the steep height on which the town is built was very beautiful, bathed in a tender morning mist. The horizon seemed illimitably distant and the plain a vast scene of verdure. To the south-west rose the wooded hills of the forest of St. Gobain, which I intended to explore before evening. At the foot of the hill we drove along a very rough causeway, over which the poor horse had to stumble, and the carriage to jolt, for about two miles, but then the real enjoyment began. We came upon a road, as smooth as any private avenue, which led through the village of Cerny, and we passed the fine castle of St. Nicholas in the forest to our right. There is a very remarkable tower or donjon, built in the thirteenth century, at Cerny. And at Bucy I remarked a very curious old

[1] M. D'Arbois de Jubainville here refers to an unpublished memoir which was crowned by the Institute in 1848, and the manuscript of which was in his possession.

[2] *Vide* a study on a Græco-Latin glossary in the Library of Laon, published by M. Miller in the "Notices et Extraits des Manuscrits de la Bibliothèque Nationale et des autres bibliothèques," vol. xxix., 2e partie. A Greek Psalter of Irish origin is now preserved in the Library of the Arsenal at Paris, No. 8047. *Vide* Montfaucon, "Palæographia Græca," pp. 235-247. See also "Proc. Royal Irish Academy," 3rd Series, vol. ii., p. 200.

church. There are ruins of an abbey here, dating, they say, from the year 1089, with a round tower for a staircase at one side. We then passed a thirteenth-century cross in the forest, and at Molinchart there is a Celtic monument formed of an immense block of sandstone. Here we plunged into the depths of the beautiful forest. The banks on the side of the road were richly carpeted with violets and ground ivy, and the music of the cattle bells, reaching us from cows grazing, unseen, far in among the trees, the opening glades, and long avenues of green velvety sward, made a rich ground to the silvery bark of the beech and birch trees, rising like shining columns illuminated by the noonday sun. How wonderful it all was! April is certainly a good time to be in a forest when there is sunlight, and sunlight such as we had this spring, for the framework of every tree is still visible against the blue, though veiled by the tender tremulous green of the bursting leaves. We came constantly on groups of wood-cutters, with their faggots tied and piled beside them; and I noticed the prevailing colour of the women's dress was blue. At half-past two we drove into the quiet village, with its lofty church dedicated to the patron of the place, our Irish pilgrim from Lough Corrib. It stands on a hill, and forms a striking object from the road approaching the village from another side of the forest. I first called on the curé, who was just starting on a visit into some distant part of the parish, but who most kindly pressed me to return next day, promising to show me all the existing vestiges of St. Gobain that he knew of. I had still six hours before me of daylight, and I determined to get something done; so I hired a guide to take me to the hermitage and cave of St. Gobain, which lay some miles distant, in the depths of the forest. We went along a delightful footpath through the trees, but I soon found that if my companion had ever had any knowledge of the place his memory was defective; so I hailed a wood-cutter working in one of those

Fig. 73.—HERMITAGE OF ST. GOBAIN.

delightful glades which opened on us now and then, and asked him to be our guide to the hermitage. I was now quite at ease, and could enjoy the flowers that brightened up the green sward on every side, *éclairs*, and bluebells, and cowslips, and marsh-mallow, and violets, and all the wild tangle of bramble and ivy in the underwood.

We reached the hermitage at last; I found that it had been occupied by a monk even within the last century. It stands, as it were, on a tiny island in the middle of a pond filled with those little scarlet gold-fish which shoot like flame through the green depths of the forest mirrored in the water. Still, the cave had to be reached where the saint went for retreat and penitence, and I commenced my ascent to the rocky heights above us.

When I first saw the cave I was almost tempted to believe that it was a dolmen, but its vast size rendered that impossible. The chamber underneath the enormous rock which forms the roof, measures ten feet eleven inches wide, and thirteen feet in depth. Then three little cells, or closets, open at the back. It would be quite easy, by filling up the small open spaces behind, and by fixing a door and wooden plank in the front, to make this cave quite air-tight. Signs of recent occupation might be perceived in a heap of wood ashes at one side, and traces of smoke on the rock.

After spending some time in this extraordinary cave, we returned, through the forest, to the place where we had left the carriage, and our party by that time was increased by another wood-cutter and a forester, or wood ranger; such a splendid-looking young fellow! with his gun slung on his back, and his free step and happy laughter, he seemed to bring one back to the days of Robin Hood, or the huntsmen in "Der Freischütz."

The return to Laon from St. Gobain was very delightful, passing through that beautiful forest in the cool evening. Unfortunately I drove eastward, so the sunset was behind me; but

Fig. 74.—CAVE OF ST. GOBAIN.

I often stood up to look back at the exquisite lacework formed by the dark tree branches against the crimson and golden sky.

Next day, when I returned to St. Gobain, I went by train, changing at La Fêre, and again at Tergnier, so I did not reach my destination till half-past one. I went at once to the church, and made a study of the old and curious bas-relief on the altar

Fig. 75.—BAS-RELIEF ON ALTAR, ST. GOBAIN.

of St. Gobain,[1] which represents the martyrdom of the saint. The old man is seen seated, quietly reading his Bible under a great tree, and at the foot of a flight of steps leading up to his hermitage. A cross stands beside the lowest of these steps. Flowers peep out among the stones. In the background is the forest, the trees carved in high relief, and through their stems and interlaced branches the evil faces of the murderers are seen peering at their victim.

[1] See p. 173 *supra*.

A statue of the saint, holding a palm branch in one hand and a book in the other, surmounts the altar of his chapel. His bones are preserved in a reliquary on the high altar. The curé

Fig. 76.—STONE MARKINGS AT ST. GOBAIN.

then showed me into the crypt beneath the chancel, where the well, opened miraculously by the touch of the saint's crosier, is reverently preserved; it lies directly beneath that part of the floor of the chancel where the high altar stands. An arched doorway in the wall of the crypt shows the rude stone steps leading down to its clear waters, but I looked in vain for the inscription. Unfortunately this church is kept in very good order! The walls well pointed and clean, and all such disturbance of the smooth surface of the stone as an old inscription would produce is carefully scraped away. The ideal of such restorers of ancient buildings reminds me of the modern photographer's practice of touching up our portraits. Such men would take the rugged face of a Darwin, or the worn face of a Newman, and smooth away every line carved thereon by sad experience and by time.

I then went on to see the Pierre de St. Gobain, near the Calvary: this is the saint's stone pillow, a natural rock, said to be marked by the impressions left by the saint's head, and of his Bible (see fig. 76). The cross rises above, bearing the instruments of the passion.

When I had finished my sketch of this curious example of stone markings, a subject that I have already enlarged on in "Six Months in the Apennines," pp. 180, 285, where I found the print of Columban's hand was still held to be indented on a rock near Bobio, I returned to lunch at the bright little inn on the outskirts of the village of St. Gobain. While I was sitting at the table the baker came in, and I noticed that he had a notched stick in his hand, and that my landlady brought out another from an inner room which matched it. It was the sort of tally used by bakers of the olden time in settling with their customers. Each of them—the landlady and the baker—had a separate stick, on which, for every loaf delivered, a notch was made. Do you remember dear Sir Walter Scott's Antiquary,[1] who "was in an unco' kippage" when they sent him a baker's book for the first time, "instead o' the *nick-sticks*, whilk were the true, ancient way o' counting between tradesmen and customers"? I was delighted to find a custom that had fallen into disuse in Scotland

[1] Chap. xv., p. 205. 1829.

in the days of Scott, still practised in the depths of a French forest. My good landlady, seeing my fascination, gave me an old pair of nick-sticks to take home with me.

But my time is drawing to a close, and these letters have already run to a greater length than I intended. I have neither time nor space to follow out my original programme entirely. I had hoped to trace the footsteps of St. Etto, called by the French St. Zé, to his church on the river Sambre, and to Fisca, near Avesnes, where he founded an oratory, and to Dompierre, where his body is entombed in his episcopal vestments, with mitre and cross, and where his holy well is honoured; and also to search for the vestiges of St. Fursa's two brothers, Foillan, or Feuillan, and Ultan, or Outain, whose memory is honoured all through the country of their friend, St. Gertrude of Nivelles; but it is impossible to penetrate so far this year, at all events; I can but make one more expedition from Laon, and that is through the forest of Thiérache Nouvion to the church of Fursa's follower, St. Algise.

EXPEDITION TO ST. ALGISE.

Laon.

DEAR B.,

YOU will remember that Algise, when he left Fursa, went to a retired place on the river Oise, called Mont St. Julian, and was guided to the spot where he founded his church by a dove; that he was joined here by Enna and several other Irish pilgrims, and that, finding the number of his community rapidly increasing, he sent to Ireland for money with which to enlarge his monastery, and I hope you have not forgotten the beautiful legend of how this treasure at length reached him. I was determined to find whether any vestiges of this settlement still existed, and on inquiring, I learned that but recently the name Mont St. Julian had been changed to that of St. Algise; so I started from Laon by the train for Vervins, the nearest station to the village so called; then, taking a carriage, I drove due west through a richly cultivated country, with here and there patches of wood, the remains of the ancient forest of Thiérache. It is now called Le Nouvion en Thiérache, and is also watered by the Oise. The whole forest of Thiérache was a dependency of the bishopric of Laon, and covered the northern half of the department of Aisne. The church of Algise, formerly Mont St. Julian, lies between it and the forest of Arigny. These are all fragments, as it were, of the ancient Forêt Charbonnière. The territory of the Nervii preserved its mantle of woodland which extended along the Sambre and the Meuse, till it was united with the forest of Ardennes,[1] the ancient name of which was *Ar* and *dan*, *dean*, a

[1] See L. F. Alfred Maury, "Les Forêts de la Gaule," p. 61.

forest, Arddu, high (*altior*). It was the country where the Treviri concealed their infirm and aged from the attacks of Julius Cæsar's soldiers. Then this forest covered a vast district, comprising lands watered by the rivers Rhine, Sambre, and Aisne.[1] It seems to have greatly diminished a century after, if the account given by Strabo be correct, and even now its borders are daily reduced by the labours of the ploughman and the farmer.

At the time of which we are treating, when Fursa and his companions penetrated its recesses, the forest extended five hundred miles from the banks of the Rhine across the country of the Treviri and that of the Nervii. The Frankish kings had their royal dwelling here, during the Merovingian era, in the part called Canton of Bastogne (Belsonancus). Here it was that Childebert II. assembled the chiefs of his kingdom. The clearances, or openings, made by the Roman roads are still traceable in these forests in the district near the frontier of the Mediomatrici, which district was subdivided in the time of Charlemagne. Nevertheless, the forest seemed to lose nothing of its terrors, and produced so profound an impression on the imagination that it is constantly mentioned by the *trouvères*, who paint it in fables, such as that of the Chanson Roland, as the haunt of wild beasts of foreign and tropical climes. In the old romance of "Parthenopex de Blois," this hero and King Clovis are represented as hunting in this forest, and the writer betrays his ignorance of natural history in the most delightfully naïve manner. He describes the woods as extending to the shore of the sea, whence seafarers landing on its borders dare not penetrate its depths by reason of the elephants and lions, giraffes and dragons, by which the woods were haunted. Another romance of the Middle Ages finds olive groves in the forest of Mans, and it is to such sources, I have

[1] See Cæsar, "Com.," lib. v., ch. 3. See also "La France Littéraire," vol. xxi., p. 380.

no doubt, that we must trace Shakespeare's wonders of the forest of Arden in "As You Like It." Such anomalies as the introduction of tropical plants and animals into the northern lands he wrote of, only imply that his mind, like that of Scott, was impregnated with ancient myth and ballad poetry, not that he was ignorant of geography and natural history.

Fig. 77.—CALVARY, ST. ALGISE.

At the present day it is difficult to realize how slow was the march of progress in these times. Manners were much the same in the gloomy depths of this forest in the time of King Clovis II. as they had been in the time of the Nervii and Eburi. It was haunted by brigands. It was with much difficulty that Christianity penetrated into its recesses. The barbarous descendants of the Nervii obstinately resisted the preaching of the Gospel. Pagan superstitions linger even to the present day in the Ardennes. The horn of the wild huntsman, who still rides by night, is heard by the foresters, who see their stags, and boars, and deer fall before his invisible sword. Such legends have passed into Christian mythology, and St. Hubert himself has become the wild hunter, while he is also held to have been the first apostle in these parts.

Pentecost is marked by certain customs among the Flemish peasantry, inherited in like manner from their pagan ancestry. Thus the peasants plant trees on the eve of Whit-Sunday or Whit-Monday before the doors of their stables or their cattle stalls. Such trees have a sacred character; so also there are "Les Sapins de la Pentecôte" in the Ardennes—trees that are distinctly the heirs of the sacred trees, said also to have been prophetic, with which this forest was held to have been filled.

But to return to our saint. After about two hours of driving we saw the village called by his name;[1] but before we reached it I found a modern church, dedicated to St. Algise, on a height over the river Oise, and walking down the hill on which it stands I crossed the bridge, and turning to the left, at a distance of about a quarter of a mile along the river, I found the site of his original church, which is now converted into a Calvary, with a holy well at its side.[2]

The poor woman whom I hired as my guide told me, that on the eve of the Ascension they still bring children who have been ill through the past year to bathe them in its healing waters. This is all that is left to mark the site of the monastery. The river still flows on, and I sat on the bank for upwards of an hour. It was delicious to watch the sunlight trickling through the trees, and to listen to the happy murmur of the river, and dream of the pretty legend of St. Algise and his phantom boat.[3] I could almost think I saw the mystic coracle, drawn onwards by its unseen angel guides, float towards me, against the current of the river, and the wondering shepherds standing, awe-stricken, on the bank, until the loving master approached, who saw nothing but God's hand in it all, and knew, from what he saw, that his brother had been faithful even unto death (see fig. 78).

[1] In the Canton of Vervins, Department of Aisne.

[2] See p. 111 *supra*.

[3] See p. 112 *supra*.

This legend is interesting in many ways. The mystic boat reminds one of the ship that came from Jerusalem up the river Serchio to Lucca, bearing the *Volto Santo*, the holy face of Christ, said to have been carved by Nicodemus.

I told you of it in a letter from Lucca, in my Apennine book,[1] how the phantom ship, sail-less, rudderless, and unmanned, drifted miraculously up the river Serchio, and stopped in the midst of the city; and now I remember that a variety of the same legend exists in districts around the mouth of the river Authie. There they tell how three crucifixes, which were carved from an image of Christ commenced by Nicodemus and never finished, were miraculously wafted to their shore in a boat steered by invisible hands; and again, at Boulogne, when St. Omer entered on his episcopate, an image of Our Lady, painted by St. Luke, was brought in like manner from Palestine, two angels guiding the vessel into port.

The myth is as old as it is beautiful. In the "Odyssey" the ships of Alcinous are without pilots and without rudders after the manner of other ships, and these barques "themselves understand the thoughts and intents of man; . . . . and most swiftly do they traverse the gulf of the salt sea, shrouded in mist and cloud, and never do they go in fear of wreck and ruin."[2]

There is another resemblance also between this coracle of Algise, that drifted hither from the Irish shore, and the mystic ships in ancient legend. It was also as they were at once both a coffin and a bark; for the primitive receptacles of the dead, the funeral urns and vases, were often boat-shaped; and this is the meaning of the Welsh proverb, "Everyone will come into the ship of the earth," as also of Tennyson's

"Dusky barge,
Dark as a funeral scarf from stem to stern,"

[1] See p. 83.

[2] See "Odyssey," bk. viii., 556, p. 133; trans. by Butcher and Lang.

that bore away King Arthur on the level lake in the long glories of the winter moon; so, in like manner, the savage is buried in his canoe, that he may float away to the realm of departed souls.

It has been said that these legends of the advent of mystic vessels to our shores, laden with the symbol of a new religion, point simply to a foreign cultus brought across the sea, when a new voice is heard crying in the wilderness,

> "Ring out the darkness of the land,
> Ring in the Christ that is to be."

The symbolism still remains the same, be the vessel what it may, woven of wicker-work, bulrush or papyrus, or formed in fashion like the "gourd"

> "Of which Love scooped this boat—and with soft motion
> Piloted it round the circumfluous ocean,
> . . . . . and lit
> A living spirit within all its frame,
> Breathing the soul of swiftness into it,"[1]

as it sails onward, over rapids, sands, and shining pebbles, until at last its goal is reached, where the vessel may discharge its precious freight, and the spirit deliver its message of

> "Peace on earth, goodwill towards men."

---

[1] Shelley, "Witch of Atlas," xxxiii., xxxiv., xli.

APPENDICES.

APPENDIX I.

(Pages 6 and 7.)

A FEW notes made in Luxeuil on these Gallo-Roman inscriptions may be read with interest. Most of them are now exhibited in the Gallery of the Baths outside the town.

The first three to be mentioned are *ex voto.* (1st) To Brixia and Luxovium; (2nd) to Luxovio et Brixiæ c. i. v. l. Firmarius L.V.S.M.; (3rd) to Apollo and Sirona ide[m] Taurus.

The first and third of these inscriptions are incised in white or yellowish sandstone. The first may be read:

I. (*Lus*)SOIO ET BRICIÆ DIVIXTIUS CONSTANS V(*otum*) S(*olvit*) L(*ibens*) M(*erito*). *I.e.* "Divictius Constans is acquitted with gratitude of the vow which he made at Lussoium (Luxovium) and at Bricia."

This slab is preserved in the collection of M. Boisselet, nephew of Col. Faber, at Vesoul. It measures 10 inches high, and $7\frac{1}{8}$ inches wide. The second reads thus:

II. LVXOVIO ET BRIXIÆ G. IVL.
FIRMARIVS. V.S.L.M.

The stone itself no longer exists, but a copy of it is found in a manuscript lectionary containing homilies on the Gospels (*Homiliæ SS. Patrum in Evangelia quattuor*), probably of the ninth century. It is marked No. 495 in the collection of manuscripts sold by Libri in London in 1859.[1] I have not been able to discover where it is now.

The monk who copied this inscription, prefaced it with these words:

"Has litteras in lapidibus sculptas ita invenimus, extra positas."

"We found these letters cut in stone placed outside."

---

[1] See catalogue of the extraordinary collection of splendid manuscripts, p. 106, and plate XIII.

A comparison of these two inscriptions gives the variants of Brixia for Bricia, and Lixovius or Luxovius for Lussoius, showing the change in spelling from the fourth to the ninth century, and Desjardins thinks that the copyist was probably familiar with Brixia (Brescia) in Italy, and he adds, "L'infidélité de sa copie est prouvée d'ailleurs par le nom barbare *Firmarius :* il devait y avoir, sur le monument Firmanus."

A particular cult of the local deities was practised at Luxeuil to Lussoius and Bricia. The former gave his name to the locality, Lussovium, the latter to the river Breuchia, which flows through the vale of Annegrai and the town of Luxeuil. The waters of Luxeuil were specially placed under the protection of Lixovius and Bricia.[1]

The next monument on our list is the most interesting that has yet been found at Luxeuil. The inscription on the face of this monument is as follows:

III. APOLLINI ET SIRONAE IDE(M) TAVRVS.

"The aforesaid Taurus to Apollo and Sirona."

This inscription is engraved upon an altar of white sandstone which was discovered in 1858, during the excavations in the garden of the Baths of Luxeuil. The altar is square, measuring 1 ft. 4 in. in breadth, and 1 ft. 3 in. in depth, and 3 ft. 3 in. in height.

The inscription is on the front. Male figures are carved on each of the two sides, and a third is seen on the back. A garland of fruit and flowers, confined by a ribbon, crosses the front face below the inscription.

M. Robert, in the "Revue Celtique," tom. iv., p. 134, 144, and M. E. Desjardins, in his tract on "Les Monuments des Thermes Romains de Luxeuil," give the material from which the following notes are drawn.

The Gaulish Apollo was not only a god who cured the sick, but, as at Rome, he was a personification of the Sun. By his vivifying power the god whom the Gauls named Grannus, and the Romans Apollo, in a general way exercised a beneficent influence on health. The word Grannus is connected with the Irish Grian. Caracalla when sick invoked Grannus,[2] not as the protector of springs, but as the equal of the great god of health, Esculapius and Serapis; in vows, he was associated with Hygeia, the daughter of Esculapius, as is proved by an inscription found in the bed of the Danube.[3] The name of the goddess Sirona is found

[1] See Bourquelot, "Mém. des Antiq. de France," tom. xxvi., p. 22. "Revue Celtique," tom. iv., p. 134, 144.

[2] Dion Cassius, liv., lxxvii, ch. 15.

[3] "Corp. Inscrip. Lat.," tom. iii. nd. 5873.

on many inscriptions along with that of Apollo in Gaul, and such associated goddesses shared the attributes of their god. Hers was a fertilizing power, assisting the productions of nature, repressing evil, and acting upon thermal springs, either as a goddess of health, or as a diffuser of heat. That she presided over waters was only one aspect of her more general and extended sphere. M. Alfred de Maury has sought to confine her attributes and position to that of protectress of warm baths, converting her into an Artemis *thermis;* but M. Ch. Robert does not accept one or two of the etymologies of her name by which de Maury seeks to establish this special attribute of the goddess. Most of the places where inscriptions to this goddess Sirona are found do not appear to be thermal springs, although in three instances, Luxeuil, Fontaine, and Nierstein, they are so. And the waters of Luxeuil were not specially placed under the protection of Sirona, but rather under that of the god Lixovius, and the goddess Brixia. M. Becker, in the "Rheinische Arch. Journal" (tom. xx., p. 107), explains her attributes by saying that this goddess partook of the nature of the genius of motherhood, symbolizing the diverse forces of nature.

In Gaul it was the tendency of the provincials to transform themselves into Romans, and yet the worship of Sirona appears to have been continued by the ancient inhabitants of the soil under the empire. M. Robert gives three illustrations of a monument in Baumberg showing Apollo and Sirona, clad in a tunic, and holding her attributes —fruit in her right hand, and corn in her left. The garland of fruit and flowers on the Luxeuil monument may represent corresponding attributes.

Male figures are carved on the other three sides of the altar. That on the right is bearded, while the youth on the left has no beard. These forms are so ruined that it is difficult to trace their distinctive attributes. But they are said by M. Robert to resemble certain genii sculptured on monuments in the British Islands and on the borders of the Rhine. Yet a bearded face would hardly suit personifications of this nature. The male figure on the back is entirely naked, and is probably meant to represent a divinity. In his right hand he lifts what appears to be a knife. The left arm descended to the knee, but is half broken off. The left leg rests upon an object now destroyed, which may have been a lyre; if so, the object in the right hand would be a plectrum. From the words in the inscription, "*idem Taurus*," it would seem that the person named Taurus who raised this altar to Apollo and Sirona had already erected another, probably in partnership with some other worshipper, and that these two altars corresponded in size, one being supplementary to the other, which was raised to the special divinities of the place.

IV. EPONA.

A third religious monument of this period may be seen in Luxeuil, but without any inscription. It represents the goddess Epona, and the mere outline or frame in which the figure is set, resembles the termination of a sarcophagus.

The Gaulish divinity Epona is always represented, as in this instance, mounted on the right side of her horse. She was the tutelary goddess of horses, and many such representations of her may be seen in the Museum of St. Germain en Laye.

We now pass on to sepulchral monuments, of which we offer nine examples.

V. D.M.

TASCILLA.

2 ft. 5 in. high; depth, 1 ft. 3 in.

VI. D.M.

OXTAIAE.

2 ft. 5 in. high; depth, 1 ft. 3 in.

These two inscriptions are found on the extremities of the lids of two different sarcophagi, and may be read:

"Dis Manibus Tascilla"
"Dis Manibus Oxtaiae;"

both names of Gaulish women. These monuments are now placed in the gardens of the baths, close to the doorway leading to the fountain of Hygeia.

VII. D.M.

MARICIAINI.

This inscription may be read "D(*is*) M(*anibus*) Mariciaini," the proper name being doubtless the dialectal form of Marcianus. The figure appears to be that of a sculptor. He holds a gouge in his right hand, and in the left the funeral cup.

VIII. D.M.

MVSINLIRIIAELIIFI(LII).

This has been read "Dis Manibus Musini Lirii Ælii Filii." "To the Manes of Musinus Lirius, son of Ælius."

The figure is clothed in a toga, and holds a whip. Height of principal figure, 3 ft. 4 in.; width, 1 ft. 11½ in.; height, base, 1 ft. 8½ in. This figure is now placed in the Gallery of the Baths of Luxeuil.

IX. MEMOAMINI OLAATI.

This inscription has been read "Memo(riæ) Amini (uxoris) Olaati." Amini is the genitive of the name Aminum, a neuter termination, "which," says M. Desjardins, "was not uncommon in the time of Plautus." This monument measures 3 ft. 9 in. high; breadth, 1 ft. 7¼ in. It is now placed in the Gallery of the Baths of Luxeuil.

X. D.M.

CASSIANVS MARONIANVS FILIUS VXOR VINILLA.

Cassianus and his wife Vinilla are represented on the face of the tomb. He holds a bag or purse in the folds of his *pallium*, and a basket in his left hand. With his right he touches the top of an *alabastrum*, the lower part of which his wife Vinilla clasps in her right hand. She passes her left arm round her husband's shoulder.

A bust in the triangular space above the heads of these figures probably represents the son, Maronianus.

This fine monument measures 3 ft. 8½ in. in height, 2 ft. 9 in. wide. It is one of the additions made to the Gallery in the Baths in the year 1847, when several other *cippi* were excavated at a depth of three feet three inches in the Gallo-Roman cemetery, now covered by houses, in the centre of the town of Luxeuil.

XI. D.M.

DIVICVS Ǝ SAMILLA MATƎR.

"Dis Manibus Divicus et Samilla Mater."

The mother and son are represented above this inscription. A great part of the figures is broken away, only the busts and feet remaining. The monument was apparently 6 ft. 6 in. high, 2 ft. 8 in. wide.

The name Divictius Constans appears on a Luxeuil inscription in the Boisselet Collection. Divixtus was the name of one of the patricians of Besançon in Gallo-Roman times (see Le Clerc, *op. cit.*, p. 22).

XII. D.M.

CERIALIS DONICATI.

"Dis Manibus Cerialis Donicati."

This inscription is found on a rough pillar stone, 7 ft high, 1 ft. 11 in. wide, which was excavated at the side of the Roman way to the north of the ancient city of Luxeuil.

Could this Cerialis have had any connection with the Roman General of that name who was sent to put down the Batavian and Gaulish invasion?

XIII. D.M.

SALICILLAE VINVSTI·FIL·

"Dis Manibus Salicillae Vinusti fil(iæ)."

This inscription occurs on a monument which appears to have been the upper end of the lid of a very large sarcophagus, the tomb of a woman named Salicilla, daughter of Vinustus.[1]

XIV. D M

MIILVRONIS SPIRNVS.

Inscription on monument in the garden of M. Colle.

XV. L

SOLIN CASTI.

On monument in garden of Madame Noyon.

XVI. CENSORINI.

M. Ed. Clerc makes the following remark on this stone in his work entitled "La Franche Comté à l'époque romaine," p. 131: "Le plus remarquable est celui de Censorinus, dont la famille donna des Augustaux à la cité d'Avanche."

Many tombs are preserved in the Gallery of the Baths which bear no inscription, but still are full of interest (see Le Clerc, *op. cit.*, p. 131).

APPENDIX II.

ST. WALBERT.

(See Page 29, *supra.*)

AUTHORITY.

Life written in the tenth century by a Burgundian monk, Adso, which appears in the appendix of the fourth vol. of Mabillon and Bollandists, "AA. SS.," May 2.

ST. WALBERT was born in the beginning of the seventh century at Vinantes, or at Nanteuil-le-Haudoin, between Meaux and Dammartin. When young he earned fame in the army of Dagobert. He

[1] See "Corpus Inscriptionum de Berlin," t. 21, 22.

possessed great estates in Picardy and Ile de France, and became Count of Meaux and Ponthieu. At the French Court he had formed a friendship in early youth with Eustace, the successor of Columban in Luxeuil, and when the latter was established as head of the monastery, in the year 611, Walbert laid down his arms and became a monk under him. These arms were hung beneath the vaults of the abbey, and Adso, writing in the tenth century, records that in his lifetime the arms of Walbert still hung there.

When Walbert had finished his noviciate he retired to the hermitage we have illustrated at page 32, where he continued some time, as the monk Adso, writing in the tenth century, says: "A place is still shown, two miles from the monastery, where there is a cave, under a projecting rock, which is watered by a spring flowing gently from the earth, and here they say that he made his cell, and for no little time struggled, alone, against the temptations of the flesh and the old enemy" (see fig. 18, *supra*).

In the year 625 Eustace died, and the monks at first hoped to appoint St. Gall as his successor, as having been one of the oldest of Columban's companions, but St. Gall resisted all their entreaties, and, on his refusal, a deputation of cenobites from Luxeuil came to Walbert in his hermitage, and prayed him to become their director. The monastery then contained nine hundred monks, and he added to its glory by the wisdom and energy of his rule.

Walbert governed the abbey for forty years. When his end approached he was ministered to by his friend Migetius, Bishop of Besançon, who laid him in his grave in St. Martin's Chapel, in the north aisle of the abbey.[1]

APPENDIX III.

ANCIENT MSS. FORMERLY BELONGING TO THE LIBRARY OF THE ABBEY OF LUXEUIL.

(See page 69, *supra.*)

THERE is an Irish fragment, now preserved in Nancy, which has been described by M. Gaidoz, writing in the "Proceedings of the Royal Irish Academy,"[2] vol. x., p. 70. This manuscript consists of a

[1] See "Vie de St. Walbert, par l'Abbé J. B. Clerc." Luxeuil, 1852.

[2] "Proceedings Royal Irish Academy," tome x., p. 70. "Goidelica," tome ii., p. 509; 2ième ed., p. 54. M. Zimmer, "Glossæ Hib.," p. 262.

small piece of parchment, used as binding for another book. The matter contained therein consists of old Irish glosses, belonging to a treatise on chronological rules, such as how to ascertain what is the day of the week on which are the calends of January, and how to ascertain what is the age of the moon on the calends of January, and how to ascertain the epact on the calends of the twelve months, etc.: the value of the glosses being to furnish some examples of old Irish linguistic forms. Mons. H. D'Arbois de Jubainville has printed these Irish glosses in the "Bibliothèque de l'Ecole des Chartes," 3, 6me Série.

This appears to be the only one among the many manuscripts preserved throughout France containing fragments in the Irish language, that has been traced directly to Columban's monastery at Luxeuil, but we should not leave the subject of the earliest existing relics of this ancient foundation without indicating where the most remarkable manuscripts stolen from its library may now be found. The following notes are chiefly taken from the works of M. Léopold de Lisle.

A commentary on the Psalms, a large volume in folio, which may, perhaps, be the volume seen by the Benedictines Martene and Durand at Luxeuil in 1709, and thus described by them: "A commentary on the Psalms, of about seven or eight hundred years old, the first leaves of which are torn, which is believed by some persons to have been composed by Columban" (see "Hist. Litt. de la France," iii., 521). This is No. 4 of the collection of the Baron de Marquery, sold in Paris in 1857.

Another fine manuscript from Luxeuil, which was kindly shown to me in the National Library, Paris, in June, 1893, was the famous Gallican lectionary of the seventh century, used by Mabillon in compiling his work on the Gallican liturgy (see p. 69, *supra*).

The writing of this manuscript is described by M. Léopold de Lisle as a magnificent example of one of the most elegant forms of the Merovingian minuscule. In the illumination I observed narrow bands of interlaced design on folio 212A, and, in the opening pages, also single-line spirals. This is preserved in the Bibliothèque Nationale under the number 9427 *fonds Latin* (see p. 69, *supra*).

The oldest book belonging to Luxeuil Abbey that is known to exist was lately discovered by M. Léopold de Lisle in the library of the Chateau de Troussures in the Dept. Oise.[1] It is an example of ten homilies of Saint Augustine, belonging to the year 625, and consists of 133 leaves of parchment. It came from Beauvais, to which cathedral it was sent from Luxeuil in the eleventh century, as M. de Lisle has proved from internal evidence; and he confirms the opinion of Mabillon

[1] On the line from Beauvais to Gisors.

that this very manuscript was copied in the Abbey of Luxeuil in 625, the twelfth year of Clothair II., and that, as Mabillon believed, the scribes were at work upon it from the date of the arrival of St. Columban in Burgundy, A.D. 585 or 586.[1]

The third of the Luxeuil manuscripts which I saw contained the lives of St. Augustine, St. Gregory, and St. Jerome, written in the most beautiful characters of the ninth century. For some reasons it has been thought to be even older, as from the forms of the initial letters and the way in which one word runs into another, and the form of the letter *a* being like two *cc*. P. Martigny cites this manuscript in his new edition of the works of St. Jerome, as *Codex vetustissimus*. It contains thoughts on the spiritual life which might well be offered to the devout reader in the present day, with maxims and exhortations to prayer, mortification, study, and chastity, and the strife of the soul with envy and other passions. The life of St. Augustine is defective, wanting the first book. The life of St. Gregory is said to be by Paulus Diaconus, but is very different from that generally received as the work of this author. It concludes with a portion of the life of St. Jerome.[2]

4th. Fragments of a gospel, copied and illuminated through the efforts of Gerard, Abbot of Luxeuil, in the middle of the eleventh century.—I saw this beautiful manuscript in the National Library of Paris in June, 1893. On folio 2 St. Matthew is seen giving his gospel to an aged man, and these words are inscribed above: "Luxovie pastor Gerardus lucis amator Dando Petro librum lumen michi posco supernam." This Gerard, abbot, rebuilt and enlarged the church of Luxeuil, A.D. 1049, and the priories of Fontaines and Annegrai were rebuilt at the same time. Knowing this beforehand, from the works of Dom Grappin and M. le Canon de Beauséjour on the history of the abbey, it was deeply interesting to find, as I turned over the pages, that the favourite subjects for illustration in the lovely illuminated borders of the book were church builders engaged in the various stages of their work; thus, on folio 4, are seen men with hatchets, one making a door, another cutting down a tree, others on ladders, working at the roof. To the student of the history of ecclesiastical architecture these illuminations ought to be of priceless value.[3]

At the opening of the Gospel of St. Mark the picture of the Evangelist, with his lion, is thus inscribed: "Marcus, tuis scriptis vox est similata Leonis."

[1] See "AA.SS. ord. S. Bened.," sæc. iii., pt. ii., pp. 452, 453. "Notices et extraits des MSS. de la Bibl. Nat.," etc., tom. xxxi., 2e partie.

[2] This manuscript is No. 10863 *fonds Latin* in the Bibliothèque Nationale, Paris.

[3] This codex is marked "MS. latin 2196 des nouvelles acquisitions à la Bibl. Nat."

In December of the same year, 1893, I was kindly shown the manuscripts that have found their way from Luxeuil to the library of the British Museum. The first I saw was a commentary of the ninth century on the epistles and gospels, written by the Abbot Smaragdus, who lived in the reign of Louis le Debonnaire, and was Abbot of St. Michel, of Louvain. Were this manuscript entire, it would have been a priceless monument of antiquity, for it contained an explanation of all the epistles and gospels of the year in use on the Sundays, and during the various solemnizations of the mysteries and festivals of the successive offices of the time. It commences at the eve of the Nativity of our Lord, but now it stops short at Easter, the remainder being lost. In his preface the author explains the design he has proposed to carry out in this collection as consisting of two things. First, he will explain the allegorical meaning of the epistles and gospels; secondly, he will show the agreement and harmony of the lessons as regards times and days, actions and mysteries. But although he proposes only to give the allegorical sense, it is nevertheless true that he also gives the literal, and, indeed, often the moral meaning of his text. In order to omit nothing from the literal sense, he even records the names of villas and places where they are situated, in a kind of dictionary, and occasionally adds a short history of each place. And again, he gives an alphabetical list of the Hebrew words, with Latin translations; but only one leaf of this is left, the rest is lost. A list is given in the preface of the early Christian writers from whom his commentary is drawn, and the name of Bede occurs here, which is an additional proof that it is not older than the eighth century. It may be said, in conclusion, that the writer of this commentary displays an amount of knowledge and skill nowise inferior to those of the present day who win applause by their analysis, explanations, and commentaries.[1]

A very fine manuscript of the four gospels, also from Luxeuil, is now in the library of the British Museum. It is a folio of the ninth century, on vellum, and is complete and in good preservation. In the *capitulum* at the end of this manuscript it has been remarked that on the 1st of November there is no mention of our feast of All Saints—a festival which was established throughout Christendom in the year 835—one evidence that this manuscript was written before that period. The canons are written entirely in the finest uncial character. The text of the gospels is generally written in the most beautiful small Carlovingian characters, as is also the capitulary, so important for the history of the Liturgy.

[1] See Catalogue of the Libri MSS. This manuscript is now in the British Museum, No. 21914, Addit. MSS.

The canons of Eusebius are contained within delicately painted columns, supporting arches decorated with skilfully drawn figures and heads in the old Roman style. All these things concur to prove that this manuscript is contemporary with the Alcuin Bible, now in the British Museum, which Passavant maintained had been offered by Charlemagne himself. There is every reason to believe that this volume formerly belonged to the Abbey of Luxeuil, and on the last two pages of the volume there appear entries, in a handwriting of the tenth century, of the rents due from various places to some monastery in Lorraine. These entries are very important for the geography of western France at that period, as a great number of localities are mentioned.

Another Carlovingian manuscript from Luxeuil, which is now preserved in the British Museum, is described by Libri in the following terms:[1]

"*Sacramentarium, sive Rituale pervetustum Missæ, Baptismi Aliorumque Sacramentorum.*" 4to. Sæc. IX. (*circa* 802) on vellum.

This important manuscript was, in the opinion of Dom Martene, apparently of the reign of Charlemagne, and an examination of its contents is confirmatory of that opinion, for we are thereby enabled to fix the time as being not earlier than 800, nor later than 804. To prove this the following extract is merely necessary (reverse of leaf xv):

"Oremus et pro christianissimo imperatore nostro ill. ut deus et dominus noster subditas illi faciat omnes barbaras naciones ad nostram perpetuam pacem. Oremus semper Deus in cujus manu sunt omnium potestates et omnia jura regnorum respice ad christianum francorum romanorumque benignus imperium ut gentes quæ in sua feritate confidunt potentiæ tuæ dexteræ comprimantur."

These words can only apply to Charlemagne and his descendants, until the time of Charles le Gros, that is, from December 25th, 800, to November 11th, 887, for they alone were Emperors as well as Kings of France. Having thus definitively fixed the time of the manuscript to be within the ninth century, it becomes almost an absolute certainty that the "barbaras naciones" or "gentes quæ in sua feritate confidunt" can be none other than the Saxons, who were entirely subdued in 804. There are many other proofs, scattered throughout the services, that it must have been written prior to 809, but as these are very carefully pointed out by some learned Benedictine in his Notes, written on seven leaves of vellum prefixed, we content ourselves to referring to these as furnishing all the information needed. We add that Dom Martene deeply regretted that he had not become acquainted with this invaluable manuscript before the publication of his work, as it would have afforded some

[1] *Op. cit.*, p. 202, No. 891.

extremely curious additions to the history of the Rites and Ceremonies of the Church in the early ages of Christianity, which might be sought in vain elsewhere. Without more details we must direct attention to the ancient abbreviation 'ill.' being placed in the above-mentioned sentence, instead of the letter N used in the ninth century (but not in the early part of it) to indicate an indefinite person. But a much more important point is that the Creed, or Belief of the Apostles, which here (leaf xix) in the rubric is called "CREDO IN VNUM" does not contain the word *Filioque*, which became so celebrated in 809 for the great discussion to which it gave rise at the Concilium Aquisgranense (Council of Aix-la-Chapelle), consequently affording another proof of the antiquity of the manuscript, the word *Filioque* having been added, between two lines, by an old, but more recent hand than the manuscript itself. The whole creed shows so many material differences from the present text that, in a matter so important, we think it proper to give here at least a portion of it, premising however, that several words or letters have been erased and replaced by others in a later writing, although still of the ninth century. The words or letters erased, and now illegible, we have marked by dots (thus, ...), and the alterations or corrections which generally are inserted between two lines, by printing within two [. . . .]

"Credo ĩn unum dm patrem omnipotentem. factorem Cœli & terrae.
Uisibilium omnium et inuisibilium. Et in unum dñn ih'm xp̄m filium
dĩ unigenitum [& ex] de patre natum ante omnia secla [dñ de dō].
Lumen de lumine dñ uerum de dō uero . . . . . [genitum] non factum," etc., etc.

This manuscript is written in red and black, in very rude Carlovingian characters, having some considerable portion of it written in beautiful rustic capital letters. It belonged to the celebrated Abbaye de Luxeuil (see also No. 139, 495, etc., in the present catalogue, and the "Voyage Littéraire," vol. i. part i, p. 168). To the paleographist it affords many proofs of having been written in the very beginning of the ninth century (facsimile, p. xxvi).

The fourth manuscript from Luxeuil which I saw in the British Museum was of the eleventh century. It contains lives of the saints, notably of St. Columban, St. Eustace, St. Walbert, St. Philibert. It is marked No. 21914 fonds add. British Museum.

The fifth and last of these Luxeuil manuscripts in the British Museum consists of the works of Nicolas de Clémangis. This is a manuscript of the fifteenth century, the presence of which in Luxeuil was announced by the Benedictines Martene and Durand, "Voyage Littéraire de deux religieux bénédictins," i., 1, 168. It is marked No. 21918 Additional MSS. British Museum.

Another of the manuscripts of Luxeuil has found its way to the library of Berne, No. 87. It is a geometry of Boëtius and the scribe's name may be read on folio 17, verso. He was Constantius' head of the schools at Luxeuil, who died in the time of Milo, Abbot of Luxeuil—about the year 1023—and his death is celebrated in a poem by a certain Gudinus which appears in Mabillon's "Analecta," p. 217.

M. de Lisle mentions four other manuscripts from Luxeuil as having been seen at the sales of Libri and Baron de Marquery in London in 1857, but gives no information as to their subsequent destination. One a manuscript of the thirteenth century, marked No. 17 of the collection of Baron de Marquery contained short lives of the saints, with meditations. Another manuscript, dating from the ninth or tenth century, also containing lives of the saints, appeared at the same sale on the same occasion has been lost sight of. The third is a commentary of Bede upon the Gospel of St. Mark, a manuscript of the ninth century, numbered 139 in the sale in London in 1859. This found its way to the collection of the late Sir Thomas Phillips at Cheltenham, marked No. 16249. I do not know the present fate of this volume.

But it is most lamentable that M. de Lisle gives no account of the present destination of the manuscript No. 495 in the collection of manuscripts sold by Libri in London in 1859, of which I here quote the description given in the Catalogue of the Libri Manuscripts, page 106.

"*Homiliae SS. Patrum in Evangelia IV.* Folio. Sæc. viii. on vellum.

This venerable volume contains a collection of sermons on the Gospel for each Saint's day, commencing with that of St. Stephen. These homilies are by Saints Fulgentius Severianus, Hieronymus, Augustinus, Ambrosius, Gregorius, Magnus and Maximus, and by the Venerable Bede. The volume also contains "Relatio Egesippi de Jacobi Justi Passione;" "Sermo B. Serapionis de octo Vitiis principalibus;" "Sermo Johannis Episcopi," etc. This manuscript, written in large rude Carlovingian characters, with some mixture of uncial letters (the whole of the rubrics and quotations being in large uncial or rustic capitals, generally in red, with some large and rude initials), belonged formerly to the celebrated Abbaye de Luxeuil, in France, and contains in the beginning a very elaborate description of its contents, by the learned Benedictine Dom Victor Perrin, Keeper of the Records of the Abbey, who therein states that this manuscript is of the eighth or ninth century; and it is so rudely written that certainly it is not later than the second portion of the eighth century. Most probably at the period in which it was written this volume was used as a church service book, and it is well known how difficult it is now to find books of this kind—so important for the history of the liturgy—which have not been worn out by frequent use. This volume contains also several additions, such as "hymni," with the old music, etc., written by different hands during the ninth and tenth centuries. On the tenth leaf of the manuscript there is a note, very probably written in the ninth century, and relating to an old inscription, which we have already given at page 235.

"Has litteras in lapidibus sculptas ita invenimus, extra positas.

LUXOVICO . ET . BRIXIAE . G . IVL.
FIRMAR . IVS. V.S.L.M."

Several manuscripts described in this catalogue came from the ancient Library of the Abbaye de Luxeuil (see Nos. 140, 356, 769, 891, etc., in the present catalogue), which, as is well known, was founded by the Irish St. Columban, who first settled at Luxeuil, the inhabitants surrounding which were almost barbarians, and where the remains of a Roman colony (statues, inscriptions, etc.) were scattered about the forest. It is curious to find in the present manuscript, written perhaps at a century or a century and a half only after the foundation of that abbey, the mention of an inscription which reminds us of the state in which that country was found by St. Columban.

The fourth missing manuscript is a commentary on the Psalms, said by tradition to have been written by St. Columban, as the Benedictines Martene and Durand were informed when they saw the manuscript at Luxeuil.[1] It is a large folio, twelfth century, No. 4 of the collection of Baron de Marquery. Sold in Paris in 1857.

APPENDIX IV.

EARLY IRISH MSS. IN FRANCE.

(See page 216, *supra.*)

MANUSCRIPT IN THE LIBRARY OF LAON.

M. C. MILLER adds, in his notice of this manuscript, that there were at the Court of Charles the Bald, a number of learned Irish teachers who had brought with them a certain knowledge of the

[1] See "Hist. Litt. de la France," iii., 521.

Greek language, and, of all others, it was they who were most likely to have handled this manuscript. Among them was the celebrated Joannes Scotus Erigena, who is spoken of by M. Gidel as "the Hellenist of his time, . . . one who had read at all events the Timæus of Plato, and seems to have meditated on his doctrines. One who knew the doctrine of Aristotle; and the works of Gregory of Nazianzen, Gregory of Nyssa, St. John Chrysostom, St. Basil, and Origen were all familiar to him, while he learned astronomy in Pythagoras, and geography in Strabo."

M. Miller has added the following remarks as bearing on the question of the date of this manuscript:

"The manuscript is thus described in the 'Catalogue général des manuscrits des bibliothèques publiques des départements,' t. 1, p. 234:

"444. In folio sur vélin (*Glossarium Græco-Latinum*)—ixe ou xe siècle—Provient de Notre-Dame de Laon; avec la note: 'Hunc [immo istum] librum dederunt Bernardus et Adelelmus Deo et S. Mariæ Laudunensi, etc.' In the introduction to the catalogue, M. F. Ravaisson has identified these two names, Bernardus and Adelelmus, as belonging to two personages who occupied a high position at the Court of Charles the Bald. Among the counsellors appointed by this prince for his son Louis le Bègue in the year 877, appear the names of the Counts Adelelm and Bernard, and they are also named in the same act as executors to his will, being entrusted with the distribution of his alms, and also with the books in his treasury. 'However,' adds M. Ravaisson, 'there is a difficulty arising from the terms of the will, since he does not give the executors the power of disposing of his books at will; he directs that they should be divided between the churches of St. Denis, and Sainte Marie de Compiègne; and we must suppose that his son Louis being illiterate and less interested in books than his father, abandoned the bequest, either wholly or in part, to his two counsellors, so that they could legitimately present such books to any one of the most illustrious churches of the century. It may be added that one of the two Counts named was already possessed of the benefice of Chausse (*Cadussa villa*) in the Comté de Laon, along with two churches given by Charles the Bald to the Abbey of St. Denis.

"Amongst other volumes that formed part of this donation, another proof of the date assigned to this manuscript is brought forward. 'At fol. 309 r° we find a calculation made with letters IHCOYC. These Greek letters, taken numerically give a total of 888, 'qui numerus figuras resurrectionis aggaudet,' as is said at the end of the note. This cypher must be a synchronism answering to the year 888, otherwise it can have no meaning here. It is probable that it indicates the year in which the copyist transcribed the manuscript."

MANUSCRIPT IN THE LIBRARY OF CORBIE.

This has been described by M. Léopold de Lisle in his "Recherches sur l'ancienne Bibliothèque de Corbie." It contains an Irish book of canons.

The following is a translation by Miss Margaret Thompson from the scribe's concluding prayer:

"Upon me painting letters
May the Trinity have mercy.
Wisdom is better than gold
And counsel more precious than silver.
The dignity of beauty is destroyed with old age,
Or withers from disease, or by both is brought to dishonour."

"For me, O brother, the painter of this little volume, thou shouldst pray that God may forgive my innumerable debts. During the rule of Hael Hucar the abbot, Arbedoc the clerk himself has written these collections of scattered [jagged?] writings which have been gathered from the Holy Scriptures, or from the divine sources hither into this volume, or even from the decrees the holy fathers of a synod have framed among different races, and [in different] tongues. I entreat you all who in this assembly delight in preaching, or decreeing, or interpreting, or discoursing scripture, not to defer asking the Lord of Heaven for me, Arbedoc, that he would deign to have mercy on me, weak man, in life, in death, and after death. Peace to the reader, health to the hearer, life hereafter to the doer. May 'the Superior' keep this in the community."

MANUSCRIPT IN THE MUNICIPAL LIBRARY AT CAMBRAI.

This manuscript is a collection of Irish canons; being those of the Council held in Ireland about the year 684. A fragment of a sermon in the Irish language is inserted, which is translated by Eugene O'Curry into English,[1] and by M. Tardif into French. With the help of these two versions—the one literal, the other foreign—I venture to offer the following English version, in which the matter of the text may, I trust, be all the clearer, because freed from the archaisms of style which clog the current of thought and feeling in the original, and yet remain a true

[1] See "Bibliothèque de l'École des Chartes," 3me Série, tome 3, p. 193.

rendering of a sermon possibly read by Irish lips to an Irish congregation in France in the seventh century.

In Nomine Dei Summi.

If any man will come after me let him deny himself, and take up his Cross, and follow me.

These are the words spoken by our Lord Jesus Christ to all mankind, that they may cast their sins away from them, and gather virtues to them in their stead, bearing the Cross for love of Him so long as they have strength of soul and body to tread the path He trod. It is for this reason that He says, "If any will come after me, let him deny himself, and take up his Cross, and follow me." We follow him not if we refuse to deny ourselves—if we watch not our passions, and if we resist not temptation. It is taking our Cross upon us if we submit to condemnation and martyrdom, and all afflictions for Christ's sake. As a certain wise man says: "The Cross is so called from suffering; we bear the Lord's Cross in two ways, either when by abstinence we control the flesh, or when in sympathy for our neighbour we look on his necessities as our own; for he who shows sorrow at another's need beareth the Cross in his mind." As St. Paul hath it: "Bear ye one another's burthens, and so fulfil the law of Christ." Thus also saith the Apostle, "Weep with them who weep; rejoice with them who do rejoice:" "and whether one member suffer, all the members suffer with it; or one member be honoured, all the members rejoice with it." For, as it is the case in the human body, if one part be diseased, be it in the arm or the leg or the fingers of his hand, the whole body shares the disease; so ought it to be with us, and each member of the whole body should bear his neighbour's pain and torment as his own; as the Apostle says: "Who is weak, and I am not weak? who is offended, and I burn not?"

In the abundance of the love that cometh of God the holy Apostle speaketh: "He was diseased of the disease of others; he was slain of the slaying of others; he laboured in the labour of others." And thus should it be with all men. Each one should share the other's pain, and want and weariness, in sickness, in hunger, and in toil.

We find it shown forth in the words of the wise man that there are three kinds of martyrdom, and every affliction therein is accounted a Cross, whether we suffer the white martyrdom, or grey martyrdom, or red martyrdom. The white martyrdom is that in which a man for God's sake parts with everything that he loves, though the afflictions of poverty may reach him. The grey martyrdom is when a man in sorrow and in penitence conquers and renounces his passions. The red martyrdom is when a man is crucified with Christ and slain for His sake. To such martyrdom did the Apostles attain, while rooting out evil and establishing the law of God, and thus their bodies endured the three martyrdoms. Thus did they repent more and more; thus did they cast their passions from them; thus did they endure torment and affliction, suffering and labour, for the sake of Christ; thus having suffered the three kinds of martyrdom, they are precious before God, and this reward shall we receive if we fulfil their law.

Castitas in juventate, continentia in habundantia.

APPENDIX V.

ON WESTERN CHAMBERS IN PRIMITIVE IRISH CHURCHES.

(Page 144.)

THE occurrence of a western compartment in the primitive churches of Ireland, before and after the introduction of the chancel, is a fact the interest of which has not yet been appreciated. We have in Ireland two-chambered churches, consisting of a western ante-temple and a nave, and three-chambered, consisting of ante-temple, nave, and chancel. Mr. Wilkins, in his account of Dunwich, above quoted,[3] describes the plan of that church as having neither pillars nor side aisles; it is, he says, divided into three compartments, the ante-temple, the temple, and the sanctuary; and he adds, at p. 298, that this portico or western chamber of such ancient churches is divided from the nave by arches, "yet a continuity of roof covers the whole, as in the instance of the church of Melbourne," and it is quite evident that the *porticus* does not mean the porch or any part of the side aisles. The ground-plan given of Melbourne church shows the relative proportions of this ante-temple and nave to correspond with those in such a building as Killfursa. However, Melbourne belongs to a much later period, and has nothing of the primitive character of the

[1] See "Fragment d'homélie en Langue Celtique." M. A. Tardif. Bibl. de l'École des Chartes, tom. iii, 3e Ser., p. 193.

[2] Gal. ii., 20; v., 24; vi., 14; 2 Cor xiii., 4. I am crucified with Christ, and they that are Christ's have crucified the flesh with the affections and lusts.

[3] See Archæologia, vol. xii., plate xxvii. "Description of the church of Melbourne in Derbyshire, with an attempt to explain from it the real situation of the *Porticus* in the ancient churches," by William Wilkins, F.S.A., 1798.

Irish churches. And this western chamber has three porches and three arches leading into the nave.

It seems as if it was this western chamber or ante-temple that was generally meant by the Irish word *erdam*. Whitley Stokes gives us this explanation of the word: "*Erdam*, Cormac's *aurdam*, gen. *erdaim* seems to have been in the Irish ecclesiastical architecture what the *pronaos* or *narthex* was in the Greek," and a passage in his translation of Adamnan's Vision, as well as the instances where this word occurs in the "Annals of Ireland," prove that the word was applied to some ante-temple or entrance chamber to the church, the uses of which were similar to those of the corresponding chambers in Dunwich and Melbourne as suggested by Mr. Wilkins. It is quite clear that a chamber or chambers were erected over the western chamber in Killfursa in Galway. There are also chambers over the ante-temple of Melbourne which are divided entirely from the nave by a partition supported by arches beneath. "These," he says, "in the first instance may have been the habitations of the mansionaries or keepers of the church, who were styled Pastophori(li), Pastophorium having been the chamber or habitation where the ruler of the temple dwelt. Secondly, the lower or entrance chamber may have been the place where penitents and catechumens stood." It was also a place of interment. Bede says "King Ethelbert was buried *in Porticu Sti. Martini intra ecclesiam*," which shows that the *porticus* was within the church, and he speaks also of the burial of Archbishop Theodore, A.D. 690, and other bishops of Canterbury as in the same portion of the church; while Bingham states that "bodies were allowed to be buried in the ante-temple." (See "Antiqs. of Christian Churches" p. 290.)

Here we find this portion of the church is held to have been an ante-temple, with habitable chambers above, and it was a place allotted to penitents, and also a place of interment.

In Adamnan's Vision we read, "Then the soul was borne in the twinkling of an eye through the golden portico (*erdam*), and through the glassen veil to the land of saints, into which she was first taken when she left her body." This veil appears to correspond to the rood-screen separating the chancel or tribune from the body of the church.

In the "Annals of the Four Masters," A.D. 1156, mention is made of one of the high crosses at Kells which was placed in front of the door of the ante-temple or *erdam*, thus, "Cenannus (Kells) was burned, both houses and churches, from the cross of Doras-Urdoimh to Sifoc."

The idea that the upper chamber in this ante-temple may have been used as a muniment room seems to be supported by another passage indicating that the gospels called the Book of Kells and its shrine were kept in the *erdam*. "A.D. 1006, the great gospel of Columcille was stolen at night from the western erdomh of the great church of Ceannanus. This was the principal relic of the western world on account of its singular cover; and it was found after twenty nights and two months, its gold having been stolen off it, and a sod over it." Dr. Petrie adds, in connection with this subject, that Adamnan, in his account of the travels of Arculf in the Holy Land, describes how the fragments of the Holy Lance were kept in a chamber which, like the Irish *erdam*, was near the entrance of the building, and was, as it were, a muniment room. The passage is as follows, "The soldier's lance with which he pierced our Lord's side, and which had been broken in two pieces, is also kept in the Portico (*erdam*) of the Martyrdom, inserted in a wooden cross." See "Early Travels in Palestine," by Thos. Wright, M.A., p. 13 (Bohn, London).

APPENDIX VI.

LIST OF THE FIRST TEACHERS IN THE SEVENTH CENTURY WHO SPREAD THE COLUMBAN RULE FROM LUXEUIL.

(Page 74.)

NAME.	FESTIVAL DAYS.	MONASTERIES.
Acharius.	November 27.	Noyon (Noviomensis).
Ado.	August 24.	Jouarre (Jovara).
Adelphus.	September 11.	Remiremont (Romarici Mons).
Agilbertus.	June 24.	Paris (Parisius), Lutetia.
Agilus.	August 27.	Rebais (Rasbacis).
Amalarius.	June 10.	Trèves (Augusta Trevirorum).
Amatus.	September 13.	Sion (Sedunum).
Amatus.	October 19.	Senones en Vosges (Senones).
Ansegisus.	July 20.	Fontanella (Rotomagus).
Antoninus.	March 8 and 12.	Froideval (Frigida Valais).
Arnoaldus.	October 9.	Metz (Metis).
Attala.	March 10.	Bobio (Bovium).
Aubertus.	September 6 and 9.	Cambrai (Cameracum).
Audomarus.	September 25 and 9.	Boulogne (Bolonia).[1]
Babolenus.	June 26.	St. Maur des Fosses (Bagaudarum castrum).
Bercharius.	March 27 and October 16.	Altevillar, near Metz, Rheims.
Berthoarius.		Bourges (Betorica).
Bertin.	September 5.	St. Omer (Sithiu).[1]
Bertrannus.	January 24.	St. Quentin (Quintinopolis).

[1] St. Omer (Audomaropolis).

NAME.	FESTIVAL DAYS.	MONASTERIES.
Bertulfus.	August 19 and March 19.	Bobio (Bovium).
Burgundofara.	December 7.	Faremoutier (Farense Monasterium).
Chagnoaldus.	September 6.	Laon (Laudunum).
Chillenus Scotus.	November 13.	Arras (Atrebatæ).
Columbin.	May 31, September 13.	
Dado (Audeonis).	August 24.	Rouen (Rotomagus).
Desle (Deicola).	January 18.	Lure (Luthra).
Donatus.	August 7.	Besançon (Vesontio).
Ebertram.	November 24.	St. Quentin (Quintinopolis).
Emmo Mon.	August 27.	Sens (Senones).
Ermenfredus, A.D. 670.	September 25.	Cusance (Cusantiensis).
Eustatius, D. 625.	March 29.	Beaume.
Faro.	October 28.	Meaux (Meldis).
Frodobert.	January 8.	Moutier la celle, Troyes (Trecæ).
Gallus.	October 16.	St. Gall (Galli Fanum).
Germanus.	February 21.	Grandval (Grandis Vallis).
Gibertus.	April 7.	Crespy (Crispiacum).
Goar.	July 6.	St. Goar (Goari Fanum).
Hermenfridus.		Verdun (Virodunum).
Hildebertus.	May 25.	Tortona (Dertonæ).
Leobardus.	February 25.	St. Maur (Bagaudarum castrum).
Leodegarius (St. Leger).	October 2.	Auxerre (Autissiodorum).
Leodobod.		Fleury (Floriacum ad Ligerim).
Lua.	December 5.	Auxerre (Autissiodorum).
Lupicinus Romanus.	March 21.	Romainmoutier (Romani Monasterium).
Mellinus.	October 22.	Rouen (Rotomagus).
Mummolinus.	October 16.	St. Omer (Audomaropolis).
Nivardus.	September 1.	Rheims (Remorum).
Philibertus.	August 22.	Jumièges (Gemeticum).
Ragnacarius.	May 29.	Autun (Æduensis).
Regulus.	March 30.	Flay (Flaviacus).
Riquier.	April 26.	St. Riquier (Centula).
Rodingus.	September 17.	Beaulieu (Bellilocensis).
Romaric.	December 8.	Remiremont (Romarici Mons).
Samson.	July 28.	Dol (Dola in Armorica).
Sigebert.	July 11.	Dissentis (Desertina).
Tetelmus, martyr.	April 7.	Charenton (Carantonum).
Theodulf.		Chézy l'Abbaie (Gaudiacum).
Theofridus.	October 9.	Corbei (Corbeia Vetus, Beauvais, Bellovacum).
Ursicinus.	December 20.	St. Ursanne.
Valery.	December 12.	St. Valery (Leucaneus).
Waldebertus.	May 2.	Meaux (Meldis).
Waldelinus.		Tholey (Theologium).
Waldolenus.	November 1.	Beze (Bezna, Bosco).

APPENDIX VII.

FUNERAL CUSTOM AT CROSS ROADS.

(Page 146).

THIS Irish custom seems to belong to the worship of the Instruments of the Passion, and to be connected with the Passion of Christ. The hawthorn, and whitethorn, and blackthorn, all claim to have been used for the sacred Crown of Thorns. Sir John Mandeville says: "They maden hym a crowne of the branches of the Albiespyne, that is Whitethorn," and Giles Fletcher says:

> "It was but now they gathered blooming May,
> And of his arms disrobed the branching tree,
> To strow with boughs and blossoms all thy way;
> And now the branchlesse trunck a crosse for thee,
> And May, dismaid, thy coronet must be."

The form of procession, carrying in our hands ivy, sprigs of laurel, rosemary, or other evergreens, is said to be emblematic of the soul's immortality. So this bearing of the cross to the point where, at the meeting of four roads, that road is chosen which leads directly to the grave, is emblematic of the soul's submission; while the laying down the cross upon the thorny branch that made the Saviour's crown is an instance of Christian symbolism still lingering among our peasantry that ought not to pass unrecorded.

I find that a very similar practice still exists in France. This is noted by M. F. Darsy in the "Mémoires des Antiquaires de Picardie," vol. xv., p. 165. After describing other religious customs in the valley of the river Bresle, dept. Somme, he says: "The foreign traveller may often be surprised to find a large number of little wooden crosses fixed into the earth, at the foot of the crucifix which generally stands at the cross roads, or at the entrance to a village, and he will fail to guess the cause. But the good peasant of the place will tell him that each of these crosses has been placed there when, in carrying the dead toward the cemetery, the procession has passed near the crucifix."

The church of St. Germain l'Ecossais, in the Canton Gamache, where this practice continues, was founded by a Scotic pupil of St. Germanus of Auxerre, to whom the saint gave his own name at baptism. He is honoured on May 2nd, in the Martyrologies of Amiens, Eu, and of St.

Germain des Prés, etc. He is titular of the churches of St. Germain d'Amiens, St. Germain sur Bresle, St. Germain d'Argoule in the Somme, and of a chapel at Ribemont in the Aisne, etc.

He is represented in art as holding the seven-headed hydra with his stole, being said to have captured this monster on landing in Normandy. His life is contained in a MS. in the library of Amiens, No. 465, and in two MSS. in the Vatican Library.

It was on the shores of Picardy, to north and south of the embouchure of the Somme, that many of the early Irish pilgrims and missionaries landed, including St. Columbanus and his followers; also St. Fursa and his disciples, besides many others of lesser note, such as Caidoc, Fricor, Fiacra, and Cadroc. In such community of old religious customs as this practice here recorded, we may possibly trace a result of the passage to and fro of these early travellers.

In a letter from Mr. Wentworth Webster, written at Sare Basses, Pyrénées, on April 28th, 1894, he gives an instance of the custom of depositing crosses carried in procession at cross roads, as recorded in the Codex Calixtinus of Compostella, published by Professor Vinson in the "Revue de Linguistique" (tom. xx., January 15th, 1882, p. 15). The passage runs as thus translated:

"At the top of the same mountain there is a place called Crux Caroli,[1] because Charles, with his army, when going into Spain long ago, made a road over it with picks and spades, and other tools; and he first erected the sign of the Lord's Cross on it, and afterwards bent his knees to God, his face turned towards Galicia, and poured out prayers to St. James. Wherefore pilgrims bending their knee there towards the country of St. James are accustomed to pray, and each one of them fixes up a standard of the Lord's Cross. A thousand crosses may be found there, whence the first station of prayer to St. James is held there."

This extract stamps the custom with antiquity, as well as pointing to a wider range than I was prepared for. It is here shown to have extended to the Basque countries, and to have been a practice in existence before the twelfth century. The place named Crux Caroli has been identified as a spot at the junction of the old Roman road, with the path coming from Valcarlos, near the chapel of Ibañeta. This

[1] "In summitate vero eiusdem montis est locus, quod dicitur Crux Caroli, quia super illum securibus et dolaliris et fossoriis coeterisque manuliriis Carolus cum suis exercitibus in Hispaniam pergens olim transitem fecit, signumque Dominicae crucis prius in eo cleriavit et tandem flexit genibus versae Gallaeciam Deo et Sancto Jacobi pream fudit; qua propter, peregrini, genua sua ibi curvuntes versus Sancti Jacobi patriam, ex momorant, et singuli singula vexilla Dominicae crucis infigunt. Mille etiam crucis possunt in veniri, unde primus locus orationis Sancti Jacobi ibi habetur."

chapel, according to Alphonse Vetault, in his great work on Charlemagne, p. 237, stands on the side of Mont Altabiçar, and marks the stage on which was enacted the terrible massacre of the rearguard of Charlemagne's army, when the long column of Franks, following on the ancient Roman road from Astorga to Bordeaux, were surprised by the enemy lying in ambush in the narrow defiles of Roncevaux of fatal memory, where the Basques sought to wreak their vengeance from the evil of three generations wrought by these Carlovingian leaders.

The circumstance is striking, and intensifies the interest of our subject. The great emperor, who had waited in vain on the confines of Gaul and Spain for the battalions of his rearguard, learns the mysterious catastrophe that had entombed his bravest followers in the wild gorges of the mountains, that had swallowed up Eggihard, his seneschal Anselm, count of the palace, Roland the famous governor of the Marches de Bretagne. Here he comes to plant his cross, and kneeling with his face towards St. James's shrine at Compostella (Santiago), on the far western horizon, he pours out his soul in prayer; and for centuries afterwards the pilgrims to this shrine lay down the crosses they have borne as insignia at the foot of Charlemagne's cross, which marks the spot once red with heroes' blood.

And from this passage we also learn that this was a custom not confined to funeral processions, but extended to pilgrims in procession to the shrine of their saint as they halt at the cross roads on their way. However, in a certain sense the old Irish Christian funerals may be regarded as pilgrimages to a shrine. Their goal was the tomb of the patron saint of the district, since burial near his grave here was held to be a safeguard of salvation hereafter.

It still remains to be asked: Is there no evidence of the continuance of this custom in the Basque country in the district after the date of the codex in which it is described, that is, after the twelfth century? Or is this one of the many instances in which the faithful observation and record of the antiquities and customs of Ireland proves so important, simply because she still offers relics of the past, and living instances of practices that exist elsewhere in memory alone?

APPENDIX VIII.

FESTIVALS, BIBLIOGRAPHY AND ICONOGRAPHY OF ST. FURSA.

(Page 116.)

THE memory of St. Fursa is honoured in the Irish calendars of Oengus, the Martyrology of Donegal, the Martyrology of Tallaght, the Martyrology of Marianus O'Gorman, Martyrology of Christchurch, Dublin, and Calendar of Scottish Saints, and English Calendar of Saints, as follows:

CALENDAR OF OENGUS. *January 16th.*—Pious men on Fursae's feast ascended to the kingdom—nine thousand—greatness of victory! and a score of great thousands.

Notes from Lebar Brecc. 16.—Pious ones on Fursae's feast! Others in religion went to Heaven on his feast, *i.e.*, twenty-nine thousand. Péronne in Gaul is (his), and of the Conalli Murthemni, moreover, is Fursa, *i.e.*, on the feast of pious Fursa. Mellán, now, son of Ua Cuind of Inis mair hua Chuind on Lough Corrib in Connaught, was soul-friend to Fursa.

MARTYROLOGY OF DONEGAL, p. 19. *January 16th*, B.—Fursa, Abbot. He was of the Conailli-Murthemne, as in this quatrain:

> "The father of Fursa, a pure true saying,
> Was Lochin of Dal-Araidhe;
> The mother of this son
> Was Gelgéis, daughter of the King of Connacht."

That is, daughter of Guaire Aidhne; or Gelgéis, daughter of Aed Finn, according to another book called the Martyrology of Tamhlacht. It is therefore likely that this Fursa is of the race or house of Fiacha Araidhe, from whom are [descended] the Dal-Araidhe, and they are of the race of Iriel, son of Conall Cearnach; and he it was that dwelt in France, at a place called Péronne.

MARTYROLOGY OF TALLAGHT. *January 16th.*—Dormitatio Fursaei.

MARTYROLOGY OF CATHEDRAL OF HOLY TRINITY, DUBLIN.—Furseus Abb. 17 Kal. Feb. His office was celebrated with nine lessons.

Prime xviii | b. | xvii. Kl. |	Fursei abbatis et conf. ix. lec.
	S. Fursei, abbatis et conf.
xvij Kal. Feb. (Jan. 16), p. 79.	S. Furseus. See p. xlvii.

MARTYROLOGY OF MARIANUS O'GORMAN. *January 16th.*—Fursa[1] (his brother Foillán).

THE CALENDAR OF SCOTTISH SAINTS. FURSEY, A. *January 16th*, A.D. 650.—Bishop Forbes has observed in reference to this Irish missionary: "The reputation of S. Fursey extends far beyond the limits of the Scoto-Irish Church. Not only is he one of the most distinguished of those missionaries who left Erin to spread the gospel through the heathen and semi-heathenised races of mediæval Europe, bridging the gap between the old and new civilizations, but his position in view of dogma is a most important one. He has profoundly affected the eschatology of Christianity; for the dream of S. Fursaeus and the vision of Drycthelm (Baeda, 'H. E.,' l. iii., c. 19, *l. v. c.* 12) contributed much to define the conceptions of men with regard to that mysterious region on which every man enters after death."

Fursa is also commemorated in O'Sullivan Beare's "Catalogue of Irish SS.," in "Historiæ Catholicæ Iberniæ Compendium," tom. i., lib. iv., cap. xi., p. 49, and "Officia Propria Sanctorum Hiberniæ," and the Roman Martyrology.

The memory of St. Fursa is preserved in the Irish annals of Ulster. Boyle and Roscrea, also in the Chronicon Scotorum.

ANNALS OF ULSTER, A.D. 626.—The vision which Fursa the devout bishop saw.

A.D. 647. Fursa the Pious died.[2]
A.D. 648. The repose of Fursa in Péronne.
A.D. 660. Fursa rested in Péronne.
A.D. 1086, the following lines occur:

"The seventeenth of the Kalends of Feby. (Jan. 16).
The night of the feast of Fursa fair,
Died Mael Isu Ua Brohlchain.

CHRONICON SCOTORUM, A.D. 627. The vision of Fursa was manifested.
A.D. 646. Quies of Fursa; in Péronne of France, according to some.[3]

[1] An abbot, of Conailli Murthemni. See "Félire Húi Gormain," edited with translation by Whitley Stokes, D.C.L. H. Bradshaw Soc., vol. ix., 1895.

[2] The entry at the date 647 may possibly relate to some other person of the same name.

[3] There is a marginal note in O'Flaherty's hand, of which only the following can be read. "A. D. S. Furseus. . . . Peronae obiit." Codex Cluanensis Rectius, 652. "Annals of Boyle." "Anno 653. Fursu Paruna quivit. In the year 653 Fursa went to rest at Perone." (Harris, Ware, vol. ii. "Writers of Ireland," bk. i., ch. iv., p. 35.) "Annales Eccles. Baronius," tom. viii., p. 382, record his death at the year 654. Miraeus in Belgian chronicle at 655. The name of St. Fursa is recorded in like manner by Florence of Worcester, Matthew of Westminster, and Ware.

BIBLIOGRAPHY OF ST. FURSA.

There is a life of St. Fursa in the Irish language among the Stowe MSS. No. XXXVI. p. 165, now in the Royal Irish Academy Library. It appears to be a translation made in the seventeenth century of Bede's account of Fursa. It extends to nine and a half small quarto pages.

Another Irish life of St. Fursa is to be found in a manuscript in the Bibl. Royale de Bruxelles, No. 2324, 2340, fo. 50^a, 52^b. It is described by M. Bindon in "Proceedings of the Royal Irish Academy," May 24th, 1847, as a MS. bound in *peau de truie*, the dimensions 187 mm. high by 150 cm. broad. My brother, Whitley Stokes, informs me that the Irish is very good, perhaps twelfth century, though the spelling is modernized. It is an almost literal translation of the Latin of Bede ("Hist. Eccles.," lib. iii.).

The number of Latin and old French lives of St. Fursa to be found among the libraries of England and the continent is so great that I must refer the reader to the bibliography of the saint given by that patient and laborious scholar the Rev. Canon O'Hanlon, at the opening of his life of St. Fursa, in vol. i. of his valuable work on the "Lives of the Irish Saints."

The earliest life extant is said to be that given by the Bollandists, January 16th, tom. i., p. 259. It is anonymous, and has been cited by Surius, and is said to have been composed by a pupil of Fursa not long after his death, and written about the year 665. An abstract of this is given by Bede. The second life in the MSS. Boll., ii., 35, is also anonymous, and the time of its composition is uncertain, though it is of great antiquity. The third, much fuller in detail, is attributed to Arnulfus, Abbot of Lagny, who lived in the eleventh century.

Surius printed the first life, according to Bollandus, who reprints it, having collated it with MSS. at Corbei, in Ireland, two at St. Omer, one in St. Bertin's, and others in Cambrai, while Colgan prints it from a MS. copy in Péronne.

ICONOGRAPHY OF ST. FURSA.

The relics of St. Fursa are said to have been laid in the shrine prepared for them by St. Eligius (Eloi), of Noyon, on the festival of his canonization, February 9th, A.D. 655. This was held to be the first shrine made by the artist-bishop, but no account of its material or workmanship has been preserved, and this first shrine was replaced by another, in the presence of St. Louis of France, in the year 1256. It was after this King's return from his first crusade that he repaired to Péronne in order to be present at the ceremony of the translation of the body of St. Fursa.

"In the year of the Incarnation of our Lord, 1256, fifteen days before the kalends of October (Sep. 17), Sunday after the octave of the Nativity of the Blessed Virgin Mary: In the presence of Monseigneur Louis, the illustrious King of France, and the venerable fathers, Vermond, Bishop of Noyon by the grace of God; William, Bishop of Beauvois; Watier, Bishop of Tournai; Rudolf, Bishop of Therouanne, in the presence of many religious personages, abbots, etc., and a great number of Christians assembled there, was the translation of the glorious Confessor, St. Fursa, patron of Péronne, effected, by the hands of the said Bishops in presence of the said King Louis, eye-witness, and the precious relic has been laid and inclosed in a new shrine in the church of Péronne. In memory of which we, Louis, by the grace of God King of France, have here affixed our seal with the seals of the above-named Bishops."

This new shrine was laid in the same place as the former was, between that of St. Ultan and the Holy Innocents, where it is said to have remained till 1760; and the tradition was, that a little window which was opened near the tomb was still existing then, to which the poor were accustomed to bring their offerings for the sick and bedridden, either handkerchiefs or portions of their clothing; and others were carried to this window in the faith that by passing their heads through it they will be cured of headache, giddiness, etc. It is believed that it was behind this altar that the relics of St. Beoan and St. Meldan were deposited.

In another account we read that in order to perpetuate the fame of St. Fursa, Erchenwald added a college to his church for his ecclesiastics, and while he was thus engaged, St. Eligius the artist-bishop of Noyon, and St. Aubert, the Bishop of Cambrai, arrived on the thirtieth day after St. Fursa's death, and had his body exhumed, finding it still untouched by decay. Eligius had brought with him a shrine that he had wrought meanwhile, into which the relics of St. Fursa were reverently laid and placed upon the altar. This was the day of the canonization of Fursa, February 9th, A.D. 655.

This collegiate church of St. Fursa, which has now disappeared, is represented in the Banner of Péronne to the right of the church of St. Jean. To the left the ancient Abbey of Mont St. Quentin, founded in the seventh century by Erchenwald, the camp of the Count of Nassau, extending from the river to the abbey, and the trees and hedges of St.

Radegonda's garden. The hostelry of the Lion stands near the church of St. Fursa.

The Banner of Péronne is one of the most interesting historical monuments of that city. It is preserved in the Hôtel de Ville. It is a square piece of embroidery of the time of Henry III. or IV., perhaps Francis I. St. Fursa is represented as standing in the clouds above the city, which is sustaining the famous siege of A.D. 1536. The so-called patriots of the revolution tore away the upper part of this figure, along with the arms at the corners. It is now placed in the Hôtel de Ville at Péronne. It represents the triumph, through means of the intervention of St. Fursa, of Marie Fourré and his compatriots over the troops of the Count of Nassau.

Le R. P. Simon Martin, minime, declares that the Pope gave St. Fursa, as a mark of his episcopal dignity, a simple wooden crosier (*crosse de bois*), such as had been already given to several of his predecessors. At the present day the treasurer of the collegiate church of S. Furcy carries a crosier which is said to have belonged to our saint. This may be the same as that given by the Pope, but it is now encased in silver. It was not shown to me by M. le Chanoine Leroy.

In the pier of the porch of the collegiate church of Péronne a statue of the patron saint, clothed in his episcopal costume, was to be seen.

Two pictures brought from this church, now preserved at St. Jean Baptiste, represent: one, the burial of the saint; the other, the translation of his relics before St. Louis.

St. Fursa is seen in a stained glass window at St. Quentin.

The statue of St. Fursa may be seen in a niche near his well at Frohens.

Beautiful windows in which the legends of the saint are represented were executed in 1867, by M. Bargin, for the church at Lagny. A reproduction of a picture in engraving by Leonard Gaultier, printed in 1614 at the head of the Proper of the collegiate church of S. Fursa.

M. Guenebault ("Dict. Icon.") gives another piece where St. Fursa is shown side by side with St. Fiacra.

A large engraving representing St. Fursa between two oxen, with this inscription, "The chapter of S. Jean possesses the copper of this engraving."

The following relics of St. Fursa have disappeared, but they are mentioned in the Inventories of Notre Dame de Noyon, St. Vaast at Arras, Notre Dame de Long Pré, and St. Pierre of Abbeville:

The chasuble and stole of St. Furcy were formerly preserved at Lagny along with the pastoral staff carried by the treasurer of the college in various solemn processions.

Relics of St. Fursa are preserved in the churches of St. Sepulchre at Abbeville, of Beausart, Bernaville, Frohen, and Mont St. Quentin.

The name of St. Fursa is inscribed in the Carlovingian litanies at seven different dates.

The attributes of St. Fursa in art are a crown and sceptre at his feet, an angel, two oxen crouching, and occasionally a springing fountain.

Adamnán's Vision.

(Reprinted, with a few corrections and additions, from "Fraser's Magazine" for February, 1871, pp. 184-194.)

THE original of the following piece is found in pp. 27*a*-31*b* of the *Lebor na huidre* ("Book of the Dun Cow"), a manuscript in the library of the Royal Irish Academy, the scribe of which was murdered at Clonmacnois in the year 1106. The Irish text has been edited by Prof. Windisch in his "Irische Texte," i., 169-196.

There are two other copies of Adamnán's Vision—one in the *Leabhar Breacc*, a manuscript of the fifteenth century, also in the Academy's library; another in the Bibliothèque Impériale, Ancien Fonds, No. 8175. Extracts from the *Leabhar Breacc* copy are printed in O'Donovan's Grammar, pp. 119, 341, 349, 350, 370, 381, 382, 440-442, and in Petrie's "Round Towers," p. 439. The whole is edited in the "Irische Texte" above cited. The first two sentences of the copy now translated are a paraphrase of Psal. cxlvi. 5, 6, and the piece may be regarded as a sermon on that text. It has, however, some literary merit, and is, besides, one of the strangest of those mediæval visions which begin with that of the Irish saint Fursae (Beda, "H. E.," iii., 19), and culminate in the "Divina Commedia."

Though the Old-Irish tenues are, as a rule, still untouched, the language of our Vision is marked by many of the characteristics of Middle-Irish—confusion of *e* and *i* in desinence: putting *ae* for *oe*, *nd* for *nn*, *ur* for *air*, *er*, and *ll* for *ld*, *ln*: prosthesis of *f*: metathesis of *cs* and *ts*: verbal endings in *-enn*; and other such corruptions which need not now be specified. The piece cannot therefore be older than the eleventh century. Its composition has been ascribed to Adamnán, ninth abbot of Iona, who died in the year 703. But that such ascription is erroneous appears first, from the philological evidence above adduced; next, from the author's mention of tithes, which (according to the late Bishop Reeves) were unknown in Ireland until after 703; thirdly, from his reference to the imperial edict of donation, a forgery (according to Muratori) of the period between 755 and 766; and, fourthly, from his anachronism about the meeting at which Irishwomen were freed from liability to go to battle.

In the translation everything has been sacrificed to literalness.

MAC DÁ CHERDA.

ADAMNÁN'S VISION THIS BELOW.

HIGH and admirable is the Lord of the Elements, and great and marvellous are His power and His might. He is gentle and He is kindly, He is merciful and He is loving; for He calls up to Him unto Heaven the folk of charity and of mercy, of gentleness and of forgivingness. But He bows down and prostrates to Hell the impious, unprofitable flock of the sons of cursing. Hidden things and divers rewards of Heaven He gives to the Blessed, and He bestows a many divers torments on the sons of Death.

Now (there were) multitudes of Saints and of just ones of the Lord of the Elements and of Apostles and disciples of Jesus Christ unto whom were shown mysteries and hidden things of the kingdom of Heaven in that wise, and the all-golden rewards of the Just, and unto whom besides were shown Hell's divers torments with those that are therein. To Apostle Peter sooth was shown the four-cornered vessel that was let down from Heaven with four ropes thereout.[1] Sweet as any music was the hearing of it. Apostle Paul, again, was caught up to the third heaven, and heard the unspeakable words of the Angels and the admirable converse of Heaven's family.[2] Moreover then all the Apostles were brought on the day of Mary's death, and saw the tortures and piteous punishments of unhappy men, when the Lord commanded the Angels of the Sunset to open the earth before the Apostles that they might see and contemplate Hell with its many torments as He Himself foretold to them a long while before His Passion.

Now, what is said here was shown at last to Adamnán grandson of Tinne, to a high sage of the west of the world, when his soul went

[1] See Acts x. 11.   [2] 2 Corinthians xii. 2, 4.

forth from his body on the feast of John Baptist, and when she was taken to Paradise with angels of Heaven, and to Hell with its rabble-host.

Then, when the soul parted from the body, to her forthwith appeared an angel that had borne her fellowship while she was in flesh, and he took her with him first to behold the Kingdom of Heaven.

Now this is the first land whereto they came, the land of the Saints. A land fruitful, shining is that land. Assemblies divers, wonderful, there, with cloaks of white linen about them, with hoods pure-white over their heads. The Saints of the east of the world in their assembly apart in the East of the land of the Saints. The Saints of the west of the world likewise in the west of the same land. Furthermore, the Saints of the north of the world, and of the south of it, in their two vast assemblies south and north. Every one then, who is in the land of the Saints, is nigh unto the hearing of the melodies and to the contemplation of the Vessel wherein are nine grades of Heaven [1] according to their steps and according to their order.

As to the Saints, again, at one time they sing marvellous music, praising God. At another time they are silent at the music of Heaven's family: for the Saints need not aught else but to hear the music whereto they listen, and to contemplate the light which they see, and to sate themselves with the odour which is in the land.

A wonderful realm there is too, south-east of them, face to face with them, and a veil of crystal between them (and it), and a golden portico to the south thereof. Through this they perceive the form and separation of Heaven's family. Howbeit, there is neither veil nor darkness between Heaven's family and the Saints, but they are in clearness and in the Saints' presence on the side over against them continually.

A fiery circle furthermore (is) round about that land, and thereinto and thereout (fareth) every one, and it hurteth not.

The twelve Apostles, however, and Mary the pure Virgin in her assembly apart around the mighty Lord. Patriarchs and Prophets and disciples of Jesus anear to the Apostles. But there are other holy virgins to Mary's right, and a space not long between them (and her). Infants and children around them on every point, and music of the birds of Heaven's family enrapturing them. Bright troops of the souls' comrade-angels in lowliness and in attendance between those assemblies

[1] Seraphim, Cherubim, Thrones: Dominions, Virtues, Powers: Principalities, Archangels, Angels—a celestial aristocracy created by the pseudo-Dionysius the Areopagite, whose works the author of the Vision may have known through the Latin translation of his countryman Johannes Scotus Erigena.

in the King's presence always. Yea, no one in this present world could set forth or tell of those assemblies as of a truth they are.

The troops and the assemblies, then, that are in the land of Saints as we have said, ever are they living in that great glory until the Great Meeting of Doom, so that on the Day of the Judgment the Righteous Brehon may range them in the stations and in the places wherein they shall abide beholding God's countenance without veil, without shadow between them (and him) through the ages of ages.

But though great and though vast are the sheen and the radiance that are in the land of Saints as we have said, vaster a thousand times is the splendour that is in the plain of Heaven's family around the Throne of the Lord Himself. Thus, then, is that throne, as a canopied chair with four columns of precious stone beneath it. Yea though there should not be rapture to any one save the harmonious singing together of those four columns, enough to him there were of glory and of delightfulness. Three noble Birds in the chair before the King, with their mind on their Creator for ever: that is their office. They likewise celebrate the eight hours of prayer, praising and magnifying the Lord, with chanting of Archangels coming thereon.

From the birds, then, and from the Archangels (is) the beginning of the music, and thereafter answer them all Heaven's family, both Saints and holy virgins.

A vast Arch, furthermore, above the head of the Dignified One in His royal chair, like an adorned helmet or a king's diadem. If human eyes saw it they would melt away forthwith.

Three Zones[1] all around Him between them and the host, and what it is they are is unknown by setting-forth.

Six thousand of thousands with shapes of horses and of birds around the fiery chair flaming without limit without end.

Then, to tell of the mighty Lord who is on that throne cometh not unto any one unless He Himself should do it, or unless He should speak unto the ranks of Heaven. For none will relate His ardour and His strength, His redness[2] and His exceeding clearness, His splendour and His delightfulness, His munificence and His firmness, the multitude of His Angels and Archangels chanting music to Him, His multitu-

[1] They symbolize, probably, the Three Persons of the Trinity: cf. the Divina Commedia, ed. Carlo Witte, "Paradiso," xxxiii. 115:

> "Nella profonda e chiara sussistenza
> Dell' alto lume parvemi *tre giri*
> Di tre colori e d' una continenza."

[2] God's redness symbolizes Divine love, creative power, royalty.

dinous messengers to Him and from Him with exceeding brief answers to every troop in turn, His smoothness and His great gentleness towards some, His roughness and His great harshness towards other folk of them.

If any one were always beholding Him, around Him, from East and from West, from South and from North, he will find on every side with Him a face illustrious, more brilliant seven times than is the sun. Yea, he will not see a man's form on Him of head or of foot, but as a fiery cloud flaming throughout the universe, and every one in trembling and in terror before Him. All-full of His light are Heaven and Earth, and radiance like a king's star all around Him. Three thousand divers melodies (there are) of every choir that is at choir-singing about Him. Sweet as the many melodies of the world is every single melody of themselves apart.

The City, then, wherein is that throne, thus it is, and seven walls of crystal with divers colours around it. Loftier is each wall than the other. The platform and lowest base of the City are of bright crystal with the sun's countenance upon it, made changeful with blue and purple and green and every hue besides.

A family beautiful, very meek, very gentle, again, without absence of any good thing in them, are they who dwell in that City. For none reach it and none dwell in it continually save only pure saints or pilgrims devoted to God. Their array, however, and their ranging, it is hard to know how it happened, for there is not a back of any of them, or his side, towards another. But it is thus the unspeakable might of the Lord hath arranged them and kept them, face to face in their ranks and in their circles equally high all round about the throne, with splendour and with delightfulness, and their faces all towards God.

A chancel-rail of crystal (there is) between every two choirs, with excellent adornment of red gold and of silver thereon, with beautiful ranks of precious stone and with changefulness of divers gems, and with stalls and crowns of carbuncle on the rails of that chancel. Three precious stones, then, with a melodious voice and with the sweetness of music between every two chief assemblies, and their upper halves as flambeaux aflame. Seven thousand angels in the forms of chief lights irradiating and undarkening the City round about. Seven thousand others in its very midst flaming for ever round the royal City. The men of the world in one place, though they be very numerous, the odour of the top of a single light of those lights would suffice them with food.

Whosoever, then, of the men of the world do not reach that City (at once) from their life, and for whom the possession of it is destined after the Judgment of Doom, it is in these they make their dwellings, changefully and restlessly, in heights and in hills, in moors and in morasses (?), until Doom shall come to them.

Even thus are those hosts and the assemblies, with a comrade-angel of every single soul that is therein at lowliness and attendance upon her.

A veil of fire and a veil of ice in the chief gateway of the City before them, and they a-clashing top against top for ever. The sound and noises, then, of those veils coming together are heard throughout the universe. Adam's seed, if they should hear that sound, trembling and terror intolerable would seize them all before it. Sad, now, and troubled are the sinners at that sound; but if it be on the side towards Heaven's family nought is heard of that rough thunder save full little only, and sweet as any melody that is.

Great, then, and it is a marvel to tell it, the position of that City, for little of much is that which we have told of its divers orders and of its marvels.

Rare, therefore, is it for the soul, after commune and dwelling with the flesh, with its sleep, and with its ease, and with its freedom, and with its happiness, to advance and go to the Creator's throne unless she fare with guidance of angels. For hard it is to climb the seven heavens, for not easier is one of them than another. For there are six gates of protection before the human race up to Paradise. A gatewarden, furthermore, and a guardian from Heaven's family, have been set to guard each gate of them.

The gate, then, of the heaven that is nearest hither, thereon hath been set Archangel Michael, and two virgins by him with iron rods in their laps to scourge and to beat the sinners, so that there the sinners meet with the first yell of pain, and with the first suffering of the path whereon they go.

The gate, in sooth, of the second heaven, Archangel Uriel is guardian thereto, and two virgins before him with fiery scourges in their hands. It is with these they scourge the sinners across their faces and across their eyes. A fiery river, moreover, hath been set, with great flame thereon, before that door. Abersetus, sooth, the name of the angel tending that river, which tries and washes the souls of the saints from the measure of guilt that cleaves to them, so that they become as pure and as bright as the splendour of a star. There, likewise, hath been set a shining well with bloom and odour to cleanse and purify the souls of the just. It raveneth, however, and burneth the sinners' souls and taketh nought from them, but it is an increase of pain and penance that cometh to them there. And then thereout arise the sinners with sorrow and full great gloom, the just, however, with delight and joyousness, to the gate of the third heaven.

A fiery furnace likewise, flaming continually, is there. Twelve thousand cubits it is that its flame reaches aloft. Then the souls of the righteous fare through that furnace in the twinkling of an eye. It bakes, however, and burns there the sinners' souls to the end of twelve years. Thereafter the angel of fellowship takes them to the fourth gate.

Thus, then, is the gate of entrance of the fourth heaven, with a fiery river around it like the river aforesaid. A flaming wall likewise surrounds it, the breadth of its fire is measured at twelve thousand cubits. Howbeit, the souls of the righteous pass over it as if it were not at all, and it detains the souls of the sinners for a time of twelve years, in wretchedness and in punishment, until the angel of fellowship takes them to the gate of the fifth heaven.

A fiery river moreover is there also, but different is it from the other rivers, for there is an especial whirlpool in the midst of that river, and it whirls the souls of the sinners round and round,[1] and holds them to the end of sixteen years. Howbeit, the righteous fare over it forthwith without any delay. When afterwards it is time to release the sinners thereout, the angel smites the river with a hard rod of a stony nature, and lifts the souls up with the end of the rod. Thereafter, too, Michael bears the souls to the gate of the sixth heaven.

However, it is not told (that there) is pain or punishment for the souls in that gate, but they are illumined there by a light and by radiance of precious stones. Then Michael passeth thereafter to the angel of the Trinity, and they both show forth the soul in the presence of God.

Huge, then, and innumerable the welcome of Heaven's family and of the Lord Himself to the soul at that time if she be innocent, righteous. If, however, the soul be unrighteous, and if she be imperfect, she getteth roughness and bitterness from the mighty Lord, and he saith to Heaven's angels "Seize with you, oh Heaven's angels, this impious soul, and bestow her into Lucifer's hand to drown her and to hide her away in the deep of Hell for ever and ever."[2]

There, then is severed that wretched soul, fearfully and bitterly and horribly, from the presence of Heaven's kingdom and of God's countenance. It is there, too, she casts forth the sigh that is heavier than every sigh, at coming into the Devil's presence after beholding the delight of Heaven's kingdom. It is there she is severed from the safe-

[1] Cf. "Inferno," vii. 22:

"Come fa l' onda là sovra Cariddi,
Che si frange con quella in cui s' intoppa,
Cosl convien che qui la gente riddi."

[2] Cf. "Seize ye him and drag him into the midfire," Koran, sura xliv. 47.

keeping of the Archangels with whom she came to Heaven, and it is there, also, the twelve fiery dragons swallow every soul, each after the other, so that the undermost dragon puts her from him into the Devil's mouth. It is then she gets all-fulness of every evil with the Devil's presence for ever and ever.

Now when the angel of fellowship had shown to Adamnán's soul these visions of Heaven's kingdom and the first adventures of every soul after coming forth from her body, thereafter she took her with him to visit lower Hell with the abundance of its pains, and its tortures and its punishments.

This then is the first land whereto he came. A land black, scorched (is) it, bare, seared, without torture there at all. A glen full of fire on the hither side of it. A vast flame there that comes over its brinks on every side. Black (is) its lowest part. Red its middle and its upper part. Eight monsters there, their eyes like fiery gledes.

A vast Bridge besides, across that glen. It stretches from the one brink to (the) other. High its middle part, low, however, its two extremities. Three hosts endeavour to wend across it, and not all pass. For host of them, broad is the bridge from beginning to end, so that they go all-safe, without terror, without dread, over the fiery glen, Another host faring towards it, narrow it is for them at the beginning, but broad at the end, so that afterwards they go over the same glen in that wise after great peril. The last host, however, broad for them at the beginning is the bridge, narrow and strait at the end, so that they fall from the middle of it into the same glen perilous, into the throats of the eight red-hot monsters there who make their abode in the glen.[1]

[1] This bridge has already been compared by M. Pictet (*Origines indo-européennes*," ii. 521) with the *Chinvató peretus* ("bridge of the gatherer") of the Zend-Avesta, "which the souls of the pious alone can pass, while the wicked fall down from it into Hell" (see Haug's "Essays on the Sacred Language . . . of the Parsees," pp. 156, 169, 213, 216, 217, 266, his account of the "Ardâi vîrâf-nâmeh" in Trübner's "Record," April 25, 1870, and Justi's "Handbuch der Zendsprache," 111). M. Pictet also mentions the bridge over Giöll, across which Hermódhr rode to rescue Baldr from Hel: cf. the "brigge of paradis." *Sir Owain* cited by Scott, "Minstrelsy," 1830, ii. 360, and see Grimm, "Deutsche Mythologie," 2te Aufl. 794: Milman, "History of Latin Christianity," i. 474: "Des Vaters letzter Wille, Volksmährchen der Serben," Berlin, 1854, s. 131: Delepierre, "Le Livre des Visions," pp. 24, 52, 66; and Sale's Koran, 65. The bridge in Frate Alberico's vision is more like that in Adamnán's: "He saw here a great burning pitchy river, issuing from hell, and an iron bridge over it, which appeared very broad and easy for the virtuous to pass; but when sinners attempted it, it became narrow as a thread, and they fell over into the river, and afterwards attempted it again, but were not allowed to pass until they had been sufficiently boiled to purge them of their sins," Longfellow's "Divine Comedy," London, 1867, p. 235. No mention is made of this bridge in the

These are the people for whom that way was easy: folk of chastity, folk of devout penitence, folk of red martyrdom[1] willingly suffered for God. These, then, are the crowd for whom the way was narrow at the beginning and for whom thereafter it was broad at the end, the tribe who are constrained by compulsion to do God's will and thereafter turn their compulsion into willingness to serve God. But it is for these for whom the bridge was broad at the beginning and for whom it was narrow at the end, for the sinners who listen to the preaching of God's word and after hearing it fulfil it not.

Likewise there are vast hosts in weakness on the shore of the Eternal Pain at the hither side of the lightless land. Every alternate hour the pain ebbs from them, the other hour it flows over them. They, then, who are in that wise are the people whose good and whose evil are equal. And in the day of Doom it shall be judged between these, and their good shall quench their evil on that day, and thereafter they shall be borne to the Harbour of Life in presence of God for ever and ever.

Then another great crowd is there in the neighbourhood of that folk, and their pain is vast. Thus then are they: tied to fiery pillars; a sea of fire round them up to their chins; fiery chains round their middle in shape of serpents; their faces blaze above the pain. It is these then that are in that pain: sinners, and parricides, and destroyers of God's Church, and merciless managers of church-lands,[2] who are in presence of

Tidings of Doomsday (*scéla lái brátha*), *Lebor na huidre*, 31*b*—34*a*. According to this homily, after having been a thousand years in the fire of Doom ("for that is the duration of Doomsday, as the commentators on the holy canon declare"), the sinners part from Heaven's family:—"Not happy, now, is the road of those sinners: they get not drink nor food, but constant hunger, and great thirst, and great cold. It is they that are thereafter borne to the Devil's house with sound of despair, with heavy, yearning sighs. Miserable is the cry and shout, wailing and shrieking, woe and handsmiting of those sinful folks there, at the dragging of them to hell's torment. . . . They will sit thereafter a merciless seat on glowing coals of great fire before the King of Evil in the Glen of Pains, a place wherein they shall have heavy punishments."—*Revue Celtique*, iv. 253.

[1] "Red martyrdom."—"This is the red martyrdom: to endure a cross and destruction for Christ, as happened to the apostles in the evil ones' persecution and in teaching God's law."—Cambray Sermon, Zeuss, G. C. 1008, where *bán-martre* ("white martyrdom") and *glas-martre* ("blue martyrdom") are also explained (see page 251, *supra*).

[2] *Airchinnig.* Hence it seems that the *airchinnech* (=W. *arbennig*) sometimes performed not only the functions of the *mansionarius*, or manager of Church glebes (Todd, "St. Patrick," pp. 160-165), but also those of the *sacrista* or keeper of sacred things. Note that a *ban-airchinnech cilli caillech* (princeps femina cellæ sanctimonialium) is mentioned in LU. 22*a*. (woman-presidents are mentioned in the Laodicean canons), and that in the Tripartite Life, Eg. 2. a. B, it is said of Pope Celestine *isé immorro airchindech róbæ hi Roim isindaimsirsin* ("he is the *airchinnech* who was in Rome at that time").

the Saints' relics, over gifts and tithes of the Church, and who make of the goods possessions for themselves rather than for the guests and the needy of the Lord.

Yea, great hosts are there standing up continually in jet-black mires as far as their girdles: short icy cowls around them. They rest not and halt not for ever, but the girdles (are) burning them both in cold and heat. Hosts of fiends all around them, with fiery maces in their hands beating them on their heads,[1] and they in continual strife with the fiends. All the faces of the wretched ones towards the North, and a wind rough, bitter, right into their foreheads, along with every evil. Showers red, fiery,[2] pouring on them every night and every day, and they cannot shun them, but have to endure them for ever and ever in weeping and in lamenting.

Some of them had streams of fire in the holes of their faces.[3] Others, nails of fire through their tongues. Others, (with like nails) through their heads from the outside. It is they then who are in that pain, to wit, thieves and liars, and folk of treachery and blasphemy, and robbers, and raiders, and false-judging Brehons, and folk of contention, and witches, and satirists, men who mark themselves to the Devil, and Readers[4] who preach heresy.

There is another great multitude in islands amid the sea of fire. A silvern wall around them of their garments and of their alms. Now that host are they who do mercy without neglect, and yet who are in laxity

[1] Cf. "Inferno," xviii. 35:

"Vidi demon cornuti con gran ferze,
Che li battean crudelmente di retro."

So in the Koran, sura xxii. 21: "All that is their bowels, and their skins, shall be dissolved, *and there are maces of iron for them.*"

[2] *Frassa derga tentide:* cf. "He shall rain upon the ungodly snares, fire and brimstone," Ps. xi. 7, and "Inferno," xiv. 28, 40:

"Sopra tutto il sabbion d'un cader lento
Piovean di foco dilatate falde,
Come di neve in alpe senza vento.
. . . .
Senza riposo mai era la tresca
Delle misere mani, or quindi or quinci
Iscotendo da sè l' arsura fresca."

[3] Cf. summe ther wepeth and alle heore teres beoth berninde gleden, "Old English Homilies," 1st ser. 43.

[4] *Fir légind* = viri legendi. The *fer légind* seems to correspond with the *anagnóstés* and *lector* of the Greek and Latin Churches. The *fer-léginn* of Turbruad (Turriff) is mentioned in a charter in the "Book of Deir" (*Goidilica*, 51). See also Reeves' "Columba," 196, 365.

and in lust of their flesh to the limit of their death, and their alms help them in the middle of the sea of fire till Doom, and after Doom they will be sent to the Harbour of Life.

Moreover another great multitude is there, with red fiery cloaks[1] around them reaching to the ground. Their trembling and their shout are heard throughout the firmament. An inscrutable crowd of fiends hiding them away, and having in their hands stinking dogs, half raw, commanding the sinners to consume them and to eat them. Red, fiery wheels[2] aflaming for ever round the sinners' throats. They are brought up to the firmament every alternate hour. They are cast down into Hell's deep the other hour. [Little children (are) maiming them always.] Now they who are in that pain are men ordained who have trangressed their orders, and sham-believers, and liars who lie and befool the crowds and take on them(selves) wonders and miracles which they cannot do for them. The little children, however, who are maiming the men ordained, to wit, those are the folk that were entrusted to them (the men ordained) for teaching, and they taught not the children and rebuked them not concerning their sins.

Then another vast crowd is there, east and west of them, without standing still, over the fiery flagstones, fighting against the hosts of the fiends. Many to count then are the showers of arrows red-flaming towards them from the fiends. They come in their running without breaking off, without resting, till they reach black lochs and black rivers to quench those arrows therein. Miserable then and wretched are the shouts and the lamentations which the sinners make in those waters, for it is an increase of pain that they have. Now they that are in that pain are dishonest artisans and clothmakers and traders, the false-judging Brehons of the Jews and of every (folk) besides, and impious kings, wrongful managers of churchlands, incestuous fosterfathers, adulterous wives, and messengers who ruin them in their misdeeds.

Then there is a wall of fire on the far side of the Land of Pains: more horrible and more bitter it is seven times than the Land of Pains itself. Howbeit souls do not possess (it) until Doom, for with fiends only is its sovranty until the Day of Doom.

Woe then (to him who) is in those pains dwelling along with the Devil's family! Woe (to him that) heedeth not that family! Woe (to him) over whom shall be for lord a fiend fierce, contemptible! Woe

[1] *Cassla derga tentide.* So in the Koran, sura xxii. 20: "but for those who have disbelieved, garments of fire shall be cut out."

[2] The fiery wheels (*rotha*) remind one of the description of Charon ("Inferno," iii. 99), "che intorno agli occhi avea *di fiamme rote.*"

(to him) who shall be listening to the wail and to the lamentation of the souls in wretchedness and complaining to the Lord about the coming to them of the Day of Doom swiftly, if perchance they might get any coolness in the Judgment, for until Doom they get not any rest save three hours every Sunday![1] Woe (to him) unto whom that land were a rightful heritage for ever! For thus it is. Fells hollow, thorny there: plains bare then, they are parched: and lochs stinking, monsterful: ground rough, sandy, it is exceeding rugged, icy; flagstones broad, fiery, amidst it: seas great with awful storms, wherein are the Devil's resorts and abode continually. Four vast rivers[2] across the middle of it: a river of fire, a snowy river, a poisonous river, a river of black dark water. In those it is that the vehement hosts of the fiends bathe themselves after their delight and their enjoyment in torturing the souls.

Now when the holy hosts of Heaven's family sing the harmonious choirsong of the eight times of prayer,[3] joyfully and blithely praising the Lord, it is then the souls utter shouts wretched, miserable, at the ceaseless striking of them by the troops of the fiends.

Those then are the tortures and the punishments which the Angel of fellowship showed unto Adamnán's soul after visiting the kingdom of Heaven.

Then the soul was borne in the twinkling of an eye through the golden portico[4] and through the crystalline veil to the land of the Saints, into which she was first taken when she left her body.

Then when she bent her mind on staying and on tarrying in that land, she heard behind her through the veil the voice of the Angel who was ordering her to fare back again to the same body whence she had come, and to relate in meetings and assemblies, and in gatherings of laymen and clerics, Heaven's rewards and Hell's pains, as the Angel of fellowship had shown unto her.

[1] See "Old English Homilies," 1st series, p. 44, for a legend of St. Paul and Michael the Archangel obtaining from the Lord rest for the souls in hell "from non on saterdei a tha cume monedeis lihting."

[2] *Cethri srotha*, a reminiscence, perhaps, of the classical four (Phlegethon, Styx, Acheron, Cocytus), which both Dante and Milton have recognized in their geography of Hell, and with which the scholiast on the "Liber Hymnorum" (ed. Todd, p. 214) was slightly acquainted. "The four rivers around Mount Zion burning the souls" are mentioned in LU. 17*a*. So in the Tripartite Life, Eg. 7*a*. na .iiii. srotha tened immon sliab.

[3] The eight canonical hours are also mentioned above. They were matins, prime, terce, sext, none, vespers, compline, nocturn.

[4] *Erdam*, Cormac's *aurdam*, gen. *erdaim*, seems to have been in the Irish ecclesiastical architecture what the *pronaos* or *narthex* was in the Greek. If so, there were three doors from it into the nave, and through these the saints might well perceive the family of heaven. See Petrie's "Round Towers," 424; and Reeves' "Columba," 224*n*.

This, then, is the teaching that Adamnán was wont to use to the hosts from that time forth whilst he was in his life.

This, then, is what he used to preach in the great meeting of the men of Erin, when Adamnán's law[1] was set on the Gaels and when the women were freed by Adamnán and by Finnachta the Festive,[2] the king of Erin, and by the chiefs of Erin moreover.

These then are the first tidings which Patrick son of Calpurn[3] was wont to use, (to wit) Heaven's rewards and Hell's pains to relate unto those who believed in the Lord through his teaching, and who received their soul-friendship from him at the rising of the Gospel.

This, then, is the teaching that Peter and Paul, and the other Apostles, oftenest made. Namely, to relate the pains and rewards, for they had been shown unto them in the same wise.

This then did Silvester, Abbot of Rome, to Constantine son of Helena, chief king of the world, in the great meeting when he granted[4] the Rome[5] to Paul and to Peter.

[1] *Recht Adomnáin*, commonly called the *Cáin Adamnáin*, of which copies are preserved in the Bodleian Library, Rawl. B. 505, p. 305, and in the Bibliothèque Royale, Brussels, No. 2324-2340, fo. 78ª. The Bodleian copy begins thus:—"Five periods before Christ's birth, *i.e.* from Adam to the Flood: from the Flood to Abraham: from Abraham to David: from David to the Captivity in Babylon: from the Captivity of Babylon to Christ's birth. Women were in slavery and in oppression at that time till Adamnán, son of Ronan, etc., came." The woman that was best of women (*in ben ba dech de mnaiph*) had to go to battle, "her wallet of food on one side of her, her baby on the other side, her lance at her back, thirty feet in height, a sickle of iron at one end thereof, the which she used to put on the tress of the other woman, into the other battle: her husband behind her, a hedge-stake in his hand, beating her to battle." The MS. then tells at length how Adamnán's mother extorted from him a promise to exempt women from such liabilities. See Petrie's "Tara," p. 147, Reeves' "Columba," p. 179.

[2] Finnachta the Festive was *ardrí* (overlord) of Ireland from 675 to 695. The date of the imposition of Adamnán's law was 697, two years after Finnachta's death. Bishop Reeves ("Columba," liii.) has already pointed out the anachronism here committed by the author of the Vision.

[3] *Patraic mac calpuirnd.* So in Fiacc's hymn, 4, macCalpuirn (.i. *qui fuit sacerdos*) maic otide (leg. Fhótide), hoa deochain Odissi. Concess was his mother's name: she is said to have been of France, and a kinswoman of S. Martin of Tours: see Todd, "St. Patrick," 353, 354. She is called Concess, daughter of Ocbass of Gaul, in the Tripartite Life, B. 156*b*.

[4] See as to Silvester (*il primo ricco patre*) and Constantine's gift of Rome, "Inferno," xix. 115; and Milman, "History of Latin Christianity," i. 57. The legend of the Donation is told in a note to the "Félire" of Oengus the Culdee, January 18. Constantine sickens, and is taken to the great City. Leeches prescribe the blood-cure ("bathing by way of his joints in 300 innocent children's blood"). Peter and Paul appear to save the children, alter the treatment, order, instead, baptism and "going under the hand" of Abbot Silvester. The Emperor obeys, is, apparently, healed; and Rome thenceforward belongs to the two Apostles.

[5] *In Róim*: an instance of the individualizing article: so nom. sg. *ind Róm* "the (well-known) Rome," gen. *inna Romæ*, Z. 888.

This then is what Fabian,[1] Peter's successor, did for Philip, son of Gordian, for the king of the Romans, when he believed in the Lord and when many other thousands believed at that time. This is the first king of the Romans who believed in the Saviour Jesus Christ.[2]

These are the tidings which Eli is wont to relate to the souls of the righteous, and he under the Tree of Life in Paradise.[3] Then from the time that Eli opens the book to teach the souls, the souls of the righteous in shapes of pure-white birds[4] come there to him from every point. He relates to them then, first, the rewards of the righteous, the delightfulness and pleasures of Heaven's kingdom, and they are right glad at that time. Thereafter he relates to them Hell's pains and punishments and the banes of the Day of Doom; and greatly manifest is a countenance of sorrow upon himself and upon Enoch, so that those are the Two Sorrows of Heaven's Kingdom. Thereafter Eli shuts the book, and the birds utter a great cry of lamentation at that time, and beat their wings against their bodies, so that streams of blood come from them for fear of the pains of Hell and of the Day of Doom.

Since, then, it is the souls of the Saints unto whom is appointed eternal possession of the kingdom of Heaven, that make that lamentation, meeter were it for the men of the world though it were tears of blood that they shed in having heed of Doomsday and the pains of Hell.

It is then the Lord will pay His own wage to every one in the world, to wit, rewards to the righteous and pains to the sinners.

Then, in that wise the sinners will be plunged in a depth of eternal pain, into which the lock of God's word will shut them[5] under the hatred of the Judge of Doom for ever and ever.

[1] Fabian was martyred under Decius, A.D. 249. "*Philip mac Gordián.*" This is a blunder: Philip the Arab was the murderer, not the son, of Gordian the younger, and succeeded him A.D. 244.

[2] As to Philip's supposed conversion, see Gibbon, cap. xvi.

[3] As to the tree of life in Paradise and its fruits, see Apoc. ii. 7, xxii. 2, 14. As to Enoch and Elijah, see more in Grimm, "Deutsche Mythologie," 2te Aufl. 771, in the "Voyage of Snedgus and Mac Riagla," II. 21.6 (edited in "Revue Celtique," ix. 14), and in Norris's "Cornish Drama," ii. 16-22.

[4] As to the belief that souls assume the forms of doves and other birds, see Grimm, "Deutsche Mythologie," 788. Thorpe, "Northern Mythol.," i. 289. The souls of Mael-suthain's three pupils come to him *i rechtaib tri colum ngeal* ("in forms of three white doves"), O'Curry, "Lectures," 530.

[5] Cf. the "Tidings of Doomsday," LU. 33*a*: "then will be shut the sinners' three locks; to wit, a shutting of hell for ever upon them, a shutting of their eyes on the world to which they gave love, and a shutting of the heavenly kingdom against them." In a Breton canticle ("Barzaz Breiz," ii. 456) the singer says that the gates of hell have been shut and barred by God, and He will never open them, for the key is lost!

"Ann noriou zo bet sarret ha prennet gand Doue,
Ha n'ho digoro biken; kollet eo ann alc'houe."

But the Saints and the Righteous, the folk of charity and of mercy, shall be set on God's right hand to possess eternally the Kingdom of Heaven. To wit, a place wherein they shall be in that great glory, without age, without waning, without limit, without end, for ever and ever.

Thus, then, is that City, to wit, a Kingdom without pride, without haughtiness, without falsehood, without blasphemy, without fraud, without pretence, without reddening, without blushing, without disgrace, without deceit, without envy, without arrogance, without disease, without sickness, without poverty, without nakedness, without destruction, without extinction, without hail, without snow, without wind, without wet, without noise, without thunder, without darkness, without coldness—a Kingdom noble, admirable, delightful, with knowledge, with light, with odour of a plenteous Earth, wherein is delight of every goodness.

FINIT. AMEN. FINIT.

INDEX.

CHISWICK PRESS:—CHARLES WHITTINGHAM AND CO.
TOOKS COURT, CHANCERY LANE, LONDON.

www.ingramcontent.com/pod-product-compliance
Lightning Source LLC
Chambersburg PA
CBHW021116270326
41929CB00009B/908

9783337294601